Washington

John Doerper

Photography by Bruce Hands and Greg Vaughn

D0311565

COMPASS AMERICAN GUIDES
An imprint of Fodor's Travel Publications

Compass American Guides: Washington

Editor: Chris Culwell, Jennifer Paull
Designers: Fabrizio La Rocca, Siobhan O'Hare
Archival Research: Melanie Marin
Map Design: Mark Stroud, Moon Street Cartography

Fourth Edition

ISBN 978–1–4000–0738–7
ISSN 1539-3224

Although the details in this book are based on information supplied to us at press time, changes occur all the time in the travel world, and the publisher cannot accept responsibility for facts that become outdated or for inadvertent errors or omissions.

COMPASS AMERICAN GUIDES gratefully acknowledges the following institutions and individuals for the use of their photographs, illustrations, or both: Jean-Michel Addor pp. 124–125; James Chatters, 278; Dale Chihuly (photo by Russell Johnson), p. 74; Bruce Hands, pp. 8, 9, 10, 11, 16–17, 20, 45, 56, 61, 79, 80, 86, 94–95, 99, 104, 105, 107, 112, 117, 120, 129, 140, 144–145, 147, 149, 151, 188–189, 193, 197, 215, 224–225, 232, 240–241, 245, 262, 271, 286; Rocky Kolberg, pp. 204–205; Library of Congress pp. 30–31, 32, 248–249; Microsoft Corporation, p. 43; Museum of History and Industry, Seattle, pp. 34, 36, 37, 51, 52, 62, 100, 138, 141, 182, 183, 186, 238, 288–289; National Park Service, p. 33; Northwest Museum of Arts and Culture, Eastern Washington State Historical Society, Spokane, p. 22; Puget Sound Maritime Historical Society, Seattle, p. 57; Sisters of Providence Archives, Seattle, p. 212; MSCUA, University of Washington Libraries, Seattle, pp. 29 (neg. UW15572), 39 (UW2129), 41 (UW10706), 136 (UW552), 160 (UW7056), 184 (12), 185, 199 (UW21250Z), 202 (UW3939), 234 (NA4166), 236 (UW11046), 247 (UW5344), 260, 261 (11303), 292 (UW11363); Greg Vaughn, pp. 14, 19, 46, 48, 55, 63, 64–65, 69, 70, 71, 73, 75, 76, 77, 81, 82, 90–91, 93, 98, 101, 103, 110–111, 113, 116, 130, 131, 132, 134, 153, 155, 162, 166–167, 168, 170–171, 173, 177, 200, 203, 216–217, 218, 230–231, 235, 252–253, 267, 268, 269, 273, 276, 280–281, 283, 285, 303; Washington State Historical Society, Tacoma, pp. 26, 67, 72, 97, 139, 187, 194, 209.

COMPASS AMERICAN GUIDES would also like to thank Daniel Jack Chasan and Matthew Chasan for their editorial contributions to the first edition.

Compass American Guides, 1745 Broadway, New York, NY 10019
PRINTED IN CHINA BY TWIN AGE LIMITED
10 9 8 7 6 5 4 3 2 1

*The Washington Territory is interesting to tourists and
pleasure seekers for its splendid prairies covered with groves, laid out
by the greatest of landscape gardeners—Nature.
These groves rival in beauty the finest of the natural parks, and the latter
sink in significance in comparison of extent.*

—Tourist guide, 1872

CONTENTS

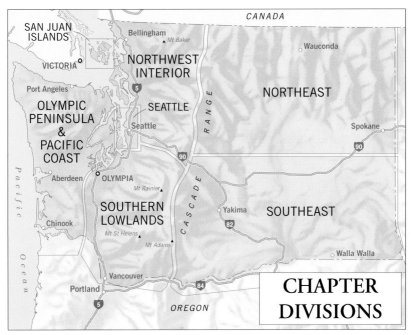

SAN JUAN ISLANDS

Bellingham
▲ Mt Baker

CANADA

Wauconda

VICTORIA

NORTHWEST INTERIOR

Port Angeles

NORTHEAST

OLYMPIC PENINSULA & PACIFIC COAST

SEATTLE

Seattle

RANGE

Spokane

Aberdeen

OLYMPIA

Mt Rainier ▲

SOUTHERN LOWLANDS

Mt St Helens ▲

Yakima

SOUTHEAST

Chinook

Mt Adams ▲

CASCADE

Pacific Ocean

Vancouver

Walla Walla

Portland

OREGON

CHAPTER DIVISIONS

Maps

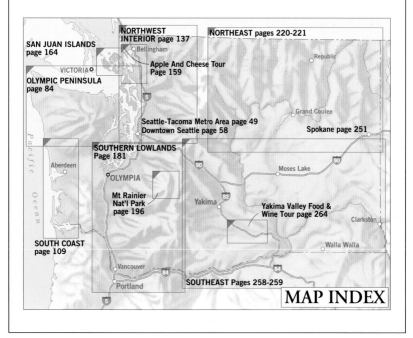

MAP INDEX

Sidebars and Topical Essays

Literary Extracts

O V E R V I E W

SEATTLE

With its sophisticated restaurants, energetic nightlife, vibrant art scene, and acclaimed opera, theater, and symphony, Seattle is an exciting city to visit and a wonderful place to live. Its big-city pleasures complement the natural backdrop of Puget

Sound's blue waters and hulking Mount Rainier. Take in views from the Space Needle, or take a harbor cruise for a unique view of the skyline. Stroll through bustling Pike Place Market or along a tree-lined street high on the slopes of Queen Anne Hill for a view across Puget Sound to the Olympic Mountains. Linger awhile with the café crowd, or grab a table at a waterfront restaurant and watch the sunset.

OLYMPIC PENINSULA AND PACIFIC COAST

The lichen-, fern-, and moss-draped trees of the Olympic Peninsula lowlands and

Olympic National Park make up the only extensive area of rain forest on the U.S. Pacific Coast. This is one of the West's most spectacular natural areas. Stately elk and black bear amble through the dense woods; bald eagles soar overhead; sandpipers and plovers have the lonely beaches all to

themselves; tall sea stacks rise from fog-shrouded surf, and trees bent by the wind writhe over rocky headlands. From Grays Harbor south, oysters thrive in estuaries. Slurp them fresh from the shell, or stop at a local restaurant and try them smoked, fried, or sauteed.

NORTHWEST INTERIOR

With their jagged, razor-sharp peaks and bluish-green glaciers, the mountains of the North Cascades are among the most majestic anywhere. Secluded valleys and wildflower meadows beckon hikers; rivers and lakes attract fishermen. Farms spreading across glaciated valleys produce some of the nation's finest apples and raspberries. Lazy rivers meander across the lowlands, ending in tidal flats teeming with shorebirds.

SAN JUAN ISLANDS

The San Juan Islands, lying between mainland Washington and Vancouver Island, are poems of sandstone and gnarled trees, a paradise for seabirds and a refuge for wildflowers. Some of the islands are barely large enough to hold a cabin; the four largest are several miles across, with streets and villages. Cliffs rise steeply from the water to pine- and fir-clad ridges, as they do on Orcas Island, or they stay low, terminating in meadows and fields, as they do on Lopez. Everywhere, you'll find sand or shingle beaches, rocky headlands, or quiet coves. The city-weary

head to Lopez, Shaw, Orcas, and San Juan Islands, which can be reached by ferry from Anacortes, on the mainland. Kayakers from around the world come here to paddle between the islands and to watch seabirds and orcas up close.

SOUTHERN LOWLANDS

On hazy days, when the sun hits them just right, the tall volcanic peaks of Mount Rainier, Mount Adams, and Mount St. Helens seem to float in the air, separated from the earth by their own shadows. Drive into the hills to get a close-up look at the devastation (and subsequent regeneration of life) on the slopes of Mount St.

Helens, stroll through a wildflower meadow on the flanks of Mount Rainier, watch birds along the banks of a quiet lowland stream or slough, or visit Washington's first pioneer settlement along the Columbia River. Take a side trip to Vancouver to see Fort Vancouver, built by the British in 1824, or visit the Maryhill Museum, one of the most isolated major museums in the United States.

NORTHEAST

This is a quiet territory, despite the agricultural bustle of vast irrigated stretches and dryland wheat fields on the Columbia Plateau. North of the Columbia River, wild woods alternate with small farms. In the center of the region, the

Columbia River backs up behind Grand Coulee Dam into 151-mile-long Franklin Delano Roosevelt Lake. Orchards in the glaciated valleys of the eastern slopes of the North Cascades produce excellent apples, cherries, and peaches. Lake Chelan, a landlocked fjord, reaches far into the heart of these mountains. The town of Stehekin, in the shadow of the North Cascade Mountains, is a popular meeting point for hikers on their way to the Pacific Crest Trail, and nearby is the town of Leavenworth, a stateside take on a Bavarian village. The economic and cultural hub of the area is the appealing regional metropolis, Spokane.

SOUTHEAST

Shielded from chilling winds by the Blue Mountains to the east and the tall hills of the Palouse to the north, southeastern Washington has an uncommonly mild climate, which may explain why Walla Walla was among the first American settlements in the state. The region boasts the state's most productive farms, where asparagus, melons, and sweet onions grow. Wine grapes are grown here, and the

deep soils of the Palouse are among the richest wheat lands in the world. The Snake River cuts through this region in a steep-sided canyon; the Blue Mountains, rich in wildlife and flowers, are perfect for wilderness camping.

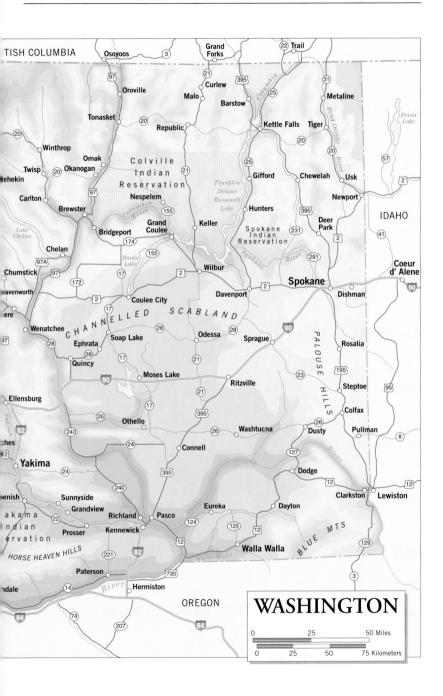

WASHINGTON

0   25   50 Miles

0   25   50   75 Kilometers

FINDING THE PERFECT SPOT

SALMON SWIMMING UP A ROAD NEAR THE LUMBER TOWN OF SHELTON! That's what the television news report said—and backed it up with a video of chum salmon, backs exposed, mistaking flooded tarmac for the gravelly shallows of a stream. The wonder of it took me back to the first time I visited Washington State.

It all began in the summer of 1975, when I was living in Davis, California, and one of my paintings was accepted in a competitive art show in Seattle. My wife and I decided this was as good an excuse for a vacation as we'd ever come up with, so off we went. Seattle was a delight. We took in the sights, rode the monorail from the Seattle Center downtown, and explored the Pike Place Market before heading out of town to find a campground. We soon discovered the perfect spot, a small county park on the Stillaguamish River, surrounded by woods that looked like scenery from *Grimm's Fairy Tales*, with a jagged, snowcapped peak for a backdrop. The next day, we drove north to Mount Baker.

Even now, three decades later, there's a spot on the Mount Baker Highway where I involuntarily take my foot off the gas pedal as the road rounds a turn: the woods open up and Mount Shuksan, a steep-cliffed, glacier-covered peak rises from a cleft. It's an incredible sight, especially on a bright day, when the sun strikes the glaciers and the ice of the crevasses radiates an unearthly blue light. At the end of the road, we found alpine lakes and ate our fill of blueberries as we hiked into the backcountry. We were in love.

The next day we explored Bellingham and made up our minds—this is where we wanted to live. Since that time, I have explored most of the state, but feel I hardly know it. There is too much to see, explore, enjoy.

After I moved to Washington State, I felt overwhelmed by the complexity of its scenery and history. To me, its map looked like a giant puzzle, with key pieces missing. Slowly, over the years, I've been filling in the pieces, and it's been a most delightful learning process.

My initial explorations took me to Whidbey Island, settled by Yankee ship captains in the 1850s. The captains came to Puget Sound for lumber, liked what they saw, and stayed.

(opposite) Hikers, skiers, and nature lovers enjoy Mount Rainier year-round.

BEAUTY UNSURPASSED

To add to the beauty, a cluster of crystalline lakes, upon which the sunbeams dance and glisten, meets the vision in several places. A ride or a drive through these natural parks is a feast of scenery to be found nowhere else in the world. In the first place there is the enjoyment of having a beautiful turf road, which cannot be excelled, beneath you; before you spread miles of flower beds, which perfume the air, their brilliant hues being contrasted and made more striking by the quiet shades of evergreen groves or dark green of the oaks, while the towering snow-clad peaks, with their cool, refreshing appearance, make up a grand background and complete a tableaux which would be difficult to surpass.

—Tourist guide, ca. 1872

Whidbey Island has a unique landscape for western Washington. There are few forests here, the land being mostly open prairies covered with wildflowers in spring. The 18th-century British explorer George Vancouver compared it to the parks of British country estates. Blue irises grow here, as do other wildflowers rare elsewhere in western Washington. The village of Coupeville, on the waterfront of Penn Cove, an inlet that almost cuts the island in half, has some of the oldest houses in the state. It's off the beaten path and has changed little in the last hundred years, as you'll note when you negotiate the narrow main street, which is so atmospheric it's often been used as a stand-in for New England villages in movies.

We explored the secluded beaches and quiet coves of the San Juan Islands, where we have fished for salmon and set pots for Dungeness crab. These islands, like Whidbey Island, lie in the rain shadow of the Olympic Mountains and are drier and sunnier than other areas of western Washington. That translates into more wildflowers and birds, making the islands a naturalist's paradise (many of the smaller islets are bird sanctuaries). Best of all, you don't need a boat of your own to explore them, as you can take a ferry to all of the larger ones. I sometimes take the ferry to get away from things. It's an ideal writer's haven: I snag a window seat, take out the old laptop computer and hack away while islands, boats, and the occasional seal, orca, or eagle drifts by. For several years, a passenger-only ferry has

(preceding pages) Rolling hills of the Palouse region in southeast Washington.
(opposite) Rosario Strait at sunset.

taken hikers and kayakers to the smaller, more remote islands of the San Juan archipelago, like Jones, Stuart, or Sucia, places otherwise reachable only by boat or seaplane.

It took me longer to start exploring eastern Washington—there was simply too much to see in the west. But I still remember my first drive to Spokane. I took back roads instead of the interstate, crossing the Cascades on Stevens Pass, dropping down past the Wenatchee apple orchards, traversing the Columbia, climbing the switchbacks to the wheat fields of the Waterville Plateau, and driving for what seemed like endless miles until I encountered the pine-studded grasslands near Spokane. On my way back, I took Route 20 through the green Methow Valley and the parklike, tree-studded alpine meadows of the North Cascades Highway.

There were several firsts on that trip. The first time I saw the white-water canyon of the Wenatchee, with its steep sides of glacier-cut rock. The first time I saw the upper canyon of the Columbia River, which is just as spectacular as the more famous gorge separating Oregon and Washington. Seeing it veiled in morning haze painted golden and pink by the rising sun is an other-earthly experience.

So are the coulees: sere, flat-bottomed Moses Coulee and Grand Coulee, a chasm of awesome proportions with straight-sided walls cut by the waters of a flood from the valleys of Montana. Dry Falls, a basalt ledge several miles wide, still marks the spot where the ice-age floods tore a gash through the rocks of the plateau before losing their strength and fanning out into a maze of smaller channels. When I visited here for the first time, I took the trail to the base of the cliff, where, in a small moist cave, I found swallows resting on a wet rock. On my way home, I drove across the vast granite shield of the Okanogan Highlands, with its park-like groves of quaking aspen, and watched hawks soar in the sky.

On other trips I have lost myself among the gnarled rocks and dense woods of the northeastern mountains, the only place in Washington visited by caribou and moose. I have cruised the gentle hills of the Palouse, a magic landscape in late spring and early summer, when the green culms of wheat change to a silky gold, and when every gentle breeze blowing up the valley ruffles the leaves, making it look like the soft fur of a vast, gentle animal.

From the Palouse, I have driven south into the precipitous canyons of the Blue Mountains and crossed the dramatic dryness of the lower Snake River Valley to the arid canyons of the northern bank, where the Palouse River falls over a basalt ledge in a tall, roaring waterfall. The state has many waterfalls, some of them well-known, like the Nooksack or Snoqualmie. Countless smaller ones are all but undiscovered, sparkling jewels awaiting the unsuspecting hiker.

I learned over the years that Washington is not as wet as I thought: it has a dry season and a wet one. Summer is mostly sunny and warm. Winter is cold. But what makes the state unique is the complexity of its climates: the wet parts of the state are not just soggy rain forests and the dry side arid desert. Small prairies alternate with forests in the lowlands and islands of the west. East of the Cascades, dry grasslands lead into moist valleys of tall cedars, dense hemlock, and lacy vine maple where cold brooks burble in beds of moss-covered boulders.

The kaleidoscopic variety of mountains and valleys, forests and prairies, sunshine and rain, is what makes Washington a state for all seasons. It's one reason why I continue to explore the state, knowing that I will always find something new.

(opposite) Llama trekking along the Pacific Crest Trail in the Mount Adams Wilderness Area.

H I S T O R Y

WHERE DO YOU START? A time long before the slow docking of microcontinents from the west that added the Okanogan Highlands, the area now covered by the North Cascade Mountains, the San Juan Islands, and the Olympic Peninsula? With the rise of the Cascades a couple of million years ago? When the great glacier that carved Puget Sound 15,000 years ago pushed south and buried what is now Seattle under 3,000 feet of ice?

Or does it make more sense to start with people? The oldest sign of human presence in Washington was found at the Manis site, near Sequim, on the Olympic Peninsula. There, quite by chance, a backhoe excavating a farmer's duck pond unearthed the 12,000-year-old remains of a mastodon. Embedded in one of the hairy elephant's massive ribs was a bone spear point. Other ribs showed marks of butchering. Artifacts up to 10,000 years old have been found at the Marmes rock shelter in eastern Washington, not far from Palouse Falls. Evidence suggests that people were catching and eating salmon beside the Columbia River 9,000 years ago.

■ EARLY SETTLERS AND EXPLORERS

No one really knows who those early salmon eaters or mastodon killers were. We do know that before European culture arrived, the Makahs, a tribe of Native Americans, paddled long cedar canoes into the open Pacific to hunt whales, that tribes along the Columbia River speared salmon above the rapids at Kettle Falls, and that the Snoqualmie tribe ran a trade route through the Cascades. Archaeologists have learned that tribes of Native Americans in the eastern Cascades set slow fires in forests to clear them of underbrush, making it easier to hunt among the pines. We also know that these people spoke a variety of different languages along the mid-Columbia River. We also know that none of them carved the great Northwest Coast totem poles—those were actually produced farther north, along the coasts of British Columbia and southeast Alaska.

Pioneer settler James Swan, who spent time among the Makahs in the mid-19th century, reported that Makah children's "chief pleasure is to get into a little

Nez Percé man and woman in Spokane, date unknown.
(Northwest Museum of Arts & Culture/Eastern Washington State Historical Society)

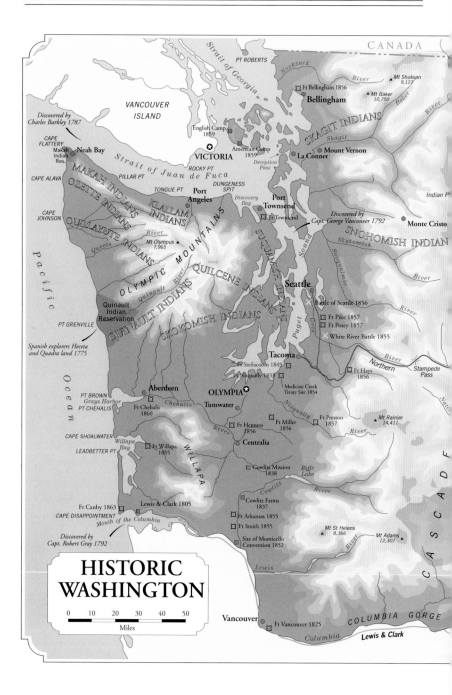

CANADA

PT ROBERTS

Nooksack River

Mt Shuksan 9,127

Ft Bellingham 1856

Mt Baker 10,750

Bellingham

Baker River

VANCOUVER ISLAND

Discovered by Charles Barkley 1787

SKAGIT INDIANS

Skagit

English Camp 1859

CAPE FLATTERY

Makah Indian Res.

Neah Bay

VICTORIA

American Camp 1859

Deception Pass

La Conner

Mount Vernon

Strait of Juan de Fuca

ROCKY PT

PILLAR PT

CAPE ALAVA

TONGUE PT

DUNGENESS SPIT

Discovery Bay

Port Townsend

Indian P

KLALLAM INDIANS

Port Angeles

Discovered by Capt. George Vancouver 1792

Monte Cristo

CAPE JOHNSON

Ft Townsend

SNOHOMISH INDIAN

MAKAH INDIANS

Skykomish

OZETTE INDIANS

River

Snoqualmie River

QUILLAYUTE INDIANS

Queets River

Mt Olympus 7,965

Pacific

OLYMPIC MOUNTAINS

Quinault River

QUILCENE INDIANS

Seattle

Battle of Seattle 1856

River

SUQUAMISH INDIANS

Ft Pike 1857

Ft Posey 1857

Quinault Indian Reservation

QUINAULT INDIANS

SKOKOMISH INDIANS

White River Battle 1855

PT GRENVILLE

Puget

Sound

Spanish explorers Heceta and Quadra land 1775

Tacoma

Ocean

Ft Steilacoom 1849

Northern

River

Stampede Pass

Ft Nisqually 1833

Ft Hays 1856

PT BROWN

Grays Harbor

PT CHEHALIS

Aberdeen

Medicine Creek Treaty Site 1854

Ft Chehalis 1860

OLYMPIA

Chehalis River

Tumwater

Nisqually River

Ft Preston 1857

Mt Rainier 14,411

CAPE SHOALWATER

Ft Henness 1856

Ft Miller 1856

River

LEADBETTER PT

Willapa Bay

Ft Willapa 1855

Centralia

WILLAPA

CASCADE

Cowlitz Mission 1838

Riffe Lake

Ft Canby 1863

CAPE DISAPPOINTMENT

Lewis & Clark 1805

Cowlitz Farms 1837

Cowlitz River

Mouth of the Columbia

Ft Arkansas 1855

Mt St Helens 8,366

Mt Adams 12,307

Discovered by Capt. Robert Gray 1792

Ft Smith 1855

Site of Monticello Convention 1852

River

Lewis

HISTORIC
WASHINGTON

0 10 20 30 40 50
Miles

Vancouver

Ft Vancouver 1825

COLUMBIA GORGE

Columbia

Lewis & Clark

Strait of Georgia

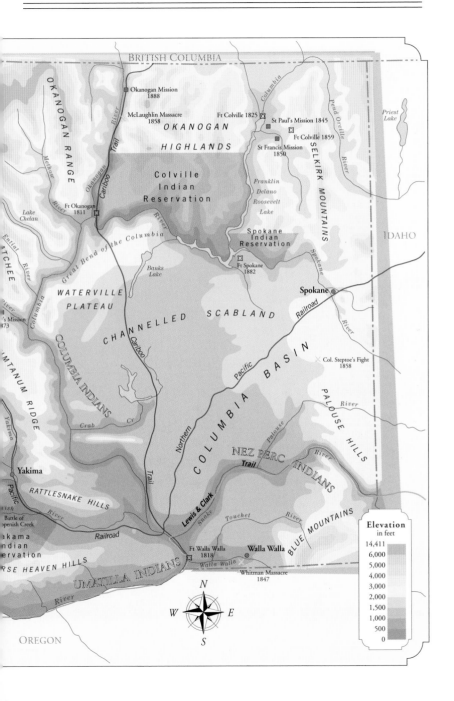

canoe, just large enough to float them, and paddle into the surf." Their elders were whalers; Swan suggested, "they are…to the Indian population what the inhabitants of Nantucket are to the people of the Atlantic coast."

We also know that Spaniards sailed along the coast in the 18th century—and possibly as early as the 16th—establishing a short-lived post at Neah Bay. There are detailed records of Capt. George Vancouver's visit, when he explored the coast for England, naming Mount Baker, Mount Rainier, Puget Sound, and any number of other mountains, islands, and points for his shipmates and friends. Later, New England merchant Capt. Robert Gray, trading sea otter skins with China for Boston investors, took the first sailing vessel into the mouth of the river that bears the name of his ship, *Columbia Rediviva.*

The best-known explorers of the area were Meriwether Lewis and William Clark, sent west by President Thomas Jefferson to "explore the Missouri river, &

Makah Indians land a whale through the surf at Neah Bay. Sealskin floats hinder the whale's diving and keep it afloat after death. (Washington State Historical Society)

such principal streams of it, as by it's course & communications with the waters of the Pacific Ocean, may offer the most direct & practicable water communication across this continent." The pair entered Washington along the Snake River in 1805 and reached the Pacific that fall at what is now Fort Canby State Park. Lewis and Clark, 29 and 33 years old, respectively, when they started their two-year journey, were men of very different personalities and interests. "Although Lewis enjoyed eating dog meat and Clark hated it, and Lewis craved salt and Clark dismissed it as a luxury, and Lewis liked eating black currants and Clark favored yellow ones, the two explorers otherwise formed a perfectly harmonious relationship," Frank Bergon has written in an introduction to their journals. "Clark had more experience in actual battle, against the Creek and Cherokee Indians, but both men were archetypal American frontiersmen, whose characters had been forged in confrontation with the wilderness."

Jefferson wanted them to record the appearance and nature of the wilderness they passed through on this journey and the people who lived in it. No one knew who those people were. Jefferson wrote to Lewis: "As it is impossible for us to foresee in what manner you will be received by those people, whether with hospitality or hostility, so is it impossible to prescribe the exact degree of perseverance with which you are to pursue your journey. We value too much the lives of citizens to offer them to probable destruction."

Soon after Lewis and Clark passed through what was for them unknown country, fur traders employed by the British Hudson's Bay and North West Companies trekked regularly between what is now the interior of British Columbia and the mouth of the Columbia River.

There is often no clear division between the past and the present. The Makahs were still whaling from dugout canoes at the start of the 20th century, and Yakamas and other

A basketry hat made of split spruce root and black-dyed cedar bark depicts a whale hunt scene.

INDIAN CUSTOMS

On arriving among [the Indians ashore] we were exceedingly surprised to see that they had almost all flattened heads. This configuration is not a natural deformity, but an effect of art, caused by compression of the skull in infancy. It shocks strangers extremely, especially at first sight; nevertheless, among these barbarians it is an indispensable ornament: and when we signified to them how much this mode of flattening the forehead appeared to us to violate nature and good taste, they answered that it was only slaves who had not their heads flattened. The slaves, in fact, have the usual rounded head, and they are not permitted to flatten the foreheads of their children, destined to bear the chains of their sires.

The Indians of the Columbia are of a light copper color, active in body, and, above all, excellent swimmers....The men go entirely naked, not concealing any part of their bodies. Only in winter they throw over the shoulders a panther's skin....

[The women] anoint the body and dress the hair with fish oil, which does not diffuse an agreeable perfume. Their hair (which both sexes wear long) is jet black; it is badly combed, but parted in the middle, as is the custom of the sex everywhere, and kept shining by the fish-oil before-mentioned. Sometimes, in imitation of the men, they paint the whole body with a red earth mixed with fish-oil. Their ornaments consist of bracelets of brass, which they wear indifferently on the wrists and ankles; of strings of beads of different colors (they give a preference to the blue), and displayed in great profusion around the neck, and on the arms and legs; and of white shells, called Haiqua, which are their ordinary circulating medium....Although a little less slaves than the greater part of the Indian women elsewhere, the women on the Columbia are, nevertheless, charged with the most painful labors....

—Gabriel Franchère, *Narrative of a Voyage to the Northwest Coast of America in the Years 1811, 1812, 1813, and 1814*

inland tribes were still dip-netting salmon from platforms above Celilo Falls until 1957, when the Dalles Dam flooded the falls and are still dip-netting on the Klickitat River. The first non-Indians who sought and finally found a route across the Cascades used Indian trails and Indian guides, and I-90 basically follows that route today. As late as the 1960s, one old woman on the Colville Indian Reservation was still setting fires in the pine forests to clear away the brush.

Still, those early explorations, those millennia of fishing and whaling and knowing the land, did not lead in any direct way to the development of the cities and agriculture and industry that exist in Washington today, or that existed here even a century ago. Native Americans can claim some continuity with that past, but for society as a whole, links with the pre-European past are largely imaginary.

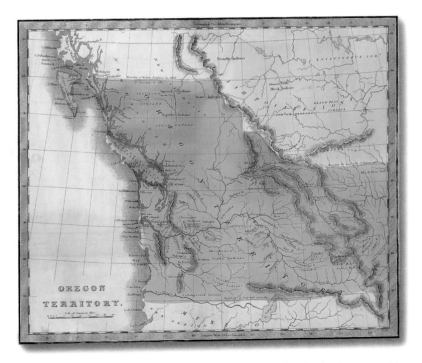

A map of Oregon Territory before the settlement of U.S.–Canadian border claims in 1846. (University of Washington Libraries)

History Timeline

1592 A Greek navigator, sailing for Spain and using the name Juan de Fuca, claims to have discovered a vast strait. Two centuries later, Bruno Heceta and Juan Francisco de Bodega claim the Washington coast for Spain.

1778 In search of the fabled Northwest Passage, British explorer Capt. James Cook sights and names Cape Flattery.

1787 Strait of Juan de Fuca entered and named by Capt. Charles W. Barkley.

1792 British sea captain George Vancouver explores Washington waters and names waterways and landmarks, many in honor of his crew members—Peter Puget, Peter Rainier, Joseph Whidbey, Joseph Baker. The same year, Bostonian Robert Gray is the first to sail into the mouth of the Columbia River. He names it after his ship, the *Columbia Rediviva.*

1805 American explorers Lewis and Clark enter Washington from the east and follow the Columbia downriver to the Pacific Ocean.

1812 Fort Spokane established by John Jacob Astor's Pacific Fur Company.

1819 Spain relinquishes all claims to Oregon Country.

1825 John McLoughlin establishes Hudson's Bay Company's Fort Vancouver.

1828 Jedediah Smith leads fur traders from California to the Columbia River.

1836 Marcus and Narcissa Whitman establish a mission near Walla Walla, which they run until they are massacred by the Cayuse Indians in 1847.

1846 England agrees to set the border between western Canada and the United States at the 49th parallel.

1852 Seattle founded by the Denny party.

1853 Washington Territory established. Population: 3,985.

1854 Medicine Creek Indian Treaty signed.

1856 Seattle besieged by Indians. Martial law declared on Puget Sound.

1858 Colonel Steptoe defeated by Indians. Colonel Wright defeats Indians in eastern Washington. Indian Wars end.

1864 Asa Mercer travels east and convinces marriageable women to settle in Washington Territory, where men are eager for wives.

1873 Tacoma chosen as western terminus of Northern Pacific Railway.

1889 Washington State is admitted to the Union. Fires devastate Seattle, Spokane, and Ellensburg.

1897 Gold is discovered in Alaska. Seattle becomes main terminus for Klondike miners.

1900 Frederick Weyerhaeuser starts his Northwest operation.

1906 The Mountaineers founded—an outdoors club devoted to preserving and exploring mountains, forests, and rivers of the Pacific Northwest.

1916 After crashing his newly purchased plane, Bill Boeing, Sr. builds his own seaplane—the first Boeing aircraft is assembled.

1938 Bonneville Dam is completed.

1942 Jimi Hendrix is born in Seattle.

1962 The World's Fair in Seattle draws more than 9.6 million people and establishes the city's most recognizable landmark, the Space Needle.

1975 Bill Gates and Paul Allen start Microsoft.

1977 First woman governor, biology professor Dixy Lee Ray, is elected.

1980 Mount St. Helens erupts, killing 57 people.

1993 Seattle hosts the Asia Pacific Economic Cooperation conference.

1996 Nine-thousand-year-old skeleton discovered along the Columbia River becomes one of the 20th century's most important archaeological finds.

1999 Protesters overwhelm police at the Seattle Conference Center during a meeting of the World Trade Organization.

2000 Experience Music Project, a museum celebrating American pop music, opens.

2001 On February 28, a 6.8 earthquake rocks Olympia, Seattle, and Tacoma, killing one person, injuring 407, and creating billions of dollars in damages.

2004 Republican Dino Rossi loses the governor's election to Democrat Christine Gregoire on recount by 133 votes.

THE SEATTLE WATERFRONT

HISTORY

Soapy Smith sashays up to the bar of his saloon in Skagway, Alaska, in the company of his minders, just months before his death at the hands of vigilantes. (Library of Congress)

SOAPY SMITH

It was along [Seattle's] Skid Road that the most famous of Alaska's bad men, Soapy Smith, rounded up the gang that eventually operated the town of Skagway as its private enterprise. Soapy Smith—like Erastus Brainerd—was a part-time genius. He took a weird bunch of individualists, men who went by the names of Fatty Green and Kid Jimmy Fresh, Yank Fewclothes and Jay Bird Slim, and organized them into a syndicate that not only ran all the gambling and robbery at the southern end of the gold trail, but even took over the United States Army Recruiting Station at Skagway during the Spanish-American War and assigned men to pick the pockets of the recruits who were taking their physicals. Soapy did not profit personally from his endeavors. When he was killed in a duel with the civil engineer who had laid out the town (and who, like Soapy, felt a proprietary interest in Skagway) Soapy's estate was a hundred dollars in cash and a satchelful of marked cards.

—Murray Morgan, *Skid Road*, 1981

■ AMERICANIZATION OF WASHINGTON

Modern Washington starts with the Missourian Michael Simmons setting up the territory's first sawmill at Tumwater Falls in 1848; with the pioneer Boren and Denny families shivering through the winter of 1851 in log cabins at Alki Point; with oystermen living in shacks on Willapa Bay in the early 1850s; or maybe earlier, with Marcus and Narcissa Whitman setting up their mission near Walla Walla in 1836.

In 1846, the United States and Great Britain settled the boundary of the Oregon Country, giving the United States clear title to the current states of Washington, Oregon, Idaho, and part of Montana. Washington Territory split off as a separate entity in 1853. The first territorial governor, Isaac Stevens—who'd finished first in the West Point class of 1839 and fought at Chapultepec in the Mexican War—negotiated treaties with the Indians that gave the United States title to most of the land in 1854, 1855, and 1856. The treaties were negotiated in traditional Chinook jargon, a trade language used at the time by Pacific Northwest Indians, and it is not clear what the Indians thought they were getting. Whatever they thought, Indians who didn't like the treaties or their results were defeated in sporadic fighting from 1855 to 1858.

People grew crops and raised livestock in Washington from the beginning. Indeed, the Hudson's Bay Company ran a farm at Fort Nisqually, north of the Nisqually Delta, and the company's Fort Vancouver on the Columbia River may have been the first place in Washington where people raised apples or grapes. But mostly, Washington was founded by people who mined the territory's rich natural resources.

Ships' crews and early settlers cut old-growth trees beside the salt water of Puget Sound, sawed them into lengths, and loaded the logs onto sailing ships, which hauled

Drawing of Fort Vancouver (1851), by George Gibbs. (National Park Service)

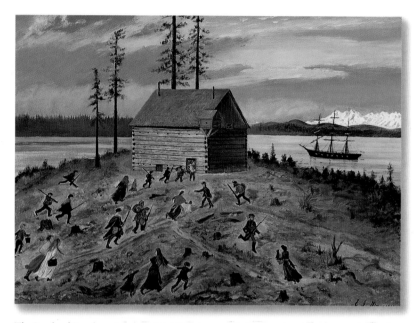

The Battle of Seattle on January 26, 1856, between Indians and early settlers, as depicted in a painting by Emily Inez Denny. (Museum of History and Industry)

them south to San Francisco Bay. In 1853, the Pope & Talbot Company built a mill at Port Gamble, on Hood Canal, just to cut lumber for the San Francisco market. Some of the Douglas firs felled by these early loggers were huge, larger than the few giants surviving in Pacific Northwest forests today and larger than California's coast redwoods. A few of these trees reached a trunk diameter of 15 to 18 feet and were 380 to 415 feet tall.

Because these trees were so huge, and the equipment to move them still primitive, loggers stayed close to water, so that logs could be transported via ships. Ox teams dragged portions of Douglas fir trunks along tracks of peeled and greased logs called skid roads. Oxen couldn't drag an old-growth log far, and they couldn't drag one up a steep hill at all.

Coal proved equally difficult to haul. To transport the first load of coal from Issaquah, now 20 minutes by freeway from downtown Seattle, in 1864, a Seattle blacksmith built a scow, hired a crew of Duwamish Indians, poled up the Duwamish and Black Rivers, sailed across Lake Washington, cut his way through

Washington Habitable? Never!

Not everyone was enthusiastic about extending U.S. territories to the Pacific Coast, as this address to the U.S. Senate in 1843 illustrates:

Does any man seriously suppose that any state which can be formed at the mouth of the Columbia River, or any of the inhabitable parts of that territory, would ever become one of the states of the Union?…Even in the most sanguine days of my youth I never conceived the possibility of embracing within the same Government people living five thousand miles apart.…Have you made anything like an estimate of the cost of a railroad running from here to the mouth of the Columbia? Why, the wealth of the Indies would be insufficient.…To talk about constructing a railroad to the western shore of this continent manifests a wild spirit of adventure which I never expected to hear broached in the Senate of the United States.

—Sen. George McDuffie, address to the
U.S. Senate, January 25, 1843

logs and brush up the Sammamish Slough, sailed the length of Lake Sammamish, loaded the coal, then turned around and followed the same path back to Seattle. The trip took 20 days.

The first rails laid in Washington were used to haul logs, coal, or wheat to the water's edge or to farther destinations. But the early railroads had nothing like the impact of the first transcontinental railroads, which transformed Washington's economic relationship with the rest of the country and made it possible to develop vast areas east of the Cascade Mountains.

■ Railroads

From a 21st-century perspective, it's hard to appreciate how important, or how powerful and corrupting, the railroads were. "The generation between 1865 and 1895…was mortgaged to the railroads," wrote Henry Adams, "and no one knew it better than the generation itself."

Washington cities were as eager as Congress to reward, or bribe, the railroad builders. Seattle offered the Northern Pacific Railway 3,000 acres and a quarter of a million dollars in cash and bonds if it would lay tracks to Elliott Bay. Tacoma

The laying of the last rail on the Great Northern Railway's main line just west of the Cascade summit in December 1892. (Museum of History and Industry)

offered the railroad two miles of waterfront and 2,700 acres in a solid block if it would lay them to Commencement Bay instead. Tacoma won.

But Tacoma's glory days didn't last. Seattle had already become the supply center for mill towns and logging camps all around Puget Sound, and had started supplying Alaska. Even when Tacoma got the railroad, Seattle never lost its crass frontier optimism. After most of downtown Seattle burned in the great fire of 1889, the city rebuilt itself in brick.

Seattle soon had a railroad of its own. James J. Hill, a tycoon from the Midwest, completed the Great Northern Railway from St. Paul to Seattle in 1893, in time for a four-year nationwide depression. During the depression, Hill gained control of the Northern Pacific, along with its vast government land grants, and since Hill had already picked Seattle as his main western terminus, that marked the end of the city's relative eclipse.

The railroads brought some places into the economic mainstream and turned others into backwaters. Once rails became the preferred means of transportation, the Olympic Peninsula, which had been so easily accessible by ship, was cut off from most of the action. On the other hand, rails soon made it feasible to mine coal in the eastern Cascades at Cle Elum and Roslyn. Miners migrated to the eastern Cascades from much of Europe and parts of Asia. In the early 20th century,

Roslyn's population included Austrians, Belgians, Chinese, Czechs, Dutch, English, Finns, Germans, Hungarians, Irish, Italians, Lithuanians, Norwegians, Poles, Russians, Slovenes, Swedes, and Welshmen.

The rails, combined with irrigation and cold storage, made it possible to grow apples and ship them to markets in the Midwest and East. The wheat country was transformed, too. Spokane became a hub for the surrounding farm area and a supply point for mining booms farther east. Eastern Washington wheat that would once have gone down the river to Portland was loaded onto trains bound for Tacoma, where it was shipped to ports all over the world.

■ STATEHOOD AND A NEW CENTURY

Washington became a state in 1889. Eight years later, the steamer *Portland* arrived in Seattle with a "ton of gold." The Klondike gold rush was on. At least

Would-be fortune hunters crowd onto a steamer bound for Alaska during the Klondike gold rush of 1897. (Museum of History and Industry)

IMMIGRANT INQUIRIES, 1872

The first inquiries which a person desiring to change his residence from one State to another would naturally be, what advantages does the State to which I wish to emigrate possess over my own? Is it more fertile, more healthy, does it possess a more genial climate, are its resources and commercial and manufacturing advantages greater? Is it easier for the poor laborer to earn a livelihood or the poor farmer to obtain land? What facilities are offered for education and attending church? And finally, what is the character of the population, in order that I may know who are to be my future neighbors and what class of persons I shall mingle with? The person thinking of changing his home should make these inquiries, and if the advantages are in favor of the State to be adopted, one should avail himself of them. There is no portion of the country, perhaps, that offers all the advantages to an immigrant equal to this Territory.

—*Puget Sound Business Directory,* 1872

2,000 people were waiting at Schwabacher's Wharf to greet the miners who had struck it rich in the Klondike, and within 10 days, the first 1,500 people had left Seattle for the gold fields. Overnight, Seattle had become a gold rush boomtown. Already a supply center for western Washington and Alaska, now the last stop of the transcontinental railroads, and not shy about self-promotion, Seattle became the main jumping-off point for Alaska-bound miners. Men and supplies streamed north on any ship sound enough to make the voyage. Gold and discouraged prospectors streamed back. Merchants who supplied the miners did very well for themselves, as did people who built or operated ships. "The Klondike excitement will put everything that can be floated into use," wrote a Puget Sound lumber baron, "and in fact some of the boats have made on one trip almost the cost of building them." Inevitably, sin flourished, saloons proliferated, and Seattle became a center of the white slave trade.

In 1899, a new generating plant at Snoqualmie Falls began selling electricity to Seattle and Tacoma. In 1900, the railroad builder Jim Hill sold 900,000 acres of land grant timberland—given by Congress to the Northern Pacific and subsequently acquired by Hill—at $6 per acre to his St. Paul neighbor, the Midwestern lumber baron, Frederick Weyerhaeuser. The sale was the largest private land deal in American history and the start of the Weyerhaeuser empire in the Northwest. The first automobiles crossed the Cascades over the ruts and rocks of the wagon road across Snoqualmie Pass five years later. Around the same time, people started putting gasoline engines into fishing boats. When the great earthquake of 1906 destroyed San Francisco, Washington mills cut lumber to rebuild the city; in effect, Washington lumber built San Francisco twice.

To celebrate all this heady progress, Seattle staged the Alaska-Yukon-Pacific Exposition, on what is now the University of Washington campus, in 1909. President William Howard Taft attended, and the exposition marked the finish line of a cross-country auto race. The A-Y-P, as it was known, left a legacy of buildings and landscaping at the University of Washington. Drumheller Fountain, better known as Frosh Pond, and the broad walk that seems to lead straight to the snow-capped peak of Mount Rainier, were created for the exposition.

This shantytown, or "Hooverville," photographed in 1937, was a result of poverty caused by the Great Depression. (University of Washington Libraries)

WARTIME, 1942

Here are are vast soldier cities that shelter 50,000 men. Here, too, are lonely island posts manned by veterans of another war, veterans with tattooed arms, gold teeth and rheumatism. Cheerfully and lively, they scan the sea and sky for advancing enemies, betimes playing bagpipes or throwing rocks at wild bears that rob camp kitchens....This Pacific Northwest, by the Great Circle route through the Aleutians, is only about 4,700 miles from Tokyo. Its army posts, naval bases, docks, airplane factories, ship and lumber yards, mines and forests, railway terminals and fishing fleets are all possible objects of enemy attacks.

After the Aleutian thrust, Japanese U-boat shelling of Vancouver and Oregon coasts was no surprise. Portland, Seattle, Tacoma, Vancouver are all exposed to the risk of air raids. But now their all-out defense works, and grim evidence of aggressive warfare meets you at every turn....

—Frederick Simpich, Sr., "Wartime in the Pacific Northwest,"
National Geographic Magazine, October 1942

■ NEW DEAL ERA

As automobiles came into use, county and state governments began paving roads, which allowed Puget Sound residents to make trips east of the Cascades to gather fruit. Beside the Sound, companies that manufactured products from forest wood built pulp mills, giving Washington its first real manufacturing industry. Throughout eastern Washington, the Grange started pushing for public ownership of electric utilities.

Even more monumental were the changes brought by the New Deal, President Franklin Roosevelt's plan to jump-start the U.S. economy out of the Great Depression. The federal government began building huge concrete dams on the Columbia River that would transform the river into a chain of lakes, turning nearly 1,000 square miles of eastern Washington desert into the irrigated Columbia Basin Project, and giving Washington residents a cheap source of electricity. The first big federal dam was completed in 1938 at Bonneville. The largest, Grand Coulee, was finished in 1941. Dams continued to be built into the 1970s. It was a mixed blessing. In addition to generating power and irrigating the desert, the dams flooded the ancient Indian fishing sites at Kettle and Celilo Falls and reduced the river's wild salmon runs from 16 million fish in a good year to 300,000.

At the time, the bargain seemed a good one. Richard Neuberger, later a U.S. Senator from Oregon, wrote in 1938 that those who would benefit would include "thousands of farmers who pump by hand, read by kerosene lamp, cook on wood stoves, and watch their wives and daughters stoop for hours over washboards and churns." Electric lights and appliances transformed rural living. The next industry to be lured to the Northwest was aluminum manufacturing, which required vast quantities of cheap electricity.

■ WORLD WAR II AND BOEING

When World War II began, Washington's aluminum industry was available to smelt metal for the military planes produced by Boeing and other aircraft manufacturers. Even before the United States entered the war, Boeing had started hir-

Debut of a Boeing C-97 Stratofreighter, ca. 1950. (University of Washington Libraries)

ing workers and turning out more planes. In 1939, the company employed 4,000 people, many more workers than any pulp or lumber mill could employ, and just a hint of what was to come. The war made Boeing an industrial giant, employing up to 44,000 people and turning out as many as 362 B-17 bombers in a single month. And the war spawned the world's first large-scale plutonium factory, built at Hanford, in the desert of central Washington, between 1944 and 1946. Hanford provided the plutonium for the first nuclear explosion and for the atom bomb that destroyed Nagasaki.

Thousands of soldiers and sailors passed through Washington to train at Fort Lewis and other military posts, and to board the ships that would take them across the Pacific.

On a warm day in August of 1955, a huge crowd of aerospace executives from around the world gathered on the shore of Lake Washington to watch Seattle's Seafair hydroplane races. Boeing's chief test pilot, Tex Johnston, brought the company's prototype 707 jet in low over the lake and did a full barrel roll at 500 feet. Boeing's president hadn't gotten over his shock before Johnston brought the big plane back and did it again. Jets had clearly arrived. The symbolic event launched Boeing's first commercial jet and started the company's rapid rise to domination of commercial aircraft manufacturing.

The 1960s put Seattle, and Washington, into the national spotlight. The 1962 Seattle World's Fair was followed in short order by the completion of the I-5 freeway, running from Canada to the Columbia River; the arrival of the state's first major-league sports team, the Seattle SuperSonics; and the construction of newer, taller buildings in downtown Seattle.

■ MOUNT ST. HELENS ERUPTS

The 1980s started with a bang, the eruption of Mount St. Helens. The mountain exploded on Sunday morning, May 18, 1980, with a force equal to 27,000 Hiroshima bombs, killing 57 people, vaporizing whole forests, choking the Toutle River and ultimately the lower Columbia with mud, darkening the skies of many eastern Washington farming communities and filling their streets with ash.

The eruption was only one of the shocks that the new decade brought. The recessions of the early 1980s hit Washington harder than they hit many other parts of the United States. More than 100 Northwestern mills closed, eliminating one-third of the state's pre-recession jobs. Statewide unemployment climbed to 12 percent, and in some timber-dependent rural areas, it lingered above 20 percent.

Despite the layoffs and the near collapse of Seafirst, the state's largest bank, things didn't stay grim for long. The mid- and late 1980s soon brought growth, glamour, and notoriety to the state.

By the end of the decade, Boeing's Puget Sound workforce topped 100,000, and people in the Seattle area worried about the effects of unrestricted growth. Boeing wasn't the only local company making money hand over fist. Microsoft, founded in 1975 by two Seattle guys and headquartered in Redmond, became the dominant company in the increasingly huge personal computer software industry.

■ HIGH-TECH BOOM

Microsoft is one of the country's great high-tech success stories. Two local teenagers, Bill Gates and Paul Allen, met at Seattle's Lakeside Academy. Both went off to college but dropped out. They had bigger plans. Starting with little

*Early Microsoft team, including Bill Gates, bottom left, and Paul Allen, bottom right.
(Microsoft Corporation)*

more than an idea, Gates and Allen went to work on a plan to modify the BASIC computer language so that it could be used on small computers sold as hobby kits by a New Mexico firm. They returned to Seattle, bought a system from a company called Seattle Computer Resources, and made it into MS-DOS, which became the heart of most personal computers sold all around the world. Allen left the company; Gates stayed. After Microsoft went public in 1986, he became the world's youngest billionaire.

With Microsoft and hundreds of smaller companies, the Seattle area became a software development center and an axis for the new biotechnology industry. Seattle and Bellevue both developed high-rise skylines. Washington wines started winning medals in international competitions. Seattle acquired a reputation as the coffee capital of the United States. Tacoma, with vacant land and great rail connections on its waterfront, became a major container port virtually overnight, rivaling Seattle. Puget Sound had always been the main supply point for Alaska, and ships from Japan had unloaded freight in both cities in the 19th century; now, as Pacific Rim trade boomed, Seattle and Tacoma had the advantage of being the closest major American ports to Japan. Most of the foreign cargoes passing through their harbors came from Asia, and most—carrying garments, electronics, automobiles, and other products—continued on by rail or truck to the Midwest and East. Together, Seattle and Tacoma were soon shipping as many containers as the Port of New York.

Magazines began calling Seattle the nation's most livable city and the best place to do business. Inevitably, people started complaining about newcomers moving in, driving up real estate prices, and clogging the roads.

■ FISH AND FORESTS

In the 1990s, Washington found itself part of the nation's main environmental battleground. The controversy with perhaps the broadest biological and economic ramifications involved the fate of wild salmon. Salmon runs have been depleted all over Washington. Many have reached the brink of extinction.

Commercial and recreational fisheries have been sustained for years by fish hatcheries, but hatcheries have yielded diminishing returns, and they have only masked and exacerbated the destruction of the wild runs. Nature, though, has a way of

Soleduck Falls in Olympic National Park.

healing her wounds. Wherever streams, creeks, and rivers are cleaned up, and where excess fishing pressures are reduced, Pacific Northwest salmon return, as if by magic. Chum salmon are once again running in the tidewater creeks of the Salish Sea, and sockeye salmon have returned to Lake Washington and its tributaries.

As early as 1884, lumber barons began to notice that timber was becoming scarce. In the 1920s, Clarence Bagley, who had first seen Washington forests in the 1860s, noted that "our boasted heritage of inexhaustible forests is nearly dissipated. Unless the Federal government or the state takes over the gigantic task of reforesting, the lumber industry of Washington will ere long become a matter of past history."

Timber companies started reforesting during World War II, but it takes time for corporate tree farms to pay off. When private land couldn't provide enough timber to feed Washington's mills, heavy logging began in the national forests. Whole communities came to depend on public timber, and the old-growth forest kept shrinking. Generations of environmentalists were appalled, but aside from putting pressure on lobbyists to preserve specific areas as national parks or wilderness, there wasn't a lot they could do.

Until the spotted owl came along. Of course, the northern spotted owl had been there all along, but little was known about it until the early 1970s, when research indicated that it lived in old-growth forests and that its habitat was disappearing rapidly. Under pressure from courts, the federal government listed the owl as threatened in 1990. A group of environmental organizations sued to block federal timber sales in spotted owl territory. In 1991, after hearing arguments in his Seattle courtroom, U.S. District Court Judge William Dwyer enjoined all federal timber sales in western Washington, Oregon, and Northern California, observing that "the records of this case...show a remarkable series of violations of the environmental laws." The injunction lasted until the Clinton administration presented a controversial plan, in 1994, to protect old-growth habitats.

The spotted owl created a controversy when the timber industry threatened its natural habitat.

■ Today's Pleasures

People here would not be battling over the environment if there weren't a lot to fight for. But there is. Within an hour's drive of Seattle, one can be hiking in protected wilderness areas or skiing in alpine terrain. The same is true of Bellevue, Everett, Bellingham, Tacoma, or Spokane. Nature intrudes even when one does not make an effort to be a part of it. Looking up from a city street and seeing the snow on Mount Rainier, watching killer whales off the Seattle waterfront, or seeing a bald eagle swoop by has to affect your point of view. People in Washington relish conversations about trails and campsites. It doesn't seem entirely coincidental that REI, Eddie Bauer, and other retailers of outdoor clothing and gear have flourished in Seattle.

Until recently, the outdoors constituted the region's chief—some might say its *only*—attraction; except, of course, for the prospect of steady employment whenever Boeing was on a roll. In the late 1940s, the English orchestra conductor Sir Thomas Beecham called Seattle a "cultural dustbin." Those days are long gone. Not only do Seattle and other Washington cities have the requisite theaters and opera and symphony orchestras, they have acquired a certain cachet. People have been moving here from all over the country, and for a variety of reasons. Most of the current attention has focused on Seattle, which has become known as the espresso capital of the country, a center for indie rock, a cool place to be. The city has certainly earned its reputation for coffee. The drink is so ubiquitous—even dry cleaners and car washes serve espresso—and the culture grown up around it so palpable, that not long ago the *Seattle Times* ran a long article about the subculture of *baristas,* the mostly young people who make espresso at the city's many cafés and sidewalk carts.

But neither the coffee nor the music is exclusive to Seattle. The now defunct Seattle rock band Nirvana actually got its start playing in Olympia, and even Forks, an economically depressed Olympic Peninsula logging town, has a drive-in espresso stand.

Many people associate Washington with rain and months of gray, damp weather. It's true, it does rain a lot here, but when the sun comes out and splashes the mountains with light, it all seems worthwhile. People head for the mountains and take to the parks.

SEATTLE

S E A T T L E

SEATTLE SITS AMONG saltwater bays, lakes, and forested mountains. To the west, the waters of Puget Sound lap up against piers and beaches, and to the east, Lake Washington delineates the city. On most days, you can see craggy, snow-covered peaks across the Sound from downtown, as well as the snow cone of 14,411-foot Mount Rainier to the south; on a very clear day you can see 10,750-foot Mount Baker to the north. The high-rises of the downtown business district rival the city's hills in height and on most days can be seen far up and down the Sound.

The pioneer founders of Seattle envisioned a city to rival the world's greatest (they originally named it New York), but locals think of their metropolis as a collection of urban villages, each with a unique personality. Much of this has to do with the way Seattle is spread out over several hills and valleys, and split into sections by the Lake Washington Ship Canal, Lake Union, Green Lake, the Duwamish River, and I-5.

Queen Anne Hill overlooks downtown Seattle. Mount Rainier looms in the distance.

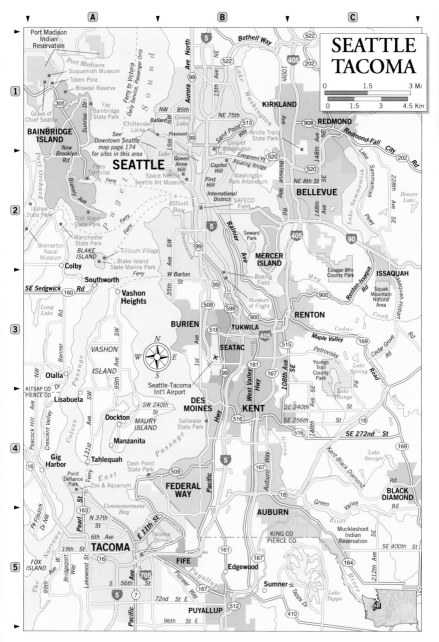

SEATTLE TACOMA

0   1.5   3 Mi

0   1.5   3   4.5 Km

Port Madison Indian Reservation

Port Madison

Suquamish Museum

Totem Pole

Bloedel Reserve

Fay Bainbridge State Park

305

Grave of Chief Seattle

BAINBRIDGE ISLAND

Sunrise Dr

New Brooklyn Rd

See Downtown Seattle map page 174 for sites in this area

Chittenden Locks

Ferry to Victoria, Daily Service, Passenger Only

Ferry Terminal

Blakely Ave

Ferry

SEATTLE

Ballard

NW NW

NW 85th

15th

Fremont

99

Green Lake

Lake Union

Queen Anne Hill

Space Needle
Seattle Art Museum

Capitol Hill

First Hill

International District

SAFECO Field

Elliott Bay

Bothell Way

Aurora Ave North

15th Ave

NE

522

5

NE 75th

Sand Point Way

513

Univ of Washington

Evergreen Pt
Floating Bridge

Washington Park Arboretum

522

405

202

100th

KIRKLAND

908

REDMOND

Redmond-Fall City

148th Ave NE

520

520

NE 8th St

BELLEVUE

Bellevue

148th Ave

202

228th Ave SE

Beaver Lake

Lake Sammamish

Lake Sammamish Pkwy

Lake Washington

Ilahee State Park

Fort Ward State Park

Manchester State Park

Bremerton Naval Museum

BLAKE ISLAND

Colby

Southworth

Tillicum Village

Blake Island State Marine Park

Ferry

Vashon Heights

SE Sedgwick Rd

160

Long Lake

Banner Rd

VASHON ISLAND

99th Ave SW

Colvos Passage

Olalla

KITSAP CO
PIERCE CO

Lisabuela

Dockton

MAURY ISLAND

SW 240th St

Saltwater State Park

Manzanita

Peacock Hill Ave NW

Crescent Valley

131st

Tahlequah

Dash Point State Park

Gig Harbor

Point Defiance Park
Zoo & Aquarium

Ferry

East Passage

509

FOX ISLAND

16

163

Pt Fosdick Dr NW

Pearl St

The Narrows

99th Ave W

Bridgeport Way

Lakewood Dr

19th St

TACOMA

N 37th St

6th Ave

Commencement Bay

Tacoma Dome

FIFE

16

S 56th St

705

5

7

72nd St E

Pacific

PUYALLUP

96th St E

512

167

Pioneer Way

Puyallup

Edgewood

Sumner

W Tapps Dr

Lake Tapps

410

164

212th Ave

Dumwamish

5

Rainier Ave

Seward Park

Boeing Field

Museum of Flight

W Barton St

35th Ave SW

99

509

599

900

MERCER ISLAND

May

Cougar Mtn County Park

90

ISSAQUAH

Squak Mountain Natural Area

Issaquah-Hobart Rd

RENTON

Renton-Issaquah Rd

900

Maple Valley

169

Cedar River

Petrovisky Rd

Youngs Trail County Park

Cedar Grove Rd

Lake Spring

Lake Youngs

SE 272nd St

169

Lake Sawyer

Kent-Black Diamond Rd

BLACK DIAMOND

Rd

18

BURIEN

1st Ave

518

TUKWILA

405

515

SEATAC

181

99

Seattle-Tacoma Int'l Airport

DES MOINES

SW 240th St

KENT

516

SE 240th St

SE 256th St

516

148th Ave SE

SE 272nd St

18

167

West Valley Hwy

108th Ave SE

Auburn Way

AUBURN

Green River

Valley Rd

Muckleshoot Indian Reservation

SE 400th St

KING CO
PIERCE CO

161

167

FEDERAL WAY

Pacific Hwy S

Green River

18

On many days, the city is shrouded in mist. Its glass-and-steel monoliths are swathed in fog, and seagulls drift like ghosts between the downtown office towers. The lugubrious "wail-honk" of a ferry horn sounds somewhere beyond the shrouded waterfront as clean-cut citizens in Eddie Bauer raincoats clutch briefcases and lattes and wait for traffic lights to change.

When the sun comes out, though, sidewalk cafés on the piers and picnic tables on the decks of Waterfront Park fill up with Seattleites who abandon their workday schedules with the speed of a sunburst. Sunlight brings out uncommon levity in the residents of the gray city by the Sound. On one sunny afternoon, I watched a staid-looking businessman in a three-piece suit, briefcase in hand, raincoat draped over his left arm, stride into the Waterfall Fountain downtown and emerge on the far side slightly moistened, with a smile.

Once you get to know Seattle, you'll learn that it hardly ever rains in summer, never mind how much residents moan and groan about the constant overcast. But perhaps Seattleites need the specter of rain to justify the energy they radiate. They never sit still for long and are always up to something, whether it's walking, running, sailing the Sound, or hiking in the mountains. Maybe it's the Scandinavian work ethic that Norwegian, Swedish, Finnish, and Icelandic immigrants brought to this area early in the 20th century. Along with that energy and industry came a lighthearted, self-mocking humor. A favorite old folk song, "The Old Settler," goes:

No longer a slave of ambition,
I laugh at the world and its shams,
As I think of my happy condition
Surrounded by acres of clams.

■ AMBITIOUS BEGINNINGS

The first settlers to establish themselves in Seattle, in 1851, were a party of Americans from the Midwest under the leadership of Arthur Denny. Though Denny never said in his autobiography what made him pull up stakes, he did admit that he wanted to find a place where he would be the first to put down roots and make a killing in real estate. When his party reached Portland, Oregon, Denny was dismayed to find a booming town of 2,000 people. He had come too late. That's when he heard about an unsettled place called Puget Sound.

The Dennys joined forces with another pioneer family, the Terrys, who hailed from New York, and together they established their new town on a sandy spit just south of Elliott Bay. They called it New York. It soon gained the epithet *Alki,* a Chinook jargon word meaning "by and by," a name the site has kept to this day. The Dennys and Terrys soon discovered that in bad weather, or at low tide, the exposed sloping beach of their site was a poor place from which to load ships. But load they did, as the town's emerging income came from lumber sold to ship captains who sailed north from another enterprising place on the coast, San Francisco.

■ SEATTLE RELOCATED

Reluctantly, the settlers picked up their belongings and moved across Elliott Bay, a less desirable place, but one where ships could sail right up to the shore. They built houses here, on steep, overgrown hillsides. It was a wet place, cut by deep ravines. Springs flowed down from the bluffs and water, seemingly everywhere, dripped from the moss-covered trees. But the trees were soon cut down. Early pictures of Seattle show mostly stumps, not trees, between the cabins. The tree cutting accelerated when Henry Yesler built a sawmill, making timber-cutting the

Yesler Way, the original "Skid Road," so called because of the log skids placed in the street to enable timber to be moved easily to the docks. Pioneer Square now exists where the flagpole appears in this photo. (Museum of History and Industry)

SEATTLE

new city's main industry. Yesler used rocks carried as ballast on inbound ships to build a wharf hundreds of feet out into the bay, so the largest ships could unload on any tide. A handsome plaque near Colman Dock marks the site of that first wharf.

Yesler's dock was also the landing place for the early steamboats that plied the waters of Puget Sound. One amusing anecdote tells of a group of legislators bound for Olympia on the *Eliza Anderson*. Wakened one morning by what they thought was the steamer's whistle, they stumbled down to the wharf on a dark, rainy morning and headed straight for the open door of a boiler room that promised warmth. But the "ship" didn't appear to move from the dock. Checking his watch and noting that it was well past sailing time, one of the legislators tapped the fireman on the back and asked, "May I ask when we are going to pull out for Olympia?"

"Olympia?" replied the fireman. "This sawmill don't run to Olympia." The legislators had mistaken the mill's boiler room for that of the steamer. By now, the *Eliza Anderson* had left, and the lawmakers had to return to the provincial capital by canoe.

The regrading of James Street allowed for the construction of the cable car system.
(Museum of History and Industry)

■ On to the Klondike

A little over a century ago, Seattle became the point of departure for prospectors heading to Alaska and the Yukon during the Klondike gold rush. The excitement started one day in 1897 with the arrival of the ship *Portland,* which happily unloaded its "ton of gold" near Colman Dock. Seattle's mayor at the time, W. D. Wood, as enthusiastic as everyone else at the thought of getting rich, immediately deserted his post to join a shipload of eager-beavers going north.

Colman and other area docks served as the headquarters of the Mosquito Fleet, the flotilla of boats that ferried passengers and freight around Puget Sound from the mid-19th century through World War II, making Seattle the hub of local trade. Vestiges of these docks—double rows of gray pilings—still march two by two into deep water at spots where steamboats used to call.

■ Colorful Characters

Early Seattle was a bit rough around the edges, a place of unlimited optimism, despite streets that sometimes became so muddy that horses and wagons might get stuck in them. When the Northern Pacific Railway snubbed Seattle in favor of Tacoma, denizens decided to build a railroad of their own. They didn't get far, but they did scare the railroad moguls into connecting Seattle to the main line.

The town's early population was lively, to say the least. Native American women sold butter clams on the sidewalks of the business district, and saloons boomed, especially in the Lava Bed—the bustling red-light district south of Yesler's mill. One of early Seattle's more colorful characters was David "Doc" Maynard, who moved to Seattle after he was kicked out of more sedate Olympia. Maynard had married a widow he met on the Oregon Trail, without first getting a divorce from the wife he had left behind in Ohio. Things became tense when his first wife sailed into port, but the two supposedly settled matters amicably, and Maynard continued to live with wife number two.

Maynard was known as a man who always helped folks in need. He had filed a homestead claim on what is now downtown Seattle but died a poor man because he sold most of his land below its value, and in some cases even gave it away, to help the budding city grow. Nard Jones reported in his book on Seattle that Maynard was given the largest funeral in the city's history when he died in 1873, and adds, "An unidentified citizen, whether friend or enemy is not known, stood up to say, 'Without Doc Maynard...Seattle would never have reached its present size. Perhaps, had it not been for Doctor Maynard, Seattle might not be here now.'"

One reason Maynard did not get along with civic-minded teetotalers like Henry Yesler and Arthur Denny is that he drank too much. In *Totem Tales of Old Seattle*, Gordon Newell and Don Sherwood record an argument Maynard had with Denny when the latter asked him to attend a temperance lecture at Yesler's hall. "'Temperance!" Doc roared. "That's the only thing I believe in taking in moderation. In fact I'm a total abstainer."

Early Seattle may have had more citizens of the Maynard ilk than of the Denny and Yesler kind, because vice prospered well into the early decades of the 20th century, despite repeated civic campaigns to stamp it out.

By 1899, most of Seattle's 40,000 inhabitants lived and worked in the 50-plus blocks of one- and two-story clapboard buildings that comprised downtown. The big fire of 1889 burned most of Seattle's waterfront business district but spared residents on the hill. The gutsy citizenry didn't sit around Yesler's cookhouse complaining, however. Instead, they erected a new downtown, of brick, and elevated the streets a full story above their previous level to solve the city's chronic sewage problem. Elevating the streets meant that many ground-floor storefronts were now belowground, thus creating Underground Seattle, a major tourist attraction.

■ PIONEER SQUARE   *map page 58, C-4*

The city's original 19th-century center was Pioneer Square. This name applies both to the triangular cobblestone park on First Avenue, where James Street meets Yesler Way, and to the ornate brick and stone buildings at the south end of downtown. The triangular square itself marks the site where Henry Yesler built the first steam-driven sawmill on the shore of Elliott Bay. First Avenue, then called Front Street, was the waterfront in those days, and logs cut on the forested ridge above town were skidded down what is now Yesler Way to the mill, where they were sawed into boards that built the embryonic city of Seattle.

Yesler Way was the original Skid Road, a label that most of the country has since corrupted to "skid row." The street got its name because logs were skidded down it but also because it marked the boundary between the city's business district and the Lava Bed red-light district to the south (called the Tenderloin after the fire, and now known as the Pioneer Square district).

The well-preserved facades of the buildings in Pioneer Square lend historical continuity to an area packed with art galleries, bookstores, and missions serving

Victorian-era buildings behind the Pioneer Square totem pole, a replica of one stolen by early Seattleites from the Tlingit Indians.

the needy. For a taste of local color, sign up for the **Underground Seattle tour,** which starts at Doc Maynard's Public House at First Avenue and James Street, across from Pioneer Square. This restored pub with its carved back bar gives you a feel for what Seattle was like in the early days; the rock bands that perform here on Friday and Saturday nights put you in touch with what's happening in Seattle now. On sunny days, you can sit at one of the tables outside and watch Pioneer Square's highlife and lowlife flow by (expect to be panhandled; it's a time-honored Seattle custom). *Underground tour, 608 First Avenue; pub, 610 First Avenue; 206-682-4646 for tour and pub.*

The **totem pole** in Pioneer Square is a replica of one that was spirited away from a Tlingit village by a "goodwill committee" of prominent Seattle citizens in 1899. When the Tlingits learned where their missing pole had gone, they demanded and received payment for their purloined property. The pole's figures relate several Tlingit tales, including one about a raven and a mink that go to sea in the belly of a killer whale.

SEATTLE

Microbrewery pub in Pioneer Square.

For a peek at Seattle's role in the gold rush of 1897, see the exhibits at the city's outpost of the **Klondike Gold Rush National Historic Park.** *Union Trust Annex, 117 South Main Street; 206-553-7220.*

At the **Waterfall Garden** (South Main Street and Second Avenue South), an enclosed courtyard, the soothing sound of a tall waterfall shuts out the noise of the city. Tables and chairs placed near the water are usually packed at lunchtime with workers from nearby offices. A few blocks to the south are two stadiums, Qwest Field, the high-tech home of the Seattle Seahawks pro football team, and Safeco Field, where major league baseball's Seattle Mariners play.

■ INTERNATIONAL DISTRICT   *map page 58, C/D-4*

Inland from the stadiums, the International District holds the city's largest concentration of Asian restaurants, food stores, and social services. Many of the area's first residents were Chinese, and their descendants have largely moved on, though some older Chinese have remained to run shops and other concerns that have been in Seattle for generations. In recent decades, people from many Asian lands, most notably Vietnam, have settled here.

The exhibits at the **Wing Luke Museum** document the lives of Asian immigrants to the Pacific Northwest. The collection includes costumes, crafts, photographs, and Chinese medicines. *407 Seventh Avenue South; 206-623-5124.*

The pan-Asian **Uwajimaya** department store sells groceries and sake, kitchenwares, garden tools, and Japanese fabrics, papers, and objets d'art. Also here are a food court and a branch of the Kinokuniya Bookstore, which specializes in Asian-language texts and periodicals. *600 Fifth Avenue South; 206-624-6248.*

■ DOWNTOWN AND THE WATERFRONT *map page 58*

From downtown hotels, it is only a short walk into the central business district. The 42-story **Smith Tower** (506 Second Avenue) was the tallest building west of the Mississippi River when completed in 1914, and it remained the tallest building in Seattle for 55 years.

High-rises dwarf the Smith Tower these days, the result of an office-building boom in the 1980s that transformed the look and feel of downtown Seattle. The

Smith Tower under construction behind the Grand Trunk Pier, where Puget Sound ferries, known as the Mosquito Fleet, docked. (Puget Sound Maritime Historical Society)

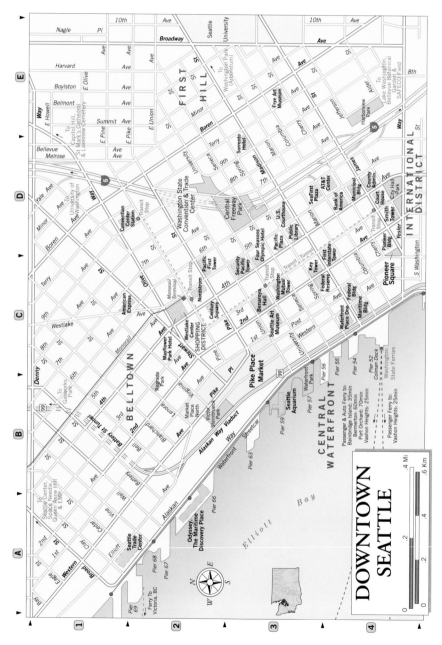

DOWNTOWN SEATTLE

city's skyline stretches north and northwest from the Smith Tower and includes another noteworthy high-rise, the 76-story **Columbia Center** (701 Fifth Avenue). At 997 feet, it is Seattle's tallest skyscraper. The skyline's most distinctive element, north of downtown, is the **Space Needle** (400 Broad Street).

■ THE WATERFRONT *map page 58, B-3/4*

Although it is no longer Seattle's economic focal point, the downtown waterfront area remains vital to the city's character. Many old piers have been transformed into shops, museums, restaurants, and amusements. **Harbor tours** depart from **Pier 55** weekdays and **Pier 57** on weekends, providing passengers with great views of the city skyline, the docks of Harbor Island, and the Ship Canal, a narrow waterway cutting a gorge from Shilshole Bay to Lake Union and Lake Washington. Some tour boats traverse the Ballard Locks, the world's second largest after those of the Panama Canal.

Many visitors stroll the mile and a half north to **Pier 70,** now a commercial complex, detouring over the harbor on the boardwalks and fishing piers of Waterfront Park, and returning on a 1927 streetcar.

On Pier 59, children can get a sense of life beneath Puget Sound in the underwater dome of the recently renovated and expanded **Seattle Aquarium** (206-386-4320). A short walk south of Pier 59 along First Avenue to the corner of University Street takes you to the newly expanded **Seattle Art Museum,** designed in a flashy postmodern style by Robert Venturi. The grand entrance hall to the five-story structure is connected to state-of-the-art galleries by an approach that makes you think you've wandered through the service entrance. The museum's extensive collection surveys Asian, Native American, African, Oceanic, and pre-Columbian art. Highlights include the anonymous 14th-century Buddhist masterwork *Monk at the Moment of Enlightenment* and Jackson Pollock's *Sea Change*.

Outside the museum you'll see the tall perpetual-motion sculpture *Hammering Man,* by Connecticut sculptor Jonathan Borofsky. The piece has had its share of adventures. When first installed, the huge steel form toppled over—fortunately not flattening any workers or pedestrians, but sustaining enough damage that the sculpture had to be shipped back to Connecticut for repairs. After it was installed a second time, a group of local artists, working under cover of darkness, fastened a huge ball and chain to one leg. Some people liked the idea, but the museum promptly removed the fetters. *100 University Street; 206-654-3100.*

Day Trips by Ferry

Puget Sound ferries are Washington State's number-one tourist attraction. On several, you can travel as a passenger or bring your car; other ferries are passenger-only. Avoid rush-hour traffic: eastbound in the morning, westbound in the afternoon and evening. A high-speed passenger-only catamaran also runs from Seattle to the San Juan Islands and to Victoria, on Vancouver Island. *Washington State Ferries, 206-464-6400, outside Washington and British Columbia; 888-808-7977 in Washington and British Columbia; www.wsdot.wa.gov/ferries*

Seattle to Bainbridge Island. The Puget Sound crossing to Bainbridge Island is popular. The big boat drops you off in Eagle Harbor, in the heart of **Winslow,** a former logging town turned suburb. The Winslow waterfront is made for walking. Pick up the fixings for a picnic at Seattle's Pike Place Market and picnic right off the ferry at **Waterfront Park.**

After lunch, walk to **Bainbridge Island Vineyards and Winery**, where Gerard Bentryn sells wines made from local grapes and strawberries. *682 State Highway; 206-842-9463.*

You can also sample the food at one of the waterfront cafés, among them **Pegasus Coffee,** at the foot of Madison Avenue, and **Bainbridge Bakers,** at Winslow Green. For trips into the interior of Bainbridge Island, or to do a loop trip and return to Seattle via Bremerton (or via the Kingston/Edmonds ferry), you'll need a car.

Seattle to Bremerton. You'll enjoy this trip if you're a navy buff, as Bremerton has one of the country's largest naval bases and shipyards. The **Bremerton Naval Museum,** near the ferry terminal, has displays going back to the days of the sailing navy. The USS *Turner Joy,* docked nearby, saw action off Vietnam and played a role in the Gulf of Tonkin affair; it's open for self-guided tours. *130 Washington Avenue; 360-479-7447.*

You can take a boat tour of the **Navy Shipyard** and a mothballed fleet through Kitsap Harbor Tours. Boats depart hourly from the boardwalk on the waterfront. *360-377-8924.*

Bremerton's waterfront has several restaurants and bars, the most notable being the **Boat Shed** on Shore Drive. You'll need a car to take a loop trip back to Seattle via the Bainbridge Island ferry. The **Naval Undersea Museum,** in nearby Keyport, has the country's largest collection of undersea artifacts, mines, and torpedoes; displays on the ocean environment; and an antique submarine. *Highway 3, Keyport; 360-396-4148.*

The **Marine Science Center,** in Poulsbo, has touch tanks for kids and a giant octopus. *18743 Front Street; 360-779-5549.*

Other Puget Sound Ferries. Additional ferries travel from Fauntleroy Cove in West Seattle to Vashon Island, from Edmonds (north of Seattle) to Kingston on the northern Kitsap Peninsula, and from Mukilteo in Snohomish County (south of Everett) to Whidbey Island.

Seattle to Victoria, B.C. (Canada). The *Victoria Clipper* runs from the Seattle waterfront to Victoria, British Columbia, and to Friday Harbor and Rosario on San Juan Island. *206-448-5000.*

A ferry crosses Puget Sound as the sun sets over the Olympic Mountains.

Benaroya Hall is the concert facility Seattle Symphony Music Director Gerard Schwarz built, or, rather, the one he got as a reward for staying in Seattle after gaining international fame (he cofounded the New York Chamber Symphony and recently became music director of the Royal Liverpool Philharmonic Orchestra). The hall, completed in 1998, takes up the entire block across Second Avenue from the Seattle Art Museum. *200 University Street; 206-215-4747.*

■ PIKE PLACE MARKET   *map page 58, B/C-3*

Pike Place Market, which perches above the waterfront, is a riot of color. Fish stalls gleam with silver-scaled salmon and red rockfish, pearly squid, and orange Dungeness crab, bright red shrimp, and blue-black mussels. Produce stalls are piled high with red and green apples, golden pears, crimson cherries, purple plums, orange chanterelles, cream-colored oyster mushrooms, and brown morels and shiitakes. It's a hectic scene, but fun. Fishmongers hurl huge salmon back and forth, joking

Pike Place Market in 1915.
(Museum of History and Industry)

Pike Place Market remains the best place to buy fresh fruit, vegetables, and seafood in the city.

with each other and their customers, who jostle with tourists. The market is one place where you'll see few people without a smile. The mood here is invigorating, but it can also be exhausting. Relax and take it easy. Treat yourself to a cup of coffee or a glass of wine, grab a window seat at a café or restaurant, and watch the freighter and shipping boats far below in Elliott Bay. Or buy picnic fixings, head down to Waterfront Park, snag a table, and enjoy an alfresco meal.

In season, you'll find fresh strawberries, raspberries, blueberries, melons, apricots, peaches, nectarines, and quinces. Cheese shops stock a sophisticated hodgepodge of cheeses, and butchers sell some of the city's best racks of lamb, steaks, and sausages. Bakeries specialize in tantalizing French, Greek, and Chinese pastries, and restaurants serve everything from plain sandwiches, spaghetti and meatballs, and dim sum to fresh fish cooked and sauced to perfection.

The market began back in 1907, when Seattle's civic leaders and businessmen, influenced by socialist ideas, started to think up ways to eliminate the middleman. In 1970, the city caught the nationwide redevelopment virus that replaced beat-up but picturesque old downtowns with Brutalist concrete structures. It looked as if

(following pages) Downtown Seattle at dusk.

HOMES AWAY FROM HOME

Seattle has its share of fine homes, cute cottages, and elegant apartment buildings, stylish architectural testaments to the rainy city's endearing way with hearth and home. But the city also has many fine hotels that carefully balance coziness and cosmopolitan panache.

The **Fairmont Olympic Hotel** (411 University Street; 206-621-1700 or 800-223-8772) has been the classiest place in town since it opened in 1929. The elaborate lobby is worth a special visit (and perhaps a drink).

The **Mayflower Park Hotel** (405 Olive Way; 206-623-8700 or 800-426-5100) isn't much to look at from the outside, but it has a handsomely appointed lobby and Seattle's most urbane bar, Oliver's, whose tall windows overlook one of the city's busiest intersections. Oliver's is a perfect place to wait out Seattle's notoriously bad rush hour over one of the best martinis in town.

The boutique **Sorrento Hotel** (900 Madison Street; 206-622-6400 or 800-426-1265) occupies a 1908 Italianate building on First Hill. The ornate lobby is a fine setting for a warming drink on a rainy day. The hotel uses the top floor dining room for private functions, but the antique elevator to it is worth a look.

the market's days were numbered. Demolition plans were derailed, however, by a local architecture professor, Victor Steinbrueck (he is memorialized by a grassy park at the market's north end), who spearheaded a grassroots campaign.

A series of ramps leads to the Hillclimb, a broad stairway flanked by shops and restaurants that extends from the cliff on which the market rests down to the waterfront. Beneath the arcade, the "down under" section of the market descends several stories to Western Avenue, where shops selling inexpensive imported olive oil, exotic spices, folk art—even parrots—can be found. The Main Arcade and the open-air vendors' stalls on the east side of Pike Place are the central arteries of the market. At the Main Arcade's north end, you'll find silver bracelets, pottery, carved wooden bowls, and other handmade objects.

Many shops have been here almost from the beginning. **Three Girls Bakery,** founded in 1912, sells wonderful breads and pastries. **De Laurenti Specialty Foods Market,** which opened in 1928, is a classic Italian deli with a great selection of olive oils, wines, and cheeses.

■ REGRADE AND BELLTOWN   *map page 58, B/C-1/2*

The streets north of Pike Place Market run almost level to Seattle Center and steep Queen Anne Hill. The Regrade hasn't always been so flat. At the dawn of the 20th century, the rounded cone of Denny Hill rose 140 feet above what is today the more level neighborhood of Belltown. The missing hill is a non-monument to city engineer Reginald Thomson, who wanted Seattle's downtown to stretch to the base of Queen Anne Hill, the result being one continuous business district. And, darn it, Denny Hill was in the way. Determined to flatten things, Thomson and his workmen, between 1902 and 1930, sluiced Denny Hill into Elliott Bay.

Today's Belltown, bounded by Queen Anne Hill, Pike Place Market, and First and Third Avenues, is worth checking out for its mix of neo-grunge attitude and bohemian chic. To get a feel for the neighborhood, check out Second Avenue near Bell Street, where you'll find restaurants, night clubs, florists, antiques dealers, art galleries, bookstores, and several impressively stocked music stores.

A few property owners fought against the Regrade, with the result that their properties were left atop sluiced-away pinnacles. (Washington State Historical Society)

Towering over Seattle Center is the **Space Needle,** the trademark structure built for the 1962 World's Fair, an event that drew John F. Kennedy and Elvis Presley. According to the "Official 1962 World's Fair Guide," the Space Needle is 606 feet tall. Its legs are 500 feet high, which puts the restaurant on its top at just above 500 feet and the observation deck a bit higher. There is an admission charge for the observation deck, but you ride free if you have a reservation for the restaurant. The top rests on a turntable mounted on a pair of twin rails and revolves 360 degrees once every hour. There are two high-speed elevators, but in case the power goes off, you'll be glad to know you can escape down two stairways—each with 832 steps. The restaurant's food does not match the view. *400 Broad Street, at Fourth Avenue; 206-905-2100.*

Seattle Center, a 74-acre cluster of buildings and gardens, has something for everyone, from operas at the Opera House to plays at the **Bagley Wright Theater** (155 Mercer Street; 206-443-2222) to big traveling shows at the exciting **Pacific Science Center** (200 Second Avenue North; 206-443-2001).

The **Seattle Children's Museum** (305 Harrison Street; 206-441-1768) is in the basement of the Center House, and the Fun Forest amusement park has carnival rides. Pro basketball's Seattle SuperSonics play in **Key Arena.** Crowds jam the Northwest Folklife Festival (206-684-7300) on Memorial Day weekend and the Bumbershoot (206-684-7337) musical extravaganza on Labor Day weekend.

All the buildings within Seattle Center looked pretty much the same until Microsoft billionaire Paul Allen commissioned architect Frank Gehry to design the ultramodern **EMP (Experience Music Project).** A museum of rock 'n' roll and blues, the unusual complex includes a Sky Church concert hall for live performances, a sound lab, exhibition galleries, and a cinema. EMP's permanent collection has more than 80,000 artifacts, including Quincy Jones's trumpet from his Seattle days, a 12-string guitar once owned by Roger McGuinn of the Byrds, and the original Stratocaster guitar used on the Kingsmen's recording of "Louie, Louie." There's also a Jimi Hendrix Gallery showcasing, among other things, the Stratocaster Hendrix played at Woodstock in 1969 and the kimono he wore at the Newport Pop Festival. You don't have to pay museum admission to enjoy the Turntable restaurant, Liquid Lounge bar, or EMP Store. *325 Fifth Avenue North; 206-367-5483.*

The Space Needle, originally built for the 1962 World's Fair, has become a popular symbol of the city.

SEATTLE

■ SEATTLE MONORAIL   *map page 58, B/C-1/2*

The Seattle Monorail whisks two million passengers each year between Seattle Center and the **Westlake Center** (1601 Fifth Avenue; 206-467-1600), a mall with several dozen stores and many restaurants. The 0.9-mile ride takes about 90 seconds. The monorail was built as a demonstration project for the 1962 Seattle World's Fair by Alweg, a German company that had designed systems for Disneyland and cities in Europe and Japan. Construction took 10 months and the cost, $3.5 million, was underwritten by Alweg.

The monorail was never meant to be permanent, but it proved such a success with residents that the city purchased the system in 1965 from the fair's sponsor. The price tag: a mere $600,000. Over the years, the monorail has become a touchstone for environmentalists and urban planners around the world who consider it a reasonably priced, eco-friendly solution to the problems of mass transit and urban pollution. With Seattle's burgeoning population causing increased car traffic, there is talk of expanding the system. Seattle voters turned down a proposal to extend the monorail to Sea-Tac airport.

Seattle Monorail, passing through EMP.

Houseboats on Lake Union near Terry Pettus Park.

■ LAKE UNION   *map page 49, B-1/2*

In the center of town, between Queen Anne and Capitol Hills, lies Lake Union. Once a center of shipbuilding and repair, the lake still has commercial shipyards, marina space, and hundreds of houseboats, as well as waterfront restaurants. A trail runs along the southern waterfront past lawns, restaurants, and docks where large yachts are moored.

Views from the lake include the clapboard houses of the Wallingford neighborhood on the north shore, sailboats crossing the lake's quiet waters, and floatplanes picking up passengers bound for Victoria, the San Juan Islands, or remote fishing spots in the mountains.

The **Lake Washington Ship Canal,** leading west from Lake Union to Puget Sound and east into Lake Washington, is a commercial waterway. Restaurants, shipyards, office buildings, and marinas crowd the shore, and fishing boats, yachts, and houseboats bob in the water. The houseboats moored along the eastern shore, once something of a floating low-rent district, have gone upscale in recent times.

SEATTLE

■ BALLARD LOCKS AND BALLARD *map page 49, A/B-1*

You can while away an enjoyable afternoon at the **Hiram M. Chittenden Locks,** known locally as the Ballard Locks, watching boats pass through. The locks were completed in 1917. Of the 75,000 boats that use them each year, most are pleasure craft, but research vessels, commercial ships, and sightseeing boats also "get a lift." On the way to the locks from the parking lot is the splendid **Carl S. English, Jr. Botanical Garden,** which contains more than 500 species and 1,500 varieties from around the world. On the south side of the locks, salmon and steelhead trout heading to their spawning grounds swim up the 21-level **fish ladder** that runs parallel to the locks. The ladder allows them to make the steep trip gradually. *3015 NW 54th Street; 206-783-7059.*

Beyond the palm trees at Chittenden is the Ballard neighborhood, homeport for most of the Alaskan fishing fleet, whose vessels have cruised north every year since the end of World War I to catch salmon. Halibut boats, crabbers, and big-bottom trawlers make the northward voyage too.

(above) Asahel Curtis photographed the launching of the lumber schooner Minnie A. Caine *in 1900. (Washington State Historical Society)*
(opposite) Customers practice climbing at the REI flagship store near Lake Union.

Dale Chihuly (foreground, right) creates one of his glass sculptures.

The Ballard area has attracted artistic types, the most famous being the innovative glass sculptor Dale Chihuly, who was born and raised in Tacoma. Chihuly studied glass-blowing at the Venini factory in Venice in the late 1960s and in 1971 cofounded the Pilchuck Glass School in Washington.

Chihuly's studio is closed to the public, but you'll find his works all over Seattle. Benaroya Hall (200 University Street) contains two light sculptures, and several of his works are usually on display at the Foster/White Gallery (123 South Jackson Street) in Pioneer Square. The lobby of the Seattle Aquarium (Pier 59) holds one of Chihuly's *Seaform* installations, and the lobby of the Sheraton Hotel (1400 Sixth Avenue) is a showcase for his white *Floral Forms #2.*

The foyer at the University of Washington's Meany Theater (Campus Parkway and 15th Avenue NE) is decorated with six of the artist's wall chandeliers, created from hundreds of red and yellow chunks of glass. Additional works can be seen at, among other places, City Centre (1420 Fifth Avenue) and at the Washington State Convention Center (800 Convention Place).

■ FREMONT   *map page 49, A/B-1*

The motto of colorful Fremont, across the Ship Canal from Queen Anne Hill, is "De Libertus Quirkus," meaning "the freedom to be peculiar." Its restaurants, pubs, stores, and giddy street sculpture make the small neighborhood well worth a stop. To get here, take Mercer Avenue off I-5, turn right at the first light, then left at the second light. Follow Westlake Avenue until you pass under the Aurora Avenue Bridge. Cross the Fremont Avenue drawbridge and you've arrived.

The bronze pedestrians in *Waiting for the Interurban* (Fremont Avenue North and North 34th Street) have been waiting for a bus since Seattle artist Richard Beyer's sculpture went up in the late 1970s. Look close and you'll see a dog's head popping out between one passenger's legs. Look even closer and you'll see that the pooch's face is a human one, said to be that of the artist with whom Beyer competed for the sculpture's commission.

The *Fremont Troll* (North 36th Street under the Aurora Avenue Bridge), a two-ton concrete sculpture of a figure crushing a Volkswagen Beetle in his left hand, is a city icon. Locals tend to love or hate the goofy behemoth, but mostly the former.

The Fremont Troll, snacking under the Aurora Avenue Bridge.

Equally eye-catching is the **statue of Lenin** (North 36th Street at Evanston Avenue) a businessperson "acquired" from a defunct Eastern Bloc country.

Locals say the **Fremont Rocket** (Evanston Avenue and Fremont Place North), a 53-foot sculpture created out of a surplus 1950s rocket, marks the center of the universe.

A great place for hanging out and sipping local brews while noshing on pub fare is the **Red Door** (3401 Evanston Avenue; 206-547-2022), one block west of the Fremont Bridge.

Near Fremont are three attractions of note. The **Woodland Park Zoo** (5500 Phinney Avenue North; 206-684-4800) has won awards for its habi-

Vladimir Lenin, liberated from a former Eastern Bloc country, holds forth in Fremont.

tats, in which animals roam free. The Asian Elephant Forest is worth a look, as is the African Savanna. The Northern Trail is a well-designed refuge for brown bears, wolves, mountain goats, and otters. **Green Lake** (East Green Lake Drive North and West Green Lake Drive North) contains jogging and bicycling trails and supports a variety of recreational activities. **Gasworks Park** (North Northlake Way and Meridian Avenue North), where summer concerts take place, occupies the site of a former gas plant. The 20-acre park is prettier than its name suggests.

■ FIRST AND CAPITOL HILLS   *map page 49, B-2*

East of downtown, across the freeway, rise First and Capitol Hills. One pleasant way to walk across to either is to follow paths through the shrubbery, flowers, and waterfalls at Freeway Park, a garden sanctuary built atop I-5.

The more southerly First Hill is sometimes called "Pill Hill" because it holds the city's largest concentration of hospitals, clinics, and medical offices. One building that stands out in this jumble of shapes is the handsome edifice of the **Frye Art Museum,** on the western slope. The Frye has a strong collection of 19th-century American and European painting. In recent years, the museum has expanded its focus to include works by contemporary American realist painters in addition to 20th-century European and Alaskan art. *704 Terry Avenue; 206-622-9250.*

Capitol Hill, north of First Hill and reached by taking Denny Avenue uphill and turning left on Broadway, has old mansions and tree-lined residential streets, and some of Seattle's best espresso shops. Broadway is, for several blocks, the city's liveliest thoroughfare.

Ordering up an espresso at Joe Bar in Capitol Hill, a neighborhood steaming with good coffeeshops.

The **Seattle Asian Art Museum** in Volunteer Park has an old brick water tower that provides great views west over Puget Sound. The museum, inside a renovated art deco building, has an admirable collection that emphasizes Chinese and Japanese, Korean, and Southeast Asian art. *Volunteer Park, 1400 East Prospect Street; 206-625-8900; also downtown at 100 University Street; 206-654-3100.*

Martial arts movie star Bruce Lee is buried in the large **Lakeview Cemetery** (north side of Volunteer Park). Buried next to him is his son, Brandon Lee, also a martial arts movie star. Lakeview, built in 1887, is also the final resting ground for many of Seattle's pioneers—Denny, Maynard, Mercer, Yesler, Boren, and Renton.

The **Grand Army of the Republic Cemetery** (12th Avenue East and East Howe Street) is a Civil War cemetery for Union soldiers, their wives and families. During World War II, the 2.3 acre-cemetery was used by the military for barracks.

St. Mark's Episcopal Cathedral, a blocky brick-and-concrete fortress with high, arched windows and a shiny copper roof, looks over the northwest edge of Capitol Hill. It is not one of the most beautiful gothic cathedrals in the country. Its bare, cavernous interior—vaulted ceilings, walls of raw concrete—was left unfinished to preserve the brilliant acoustics. *1245 10th Avenue East.*

On the southern bank of the Ship Canal, the **Museum of History and Industry** preserves pioneer artifacts that reveal much about life in Washington from the 1700s to the present. Historic pictures of 19th-century Seattle, jewelry from Indian reservations, and Boeing's first aircraft are just a few of the items on display here. *2700 24th Avenue East; 206-324-1126.*

More than 40,000 native and exotic trees, shrubs, and vines live on the 230 acres of the **Washington Park Arboretum,** whose collective greenery comprises a living museum. Oaks, conifers, magnolias, camellias, Japanese maples, hollies, and at least 130 endangered plants are protected here. Mountain ash, pine, cedar, fir, and rhododendron also grow here. *2300 Arboretum Drive East; 206-543-8800.*

The **Seattle Japanese Garden,** on 3 acres within the arboretum, has a delightful water lily-studded koi pond, waterfalls, shaded woodland walks, secluded benches, and seasonal flowers. At this rarely crowded hideaway, you can walk at a leisurely pace or sit back on a bench and relax. Despite nearby Lake Washington Boulevard, it's so quiet you can hear waterfalls splashing and koi bubbling to the surface of the pond. There's an authentic teahouse, not open to the public but reserved for *chanoyu,* or Japanese tea demonstrations. *1000 Lake Washington Boulevard; 206-684-4725 or 425-861-9109.*

Japanese garden in the Washington Park Arboretum.

SEATTLE

■ UNIVERSITY DISTRICT *map page 49, B-1/2*

West of Lake Washington and north of the Ship Canal lies the University District, home to the **University of Washington.** "U-Dub," as it's commonly called, is said to rake in more federal research and training money (for the marine sciences, cancer research, and urban horticulture) than any other public university in the United States. It's also known for big-time college football and highly publicized athletic scandals. Husky Stadium is near the Ship Canal, so fans arrive by boat.

With its small shops, restaurants, bookstores, and pubs, this neighborhood offers sharp contrast to the quiet, tree-shaded campus. Locals, not all of them affiliated with the university, hang out here till late at night.

Lake Washington was carved by the same glacier that gouged out the Puget Sound basin. The Ship Canal to Puget Sound, completed in 1916, was supposed to make Lake Washington a hub for building and repairing ships. It didn't, although wooden ships were built here during World War I and even later, and a small fleet of Alaskan whalers wintered in Kirkland for a number of years.

University of Washington crew team practices on Lake Washington.

Boeing's Museum of Flight.

■ MUSEUM OF FLIGHT   *map page 49, B-3*

One of Seattle's most engaging attractions lies south of the city between I-5 and U.S. 99 at the former headquarters of Boeing, one of the world's largest aircraft manufacturers. The company was started in 1916, when William Boeing, an heir to Midwestern lumber money who had come to Seattle to finish a yacht, decided to build airplanes. His first craft was a seaplane that made its maiden flight from Lake Union. Though Boeing, much to the chagrin of locals, moved its headquarters to Chicago in 2001, much of the development and manufacturing of its products still takes place at its plant here.

The Museum of Flight is centered around the red barn in which William Boeing built his first airplane. A huge hall inside contains airplanes—ranging in size from a biplane to a B-47—suspended from the ceiling. Also here is the original *Air Force One,* in which U.S. presidents from Eisenhower to Nixon flew. All the fancy trimmings are in place, like Jackie Kennedy's makeup parlor and Lyndon Johnson's custom-made temperature controls. *9404 East Marginal Way South; 206-764-5720.*

OLYMPIC PENINSULA
AND PACIFIC COAST

THE NORTHWESTERNMOST PART of the contiguous United States, the Olympic Peninsula, extends north between the Pacific Ocean and Puget Sound. Heavily glaciated and not crossed by any road, the Olympic Mountains form the peninsula's 7,000-foot-high spine. Short, swift rivers tumble from the mountains to the Pacific in the west, the Strait of Juan de Fuca to the north, and Hood Canal to the east. In west-facing valleys, temperate rain forests grow within a day's hike of glacial ice and the surf-thrashed rocks of Pacific beaches. **Olympic National Park,** which protects the mountains and rain forests of the peninsula's core, also has the nation's longest wilderness beach outside Alaska.

The Olympic Peninsula has been called "an island of rivers" because numerous rivers flow from its glacier-capped mountain core in four directions: north into the Strait of Juan de Fuca, east into the Hood Canal, south into the Chehalis River and Grays Harbor, and west into the Pacific Ocean. Most of these rivers bear exotic-sounding names, like Soleduck, Elwha, Dosewallips, Skokomish, Satsop, Wishkah, Humptulips, Quinault, and Hoh.

Water flows constantly and everywhere on the peninsula, but mostly during the winter rains. It falls from the clouds onto trees, and courses down mossy branches and fern-covered tree trunks to moisten fecund nurse logs on the forest floor. The water eventually finds its way to the streams, creeks, and rivers that carry it back to the sea, where the hydrological cycle starts anew.

The northeastern portion of the peninsula lies in the rain shadow of the Olympic Mountains and has some of the lowest rainfall in western Washington, which explains why the region's major towns—Port Townsend, Sequim, and Port Angeles—are popular with artists and retirees.

The human history of the Olympic Peninsula goes back at least 3,000 years, and the oldest building foundations in the region are 800 years old. Other objects show that the Makah people had a stable culture for centuries. The Makah and other Native Americans, namely the Quillayute, Quinault, and Clallam tribes, hunted seals and whales, fished for salmon and halibut, gathered wild berries, and built cultures rich in myths and rituals.

Spring wildflowers light up the shores of Lake Crescent, in Olympic National Park.

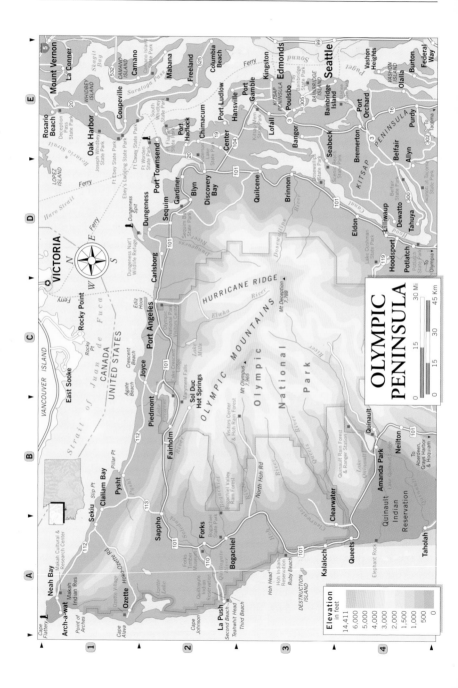

OLYMPIC PENINSULA

Warfare among the tribes ended shortly after white settlers established their forms of law and order. During the 20th century, inhabitants of this territory have also lived off the land, but to the extent that heavy logging and salmon fishing have made natural resources scarce. Fortunately, the heart of the peninsula, which includes acres of forests and rivers, has been protected from exploitation since Congress created Olympic National Park in 1938.

OLYMPIC PENINSULA

■ KITSAP PENINSULA *map page 84, D/E-4*

If you travel to the Olympic Peninsula from Seattle, a car ferry will take you to the **Kitsap Peninsula,** where a fleet of gray warships rides at anchor in Bremerton, a navy-yard town since the late 19th century.

The Kitsap Peninsula is a low, fjorded region of dense woods, picturesque harbor towns, and the U.S. Navy's largest West Coast shipyard and submarine base. The grave of **Chief Seattle,** for whom Seattle was named, overlooks Puget Sound at Suquamish on the Port Madison Indian Reservation. As a boy, the future chief saw Capt. George Vancouver's ship, *Discovery,* sailing down Puget Sound in 1792; in 1850, as tribal leader, he welcomed the first white settlers to Alki Point. This was also where, in 1854, he is said to have delivered what is considered the greatest speech ever given in the Northwest. Chief Seattle was speaking primarily to territorial governor Isaac Stevens. His speech was translated on the spot into the simplified Chinook jargon, from which it was translated into English 33 years later by Dr. Henry Smith, who had heard the original. Presumably, the ideas were Seattle's, but most of the language was Smith's. "Undeniably majestic as it is," historian David Buerge has written, "Seattle's speech does not conform to what we know of the native speaking style of the Puget Sound region." Nevertheless, the speech attributed to Seattle is a masterpiece. One of the best-known passages reads:

> Every part of this soil is sacred in the estimation of my people. Every hillside, every valley, every plain and grove, has been hallowed by some sad or happy event in days long vanished. Even the rocks which seem to be dumb and dead as they swelter in the sun along the silent shore, thrill with memories of stirring events connected with the lives of my people, and the very dust upon which you now stand responds more lovingly to their footsteps than yours, because it is rich with the blood of our ancestors and our bare feet are conscious of the sympathetic touch....

Nearby, along Liberty Bay, the town of **Poulsbo** plays up its Norwegian immigrant history. Its name means "Paul's Place" in Norwegian, and, fittingly, the town sponsors the Viking Fest in mid-May, the Skandia Midsommarfest in June, and the Yule Log Festival in November. The old mill town of **Port Gamble** overlooks the mouth of the Hood Canal, a glacial fjord on the far side of the Kitsap Peninsula. The many white buildings that dot the landscape evoke the Maine backgrounds of the founders of the Pope & Talbot Company, which sold lumber in gold rush San Francisco and built the first mill in Port Gamble in the 1850s.

As you drive over the floating bridge across the blue water of Hood Canal, it's hard to imagine that 80-mile-per-hour winds sank the bridge's predecessor in 1979. Even the new bridge is closed during particularly severe storms.

■ NORTHEAST OLYMPIC PENINSULA

Port Ludlow *map page 84, E-2*

North of the bridge is the resort town of Port Ludlow, famous for its boat harbor, golf course, and the Resort at Port Ludlow (1 Heron Bay Road; 360-437-7000) across the harbor. As you drive north toward Port Townsend, take a look around. The woods and fields of this region were made famous by *The Egg and I*, Betty MacDonald's humorous account of moving here after marrying an Olympic Peninsula chicken farmer (she didn't like the experience, preferring flush toilets and hot, running water to life in the "wilderness"). The book became a bestseller and was made into a popular film that inspired a series of movies about Ma and Pa Kettle. For fun, stop in nearby Chimacum and ask where Ma and Pa lived.

Port Townsend *map page 84, E-1*

The town got its name from Capt. George Vancouver, who named it "Port Townshend" for his friend, the Marquis of Townshend, in 1792. The first American settlers arrived in 1851, but the town didn't experience a building boom until rumors began circulating that it would be selected as the end point for a transcontinental railway. The railway never happened, but the town prospered anyway.

The **James House** (1238 Washington Street; 360-385-1238 or 800-385-1238), an antiques-filled Victorian-era inn, sits on the bluff overlooking Port Townsend's waterfront district. It's listed on the National Register of Historic Places and is just about everyone's favorite Port Townsend bed-and-breakfast. The decor of the

Clam digging along Dungeness Spit.

spacious **Palace Hotel** (1004 Water Street; 360-385-0773 or 800-962-0741) reflects the building's history as a bordello. You can easily imagine the lobby filled with music and men waiting for the ladies whose names now grace hallway plaques. The large rooms have 14-foot ceilings and worn antiques. The outstanding corner suite, Miss Marie's, has full views of the bay and the original working fireplace from Marie's days as a madam.

Many of the town's brick waterfront buildings and uptown mansions are intact today, including the 1892 **Manresa Castle** (651 Cleveland Street), a lavish mansion built by a local merchant; the 1883 **Bartlett House** (314 Polk Street); and the 1889 **Ann Starrett Mansion** (744 Clay Street), a delightfully florid survivor of the Victorian age. Most of these homes can't be toured, but the Starrett Mansion, complete with 70-foot tower, turrets, and a dramatic three-tier circular staircase, welcomes visitors.

On the road west from Port Townsend, stands of old cedar and fir still crowd the highway. Ancient stumps, some of them six feet in diameter, punctuate rain-soaked pastures, and in autumn red and yellow leaves of vine maple glow among the evergreens.

Sequim and Dungeness Spit *map page 84, D-1/2*

The highway town of **Sequim,** pronounced "skwim," has a large population of retirees, owing to the area's dry climate (it sits in the rain shadow of the Olympics). **Dungeness Spit,** possibly the largest natural sand spit in the world, juts into the Strait of Juan de Fuca, curving northeast for 5.5 miles to the lighthouse at its tip. Seabirds bob in the waters of the bay, and sea lions cruise along the exposed western shore.

The coastal forests and adjacent tidal zones are protected areas of **Dungeness National Wildlife Refuge,** where thousands of animal species—mostly birds and shellfish—gravitate. Harbor seals frolic in the waters and sometimes even on the beach, and the shallow bays south of the spit are filled with eelgrass, where baby salmon and steelhead thrive. *U.S. 101 on Strait of Juan de Fuca.*

Port Angeles *map page 84, C-2*

This former mill town has undergone a transformation. A converted railroad bed now has a paved trail with benches. There's a small aquarium now on the public pier, the **Art Feirio Marine Laboratory** (Port Angeles City Pier; 360-417-6254), with touch tanks that hold scallops, rockfish, and anemones. A viewing tower at the end of the pier is worth climbing for the sweeping views of water and land.

There are two museums in town: the **Port Angeles Fine Arts Center** (1203 East Lauridsen Boulevard; 360-457-3532), which shows the work of regional artists, and the **Museum of the Clallam Historical Society** (933 West Ninth Street; 360-452-2662), which mounts exhibits on the lifestyles, arts, and industries of the Native Americans who have inhabited this area for centuries.

Port Angeles is a mellow but memorable place that tends to attract artistic types. John Wayne berthed his boat in Port Angeles; author Raymond Carver lived here; and poet Tess Gallagher still calls this home.

Ediz Hook, at the west end of Port Angeles, is a natural sand spit that protects the harbor from dangerous waves and storms. A fine place to walk and watch shore- and seabirds, it's also good for spotting seals and gray whales. *Front Street, west past the shuttered lumber mill.*

■ OLYMPIC NATIONAL PARK   *map page 84*

Olympic National Park's grandest entrance winds 17 miles from Port Angeles to Hurricane Ridge, where you can look out over the Elwha Valley into the heart of the Olympics, or north to the Strait of Juan de Fuca. The area encompasses more than 1,300 square miles of wilderness in the heart of the Olympic Mountains. The surrounding land was set aside as forest reserve in 1897. Twelve years later, President Theodore Roosevelt established the Mount Olympus National Monument as a sanctuary for the later-named Roosevelt elk, which had been hunted nearly to extinction for its teeth, which were used as ornaments for watch fobs. Under pressure from logging and mining interests, President Woodrow Wilson reduced the protected area by half in 1915, opening much of today's park to logging and homesteading, activities that ended in 1938, when Congress created Olympic National Park. Since then, the park has expanded to include the Queets and Hoh River Valleys. Congress recently added the coastal strip, the longest stretch of wilderness beach in the United States outside Alaska.

Olympic National Park is the most geographically diverse park in America. In addition to 7,965-foot Mount Olympus, the park encompasses 57 miles of seacoast, temperate rain forests, and an array of wildlife that includes black bears, mountain sheep, bald eagles, and at least 5,000 Roosevelt elk. With more than 600 miles of trails, the park reveals itself best to travelers on foot or horseback. For

(following pages) Up to 140 inches of rain falls each year in the Hoh Rain Forest.

OLYMPIC
PENINSULA

STOLEN THRILL

There is a kind of stolen thrill, something unearned and simply granted, about the presence of the Olympics. The state of Washington makes its margin with the Pacific as if the region west of the Cascade Mountains had all been dropped heavily against the ocean, causing wild splatters of both land and water: the islands of Puget Sound and the San Juan group, streaky inlets everywhere, stretched stripes of peninsula such as Dungeness and Long Beach, the eighty-mile fjord called Hood Canal, and a web-work of more than forty sizable rivers emptying to the coast. Amid this welter the Olympic Mountains stand in calm tall files, their even timbered slopes like black-green fur to shed the wet. The region's history itself seems to step back and marvel at these shoreline mountains. The coastal Indians appear not to have troubled to travel much in them. Why wrestle forest when the sea is an open larder? White frontier-probing too went into an unusual and welcome slowdown when it reached the Olympics. Although the range sits only sixty miles wide and fifty long, not until 1889 did a six-man expedition sponsored by a Seattle newspaper traipse entirely across it and leave some of the loveliest peaks of America with the curious legacy of being named for editors. ·

—Ivan Doig, *Winter Brothers*, 1980

auto-bound travelers and campers, a few spectacular roads probe fleetingly (never more than 20 miles) into its borders.

Typically, the region experiences more rain and fog than sunshine. Beaches, tide pools, and rain forests embellish the west side of the peninsula, where heavy rains irrigate massive forests of immense red cedar, Sitka spruce, and Douglas fir. The main roads to the rain forest trailheads follow the Hoh River near Forks; the Queets River near the town of Queets; and the Quinault River, beyond Quinault Lake in the southwest corner of the park. Access roads to the beaches lead to Ozette Lake, La Push, and the southern stretch of coastline between Ruby Beach and Queets. The park keeps the road plowed in winter, and people drive up here for cross-country and downhill skiing.

(opposite) A cascading stream alongside Sol Duc Falls Trail, Olympic National Park.
(following pages) A view of the Olympics from Mount Walker on an unusually clear day.

Farther west, U.S. 101 passes through low forests to scenic **Lake Crescent,** beloved by fishermen for its plentiful trout. Close at hand are the comfortable cottages of **Lake Crescent Lodge** (416 Lake Crescent Road; 360-928-3211), built for President Franklin Roosevelt's visit in 1937. The waters at **Sol Duc Hot Springs** (Sol Duc Hot Springs Road; 360-327-3583) have been popular since pioneer days. Three sulfur pools bubble here. Their temperatures are hot, hotter, and hottest.

■ ALONG THE WESTERN STRAITS

Beyond Port Angeles, narrow Route 112 winds west along the Strait of Juan de Fuca. South and east, a blanket of snow caps the crumpled ridges of the Olympic Mountains, rising starkly from their surrounding forests. As you follow the road along the coastline, curving around rocks and trees, don't rush—this is one of the finest coastal drives in the state. Near Pysht, huge, mossy spruce trunks crowd the blacktop, and along the Pysht River look for epiphytes—air plants that grow on other plants, not in soil—dripping from maple limbs. Farther west, you'll see rocky headlands and waves breaking on stony beaches.

Neah Bay *map page 84, A-1*

Neah Bay is a sport-fishing and whaling village where the occasional totem pole reminds you that this is a centuries-old Makah settlement. It's also where the state's first European settlers came to build a home. In 1792, Spanish colonists from Mexico arrived aboard a frigate. They built a fort and a bakery, and planted a small garden, but they abandoned the area after five months. The first Americans here were traders, arriving in 1850. The Makah are still here.

Visitors need to purchase a recreation permit to hike local trails. The cost is $10 per car. The permit can be obtained at the Museum, Cultural Center, the marina, and local shops. *Route 112 from U.S. 101 at Port Angeles, or Route 113 from U.S. 101 at Sappho.*

Makahs harvest a whale. Ancient traditions dictated the division of the whale, the harpooner receiving the largest share. (Asahel Curtis photo, Washington State Historical Society)

MAKAH WHALE HUNTERS

The original inhabitants of the north coast called themselves *Qwidicca-atx,* which loosely translates to "people who live on the cape by the rocks and seagulls." Europeans found the Clallam word *Makah*—"generous with food"—easier to pronounce, and the name stuck. The Makah and their ancestors have inhabited the narrow margin between the Olympic rain forest and the Pacific Ocean for about 5,000 years. Culturally closest to the Indians of present-day British Columbia, the Makah braved the Pacific Ocean in canoes to hunt the 40-foot-long, 20-ton gray whale.

Early Makah whalers followed elaborate rituals to remove their human taint and purify their bodies for the whale spirit. The morning of the hunt, the harpooner rose at dawn, bathed in the icy water of a lake or pond, and rubbed a handful of twigs over his body until the twigs were covered with blood. He repeated this three more times, then dove beneath the surface of the water and imitated the movements of a whale, slowly, as he hoped the whale would during the hunt. Some whalers dove into the water with a corpse or skeleton strapped to their backs, offering prayers to the dead spirit, asking for help in the hunt.

Fortified with spiritual power and courage, Makah men then put out to sea in dugout canoes to stalk the whale. Paddlers brought the canoe in behind the whale, keeping out of its field of vision; when the narrow wooden boat was directly above the beast, the harpooner standing in the bow hurled his shell-tipped harpoons.

Once the first harpoon was driven in, inflated seal bladders attached to the spear kept the whale from diving too deep. When it surfaced to draw breath, more spears were thrown. When the behemoth was dead, its mouth was sewn shut to retain the gases that gave it buoyancy and to keep seawater out. The whale was towed back to shore and butchered on the beach. Its meat was eaten, its blubber rendered for oil, and its bones made into war clubs and woodworking tools.

Makah whaling ceased in 1913, but the International Whaling Commission recently granted Makah whalers permission to resume.

Makah Cultural and Research Center *map page 84, A-1*

On display here are artifacts recovered from the Ozette Village site at Cape Alava. On the whole, the objects form a kind of hymn to cedar, which the Makah used to make just about everything, including their longhouses, woven mats, blankets, hats, canoe paddles, and canoes. The museum contains replicas of the smaller cedar canoes used for seal hunting and the long canoes used for whale hunting.

The most startling display case holds knife blades made of slate, shell, and rusted metal. Where did Makah craftsmen 500 years ago get metal to make blades? Presumably from shipwrecked Japanese vessels that were carried by currents into the peninsula's waters. It is unclear how often wrecked boats from other continents drifted ashore, but there is evidence that Japanese sailors survived a shipwreck here in the early 1800s. *Route 112, 1880 Bay View Avenue; 360-645-2711.*

West of Neah Bay, **Cape Flattery,** the northwesternmost point of land in the coterminous United States, extends into the Pacific. From high ground, you can look south along the misty coast, over the dark forest and white line of breakers at the edge of the continent, to the distant sculpture garden of sea stacks at Point of

(above) Hobuck Beach on Mukkaw Bay on the Makah Indian Reservation.
(opposite) Makah sisters with grandchild in Neah Bay.

Arches. *After the Makah museum, travel west 1.5 miles to town and follow signs to Makah Tribal Center. A quarter-mile beyond the tribal center is a gravel road that leads to Cape Trail and Cape Flattery.*

■ OZETTE LAKE AND NORTHERN COAST

West of Sekiu, on Route 112, a branch road winds southwest, following the Hoko River through heavily logged hills toward Ozette Lake. Most of the land along this road is clear-cut to low stumps and slash piles as far as the eye can see.

The road ends at a ranger station on the north end of 10-mile-long Ozette Lake. You have just entered the coastal section of Olympic National Park.

Ahlstrom Prairie   *map page 84, A-1/2*

One hundred years ago, the land around Ozette Lake was settled by homesteaders, mostly Scandinavian families who built dwellings here using wood cut from

*The trunk of a felled tree serves as a bungalow in this 1907 photo.
(Museum of History and Industry)*

An aerial view of Tatoosh Island, resting just off Cape Flattery, the northwesternmost point of land in the coterminous United States.

old-growth forests. Lars Ahlstrom, a homesteader who arrived in 1902, worked his claim alone until 1958. His decades of toil are commemorated in Ahlstrom Prairie, a broad marsh crossed by the Cape Alava trail. Around the lake, the forest has swallowed all traces of the farms that once thrived here. Even on Ahlstrom Prairie, seedling evergreens are beginning the long work of reclamation.

Two 3-mile-long boardwalk trails from Ozette Lake to the long wilderness beach cut through thick rain forests, where columns of sunlight split the dense canopy high overhead, and where a soft, green light seems to emanate from trees and the earth itself.

Between the Makah Reservation, which occupies the extreme northwestern tip of the peninsula, and the big Quinault Reservation, south of Kalaloch, the whole Pacific coastline is part of the Olympic National Park, except for three small pockets of land occupied by the Ozette, Quillayute, and Hoh Reservations. The ancient forests grow down to the shore. Near the water, pale lichens beard the scaly boughs of Sitka spruce. At low tide, the beach stretches out to small, wooded

SCENT OF CEDAR

The gray log lies high up on the rocky beach, weathered until it resembles the stones on which it rests. Grab a sliver of pale wood and rip it back. Beneath the surface, it shines a rich orange-red, and a pungent odor, something you might smell after opening a jar of exotic spice, fills the air. The wood is western red cedar, and it grows in the damp valleys of the Pacific Northwest.

If you travel inland from the beach, through a dense forest of fir and hemlock, you might come upon one of these valleys. Picking your way through a swamp, you might find a long, fluted cylinder, half-submerged and covered with moss, solid to the step or touch. It too is cedar. Beyond it, a living tree rises from a fluted base three feet thick. Bark coats it in thin, shaggy vertical strips, and the branches dip and curve like the lines of a Japanese temple. The foliage is flat and multibranched, like layer on layer of horizontal bracken fern. Nearby, like an obelisk, soaring straight as a die from the forest floor, a dead cedar trunk reveals the naked, skeletal shape. Thicker at the base than the living tree, it transcends the leaning alders around it and the second-growth Douglas fir on the hill above, rising to a needle point.

It doesn't take much imagination to see this gray column as a totem in the woods. In fact, the totem poles and other magnificent wood carvings of this coast were made from cedar, which Indians also used to make walls and roofs for their houses, rope, fishing line, and canoes.

islands where surf-sculpted rocks dot the shore. Some of these landforms would look more at home in the Arizona desert than in the shallows of the Pacific Ocean. In some places, grinding breakers have worn rocks to the pitted consistency of wormwood.

Waves deposit spongy beds of sea grass along the tide line and scatter stiff stalks of bullwhip kelp in the sand. Deer and raccoon tracks show clearly in the sand, and black cormorants spread their wings to dry in the sun atop wave-shaped sea stacks—the weird-looking hives and spires of dark basalt that form close to water. The hoarse cry of a great blue heron splits the air as the bird rises with a few impossibly slow beats of its enormous wings. Mats of slick, red kelp

Driftwood on Rialto Beach.

OLYMPIC
PENINSULA

pop underfoot, and a young bald eagle flies northeast with a fish hanging limp in its talons, a pleading gull in pursuit.

Cape Alava   *map page 84, A-1*

The site of a Makah village for at least 2,000 years, Cape Alava was abandoned in the late 19th century after the U.S. government ordered village children off to school in Neah Bay. Like many long-inhabited places, the Ozette Village was built in succeeding layers. An early layer, sealed by mudslides centuries ago and exposed by winter storms in 1970, provided one of Washington's most important archaeological sites—a Pompeii of the Northwest coast. Wooden artifacts and woven baskets dating to the 1400s, perfectly preserved in their airless tomb, gave a clear picture of traditional Makah life. The archaeological excavation of the Ozette Village eventually ran out of money and was shut down, but the artifacts are preserved at the Makah Cultural and Research Center in Neah Bay, and a replica cedar longhouse now marks the village site.

Makah Indian petroglyphs on the coast, south of the Ozette Indian ruins.

Sunset off the coast near La Push.

■ LA PUSH   *map page 84, A-2*

Fourteen miles west of U.S. 101 and the town of Forks lies the fishing village of La Push, close to the mouth of the Quillayute River on the tiny **Quillayute Indian Reservation.** The coast here, accessed by Route 110, is magnificent: wind-warped cedar and hemlock and stands of lichen-whitened alder stand on steep clay banks overlooking the Pacific. **Second Beach** and **Third Beach** are reached by half-mile trails leading down from the road about a mile before town. La Push itself is on First Beach, a site occupied by the Quillayute for centuries. The town is a collection of shabby, weathered houses, an old Shaker church, and a small harbor where fishing boats bob. Salmon fishing is the chief livelihood of the Quillayute people, as it has been for millennia. Gray whales are known to play off-shore during their annual migrations, and most of the year the waves are great for surfing and kayaking (bring a wetsuit).

■ RAIN FORESTS *map page 84 A/C-2/3*

People come from all over the world to see the enchanting rain forests of the Olympic Coast. Everything here is green—innumerable hues, shades, and overlapping layers of green. There are no hard edges—moss softens everything and a thick carpet of it covers the ground. Tree roots create ripples in the green, and waves of moss seem to flow toward the trees. In fall, you might hear the high "bugling" of Roosevelt elk or see one of the big creatures slip through the trees.

Multiple layers of tree limbs, vines, and moss create a canopy overhead, and where light is able to penetrate, a tangled undergrowth of brush and small plants flourishes on the forest floor. Some old trees die and remain standing as gray, weather-bleached snags. Others fall and decay slowly, releasing nutrients for centuries. These nutrients eventually develop into nurse logs that grow above the forest floor. Because nurse logs thrive away from the suffocating duff and aggressive fungi of the forest base, they allow less hardy species, like Sitka spruce and western hemlock, to survive.

The western hemlocks that hitch rides on western red cedars can grow into substantial trees themselves, reaching diameters of 9 feet and heights of almost 200 feet. They are counted among the "Big Four" of the temperate rain forest, along with western red cedar, Douglas fir, and Sitka spruce.

Plant and animal life in the Washington rain forests equals that of tropical rain forests, though it is not as diverse. Only a few conifer species are found here, and there are even fewer deciduous ones. But the sheer size and number of these conifers, and the density of their over- and undergrowth, puts them among the tallest and thickest trees on earth. Willaby Creek Nature Trail, on the southern shore of Lake Quinault, passes through a grove of impressively lofty Douglas firs, some of them 300 feet high.

Washington's rain forests are so dense with growth it's easy to get lost while hiking through them. Stick to established trails.

On U.S. 101, just south of Forks at Bogachiel State Park, head east into the **Bogachiel Valley Rain Forest.** Past the Bogachiel River, North Hoh Road leads inland to the **Hoh Rain Forest** (off U.S. 101 at Upper Hoh Road; 360-374-6925), where the best-known rain forest trails begin. Farther south, U.S. 101 leads east to **Lake Quinault,** where you will find trailheads, campgrounds, and the **Lake Quinault Lodge** (345 South Shore Road; 360-288-2900), an impressively handsome,

Hiking in Olympic National Park—one of the world's few temperate rain forests.

96-room hotel built on the shores of Lake Quinault in 1926. Guests can boat on the lake, walk or jog on trails, or drive short distances to nearby hiking trails.

■ SOUTHERN COAST SETTING

Between Grays Harbor and the Columbia River, the mountains recede from the coast and are replaced by long, sandy beaches and dunes. The sand comes from the rivers and is moved by tidal currents. In some places, beaches have expanded; in others, they've receded. At Toke Point, near Tokeland, the sea eats into the coastline at a rate of 12 feet per year; farther out on the coast, at Cape Shoalwater, the erosion rate is 150 feet per year. Willapa Bay and its main channel have moved north about 2 miles since records were first kept in 1887.

Near Ilwaco the land is low and was used as a portage during the days when canoes were the main form of transportation. In 1876, during an unusually high flood, the Columbia River broke through and poured into Willapa Bay, diluting the salt water of the bay to such an extent that native oysters died. The beaches are windy and attract kite-fliers from all over the Northwest.

Chehalis and Chinook Indians occupied this region 200 years ago. Expert canoe builders, they braved the coastal waters and rivers in all sorts of weather and impressed American explorers Lewis and Clark with their seamanship. The Chinooks were the greatest traders on the coast, middlemen between the people of the coast and the interior. Their language became the basis for the colorful Chinook jargon, a trade language composed of Indian and European words that served as the Northwest Coast's lingua franca for more than 100 years.

By the time the exploration party of Lewis and Clark reached the mouth of the Columbia River in November 1805, the Chinook had become experts in trading with American mariners. The first to come was Yankee fur trader Robert Gray, who "discovered" the river in 1792 when he sailed his ship *Columbia Rediviva* across the treacherous bar at the river's mouth. (British naval lieutenant William Broughton soon followed in Gray's wake, claiming the river for Britain.)

The first settlers on the Washington coast were attracted by the plentiful oysters, which they shipped to San Francisco from Oysterville and from the now-vanished town of Bruceport. Pioneer settler James Swan left an interesting account of his sojourn during the 1850s in the book *The Northwest Coast; or Three Year's Residence in Washington Territory.* Willapa Bay has remained a backwater, and oyster-growing, fishing, crabbing, and logging are still the region's main industries.

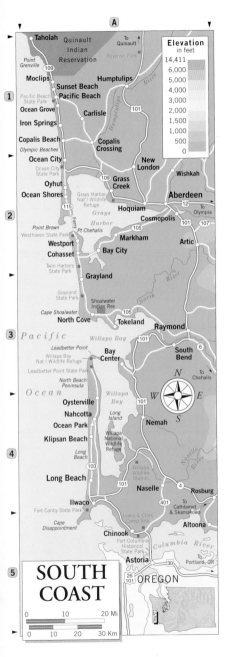

Heavy breakers and unpredictable currents at the bars of the Columbia River, Willapa Bay, and Grays Harbor made a treacherous passage for many ships. Even now, a boat occasionally comes to grief on the bars.

■ GRAYS HARBOR
map this page, A-2

Curving inland around the Quinault Indian Reservation, U.S. 101 connects the estuary and mill towns of Grays Harbor. The ocean beaches to the west have razor clams and are a popular resort destination for tourists and locals.

Grays Harbor has one of the largest estuaries on the Pacific Coast north of San Francisco. The towns of **Aberdeen** and **Hoquiam,** which stand beside the estuary, have always had plenty of lumber mills, and old pilings driven into the seabed to hold log booms still rise from the water's edge. The two towns are so close you can hardly tell when you leave one and enter the other, which might explain why they have never gotten along. Once, when the Chehalis River flooded, the city of Hoquiam built a dike across the main street to "keep the floodwaters in Aberdeen."

In recent years, Aberdeen has maintained its downtown business core while also attracting retailers to several

(following pages) Sea stacks at Ruby Beach.

OLYMPIC PENINSULA

malls, the largest of which is south of the Chehalis River. Hoquiam, with its old extractive mills still standing along the Chehalis River waterfront, seems more interested in reliving the past.

A tall, masted ship may sail across the bay, a replica of Capt. Robert Gray's other nautical charge, *Lady Washington*. It was built for the Washington Centennial in 1989 and occasionally offers rides. Oysters grow in the waters on the south side of the estuary.

Grays Harbor National Wildlife Refuge   *map page 109, A-2*
Up to one million shorebirds flock to this bird sanctuary during the spring birding season before flying off to northern breeding grounds. Dozens of species of shorebirds land here, but mostly sandpipers, dunlin, short-billed and long-billed dowitchers, and, of course, the semipalmated plover.

Grays Harbor is a designated Western Hemisphere Shorebird Reserve, and hundreds of bird-watchers show up here each year in late April for the Shorebird Festival (360-495-3289). The best months to visit the refuge are April and May,

(above) Massachusetts doesn't have a monopoly on cranberries—these berries are harvested in the Long Beach area. (opposite) A glowing sunset over Willapa Bay.

and the best times of day to come are an hour before and an hour after high tide. *100 Brown Farm Road, Olympia; 360-532-6237 or 360-753-9467.*

Westport, at the southern edge of the estuary's mouth, has a fishing and crabbing fleet, and charter boats for catching salmon and bottomfish, or for viewing whales that migrate up the coast in spring. A drive south from Westport takes you past dunes and cranberry bogs. In spring, look for wild strawberries growing in the dunes; in fall, search for wild cranberries growing in moist, boggy depressions among the sand hills. In season, you may dig for razor clams on the beaches. Westport is an active town with boating, bicycling, clam digging, and lots of fishing. There's a great boardwalk here, at the end of Neddie Rose Drive, and the town has miles and miles of beaches where you can play in the sand, wade in water, or just watch the waves.

Getting to **Bowerman Basin,** the spring and fall migratory birding mecca west of Hoquiam, is inconvenient for casual travelers, but there are turnouts on Route 109 west of Hoquiam where you can pull over and scan the tide flats of the basin with binoculars.

West of Hoquiam, Route 109 skirts the northern shore of Grays Harbor before turning inland. It does not touch the ocean again until it passes Ocean City, where you'll find **Ocean City State Park** (from Hoquiam, 16 miles west on Route 109 to Route 115 and look for signs), which is great for camping because the enormous trees provide natural windbreaks. The lagoon at the entrance has foliage so thick with lichen it looks like something out of Bayou Country. Bird-watching and beachcombing are popular activities.

■ WILLAPA BAY   *map page 109, A-3*

Willapa Bay, just south of Grays Harbor, is the cleanest estuary anywhere in the United States outside Alaska. The area produces more oysters than any other place in the United States and ranks among the top five oyster-producing spots in the world. You can't miss the town; most of it is covered under huge piles of oyster shells, which rise beside packinghouses at the water's edge.

A quick drive south from Grays Harbor takes you to the old riverside logging town of **Raymond,** where a tall wooden statue of a logger stands in a little park. Farther south, U.S. 101 runs along the waterfront of **South Bend,** known to some as "the oyster capital of the world." After passing through South Bend, U.S. 101 follows the Willapa River to Willapa Bay. A historical plaque here marks the site of

Bruceport, from which local oysters were first shipped to San Francisco in the 1850s. The forests east of this shore are true temperate rain forests, and though most of the area was logged long ago, a few giants survive in remote nooks.

After crossing the Niawiakum River, look for a sign directing you to **Bay Center,** a prime oyster habitat and one of the country's biggest oyster producers.

Parts of Willapa Bay have been protected since 1937 as a national wildlife refuge. Near the refuge's headquarters, just south of South Bend, **Long Island** supports a 4,000-year-old grove of western red cedar. The remainder of the refuge is across the bay, at the northern tip of **Long Beach Peninsula,** which separates Willapa Bay from the Pacific Ocean. This is a low fenny land of slowly meandering rivers, of reedy marshes and damp forests, of old docks and piles of oyster shells on the shore.

The peninsula, a 28-mile-long spit of land stretching north from the mouth of the Columbia River and Cape Disappointment, is the West Coast's longest uninterrupted stretch of sandy beach. Hiking and bird-watching are great here, but don't even think about swimming. The water is too cold and the surf too rough. Hypothermia and undertow account for fatalities each year.

Gray whales pass by Long Beach Peninsula two times a year: from December to February, on their migration south from the Arctic to their winter breeding grounds in the saltwater lagoons of Baja, California; and from March to May, on the return trip north. One good place to view the whales is the **North Head Lighthouse,** north of Cape Disappointment in Fort Canby State Park.

Oysterville, once the center of the local oyster industry, has houses from the 1860s and a 1906 schoolhouse. Quaint is the operative word here. Don't miss the 1892 Oysterville church, with its shingled steeple. A sign marks the site of the first Pacific County Courthouse—the seat of local government until South Bend boosters stole the records and built their own courthouse. ("Stealing the courthouse" happened surprisingly often in the early Northwest.) This small coastal community was settled in 1854, when it became a major oyster producer for San Francisco. But this was an oyster town long before that, going back to the days when Chinook Indians harvested oysters from Willapa Bay.

The lakes and marshes of Long Beach Peninsula attract migrating birds, including trumpeter swans. **Leadbetter Point State Park,** just beyond Oysterville but before the refuge at the extreme tip of the peninsula, gives you a chance to walk along a bay that looks unchanged from a century ago. Snowy plovers breed on the sandy beaches of Leadbetter Point, and shorebirds rise, skim the water, flash white undersides as they turn, and settle up the beach. Their twittering fills the air.

■ COLUMBIA RIVER

Below the steep cliffs of Cape Disappointment, the Columbia River and the Pacific Ocean growl at each other across a barrier of sand where tall breakers pound the beach. Many ships have wrecked here in the last 200 years, even

Cape Disappointment Lighthouse, built in 1856 and the West Coast's oldest functioning lighthouse, overlooks the Columbia River in Fort Canby State Park.

though a lighthouse clinging to the sheer rock has signaled the dangers of these waters since 1856. This is the beach on which Lewis and Clark first walked beside the Pacific in 1805.

Fort Canby was built on a rocky headland during the Civil War to protect the coast from Confederate raiders. The **Lewis and Clark Interpretive Center** here contains journal excerpts from the Lewis and Clark expedition and photo murals of places on the explorers' route. Despite the construction of two lighthouses and a few military bunkers, these wild headlands are little changed since Clark, "accompanied by 11 men," stood here on November 18, 1805, and recorded in his journal:

This spot, which was called Cape Disappointment, is an elevated circular knob, rising with a steep ascent 150 or 160 feet above the water, formed like the whole shore of the bay, as well as the seacoast, and covered with thick timber on the inner side but open and grassy in the exposure next to the sea.

The woods certainly remain as tangled as they were when Clark traversed them. You can walk through the crumbling concrete gun emplacements or hike to the north jetty, which guards the mouth of the river. Waves smash against the black boulders, throwing spray to the uppermost rocks, as gulls screech overhead. *Cape Disappointment State Park, 2.5 miles west of Ilwaco; 360-642-3078.*

For many years, the village of **Ilwaco,** just inside the mouth of the Columbia River, was a bustling fishing port, but with the decline of salmon stocks, the community has been forced to direct its attention to the tourists who pass through en route to Cape Disappointment, Fort Canby State Park, and North Head Lighthouse. The harbor here is a great place to watch gulls and other seabirds.

The oldest standing cannery in Washington sits on the Cathlamet waterfront along the Columbia River.

OLYMPIC
PENINSULA

A few miles up the river is sleepy **Chinook,** one of Washington's oldest ports. Once a major cannery town, Chinook takes its name from the local tribe that once controlled the Columbia River from its mouth to Celilo Falls. Chinook is a calm, quiet place where folks know their neighbors. Weathered St. Mary's Church in the nearby hamlet of McGowan was a gift to the church association by pioneer Patrick McGowan. The freestanding church has long served as a landmark for local fishermen returning home across the watery expanses of the lower Columbia River. Stop at the small picnic area west of the church and you will be following in the footsteps of Lewis and Clark, who camped here.

■ EAST UP THE COLUMBIA

If you drive from Cape Disappointment up the Columbia River (follow U.S. 101 to Route 401 then to Route 4), you'll notice dark rock pushing through the soggy ground along the riverbank. Cattle graze in wet pastures, and abandoned houses and barns mark the landscape. A sign indicates the site at which Lewis and Clark camped for 10 days in November 1805, and evidently first saw breakers driven upriver from the open sea. (The explorers actually thought they had seen the ocean before this, when they sighted the broad expanse of Grays Bay.) Clark wrote in his diary:

> We are all wet and disagreeable, as we have been for Several days.... The flood tide came in accompanied with emence waves and heavy winds, floated the trees and Drift which was on the point on which we Camped and tosed them about in such a manner as to endanger the canoes...with every exertion and the Strictest attention by every individual of the party was scercely sufficient to Save our Canoes from being crushed by those monsterous trees maney of them nearly 200 feet long and from 4 to 7 feet through.

Beyond the sign that marks a happier campsite, you pass an idyllic landscape of small rivers and an old church. From the abandoned gun batteries at **Fort Columbia State Park** you can look straight down the river to the ocean. This is a delightfully rustic backwater of old sloughs, churches, and the green superstructure of the bridge to Astoria.

At the bridge, the river road leaves U.S. 101 and turns into Route 401, the connector road to Route 4, which runs to Longview. Signs direct you to Megler, a town that no longer exists. Decaying wooden pilings in the shallow water near the river shore mark the site where Megler and its former canneries once stood.

Route 401 soon turns inland and joins Route 4 at Naselle, a wide spot in the road with a general store and not much else. **Grays River,** a tiny farming community, is where dairy cows feed on the lush grasses of the wet meadows, and where black bear, elk, and deer inhabit nearby forests. In winter, thousands of waterfowl visit the marshes. The Grays River covered bridge, built in 1905, is the only covered bridge left in Washington. The **Julia Butler Hanson Wildlife Refuge** (Route 4; 360-795-3915) protects a small herd of Columbian whitetail deer.

Running through forests, pastures, and densely wooded hills and mountains, the highway rises to 1,000 feet before dropping down to the Columbia River at the village of **Skamakowa,** whose native name translates as "fog over the waters." The description is apt, though it's really more of a fine mist than fog. The moist air and gray envelope lend a sense of mystery to the area, which has homes that date from the 1800s, a 19th-century meeting hall that now serves as an art and history center, a general store, and taverns. Skamakowa has a pleasant riverfront park, Vista Park (13 Vista Park Road; 360-795-8605), with campsites and views. In winter, look for visiting tundra swans, geese, and bald eagles along the river and in nearby sloughs.

The highway once again turns inland beyond Skamakowa and passes the small town of **Cathlamet,** whose Victorian clapboard houses rise on a slope above the Cathlamet Channel of the Columbia River. The county seat of tiny Wahkiakum County, Cathlamet got its start in 1846 as the trading post of a retired Hudson's Bay Company trader. The town is separated from the Columbia by **Puget Island,** a low, marshy expanse of dairy pastures connected to the Washington shore by a bridge, and to Oregon by the last of a once-numerous fleet of Columbia River ferries. Look for ospreys nesting on abandoned riverside pilings, and watch them fish. They hover high overhead, and then plunge down into the water feet first and usually come up with a fish in their vise-like talons.

From Cathlamet to Stella, Route 4 hugs the right bank of the Columbia River. Turnouts along the way provide opportunities for bird-watching and viewing the huge freighters that move upriver to Portland, looking like specters as they float among the willows and cottonwoods of the river's low islands. At Coal Creek Slough, Route 4 moves inland toward Longview.

HEAVENLY OYSTERS

EVERY FALL, WHEN THE LEAVES TURN GOLDEN, I know that oyster season is about to begin. I drive south on Chuckanut Drive, from Whatcom into Skagit County, turn right at the Oyster Creek Inn, and wind my way down the narrow draw of Oyster Creek to Taylor Shellfish Farms, an aggregation of shucking sheds, cabins, and cottages. I am in luck. The oysters spawned early this year. Fattened on the detritus of summer, they are back in season, plump and flavorful. But before I buy, I take a good whiff of the air.

The sea breeze is pregnant with aromas: the refreshing scent of fir boughs wafts down to the beach from the cliffs; a sharp tang of salt and kelp and marine life hovers above the tide; an earthy bouquet of fragrances rises from the mud of the shore. Thinking of the old adage that you'll know how oysters in a given bay taste by the smell of the beach at low tide, I'm getting hungry. This bay smells great. I long to become part of the shore and the sea, to imbibe it, to take some of this mystical experience home with me, and I know I can come close to doing so by eating an oyster, which is the one tangible part of all of this I can ever hope to share.

Sharing is what oysters are all about. Oysters have always been a sociable food. In 19th-century London, diners stood at bars, eating oysters raw, enhanced perhaps by a touch of cayenne pepper and malt vinegar, accompanied by crusty bread, sweet butter, and stout, the drink seemingly created to heighten the natural flavor of oysters. I am fortunate to work in an office where just about everyone loves oysters. Since I have stopped at the oyster farm on my way to work, I buy several dozen oysters in the shell to share with co-workers. But first I need to slurp a dozen from the shell, right at the farm.

Eating a fresh oyster on the seashore is to experience a poem of nature—an incarnation of the sea breeze, of the salt water reflecting the green trees, berry bushes, and herbs of the shore. But while a good oyster contains some of the aromas of the sea, it transmutes the flavor of the seawater into a magical liquor, the way a poet transforms words. The words are still there, but they have taken on a new and mystical gestalt, a life of their own. Thus the oyster liquor, though more or less briny, depending on how salty the environment in which the oyster is

Bill Webb, founder of Westcott Bay Sea Farms, poses with some gourmet varieties.

raised, is not just mere seawater that has remained behind in the shell, it is a truly special liquor.

You can easily test this by reducing both oyster liquor and seawater over moderate heat. The seawater will evaporate and leave nothing but a crust of salt and minerals; the oyster liquor will thicken into an aromatic sauce.

■ How an Oyster Should Taste

Oyster connoisseurs know how an oyster should taste, but defining this flavor with precision is as elusive as describing the flavor of a complex wine or a rare tea. Eleanor Clark, in the classic oyster book *The Oysters of Locmariaquer,* states, "the whole point is taste, you can't define it." I asked Kevin Shoemaker, general manager of Elliott's in Seattle, one of the region's top oyster restaurants, and his former chef, Tony Casad, to define the flavors of oysters. Shoemaker talked about distinguishing oysters of separate species and different growing regions by their salinity and their mineral content (how "metallic" their taste is). Casad agrees, adding that texture and sweetness are also important. Some oysters, he says, are a little creamier, like those from Westcott Bay on San Juan Island; others, like those from Orcas Island's Crescent Bays, are firmer. He also stresses the shape of the shell— whether deep or shallow—the shell color, and the way the shucked oyster looks on the half shell. "When the oysters are shucked properly, they look appealing," he adds. Shoemaker and Casad should know. At Elliott's annual "Oyster Sound Off," held each year in October, the restaurant serves more than 35 different kinds of oysters, all of them superbly fresh.

Bill Marinelli, a seafood broker who supplies about a third of those oysters, describes the flavor of oysters as "incredibly complex," and says you must judge an oyster the way you judge a fine wine. Aside from salinity and texture, you also evaluate the aftertaste, which may be fruity like watermelon, or crisp like cucumber. He describes some of the Pacific oysters he sells as "smoky." Marinelli insists that oysters, like wines, should be judged by the way they relate to other foods.

As I sit on the shore and relish the aftertaste of my farm-grown oyster, I reflect on the obvious, "forward" oyster flavors, which I compare to the cries of seabirds on the shore. Then I savor the hidden flavor elements, which are more elusive, like the song of the hermit thrush hidden deep within the shore woods. Because oysters are so delicate, I once compared the evanescence of their aroma and taste to the fleeting life of a morning glory, which opens in the morning but becomes a mere memory by nightfall. Yet, on further study, I discovered that oysters are also surprisingly sturdy. They can live out of water for up to a week, as long as their shells remain tightly closed. According to Bill Dewey, manager of Taylor Shellfish Farms, oysters can freeze solid, through and through, and come back to life when the weather warms, as long as they remain undisturbed in their beds. Despite their delicate flavor, they can hold their own against heavy flavors like vinegar, garlic, onion, and chili, perhaps in part because of their brininess.

An oyster's shape, size, and flavor are not only determined by its species, but also by its habitat. Oysters grown on rocks or racks, on long lines suspended in deep water, or in suspended trays or lantern nets, will taste cleaner than oysters grown in the silt of tide flats. Beach-grown oysters exposed to the elements have heavier shells than oysters always covered by water, and may thus stay fresh longer.

■ OYSTER SPECIES AND FARMERS

Oyster farmers on the Pacific Coast raise several different species: the native Olympia oyster, a tiny mollusk that rarely grows larger than 1.5 inches long; the Pacific Miyagi oyster, imported from Japan before World War II, but long since gone native; and the European flat oyster ("Euro-flat"), a succulent larger relative of the native Pacific Coast oyster. A few oyster farms grow a smaller, tasty sport of the Pacific oyster, the Japanese Kumamoto, though some wonder if this strain still exists in its pure form.

Pacific oysters like company, and if left alone they will settle on top of each other in dense clusters, making shucking a task for experts. For this reason, many Northwest oyster farms have traditionally sold their oysters shucked: the oysters are shucked at the farm, presorted by size, packed into jars, and shipped to restaurants and markets. Most are used in cooked dishes.

The Kumamoto, European flat, and native oyster have traditionally been sold in the shell and shucked just seconds before being consumed raw. During the last decade, advances in cultivation methods have led to the ready availability of single oysters that are easy to transport in the shell. These should not be shucked until just before they are slurped from the shell. Some oyster farms, like Samish Bay, grow only half-shell oysters; at others, almost all oysters are shucked on-site and sold in jars.

After leaving the oyster farm, I stop off the road, settle myself in a clearing with a view of the San Juan Islands, and sit down to an impromptu picnic. The office can wait.

WASHINGTON OYSTERS

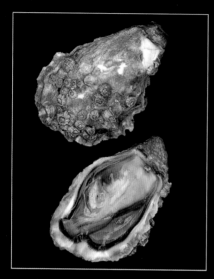

Pacific oyster, Hamma Hamma

Pacific *(Crassostrea gigas)*
Also known as Miyagi oysters, Pacifics are one of four types of the species *Crassostrea gigas* that once grew on the coast of Japan. They are now the most commonly cultivated oyster in the world. This hearty species can vary greatly depending on environment. Since there's so much range, Pacific oyster varieties are known by their growing area: a Coos Bay can be quite different from a Crescent Bay. The Pacific oyster's thick shell is fluted and usually rough. While they can grow to be quite large, these oysters are usually sold commercially when 3 to 4 inches in length. They have a firm, meaty texture and crisp, clean taste.

Olympia *(Ostrea lurida)*
The only true native oyster of the Washington coast, Olympias were enjoyed by Lewis and Clark when they reached the Pacific. Their tiny size—usually an inch or so—and sweet, mild taste make them a popular choice for the first-time raw-oyster eater.

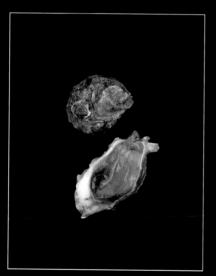

Olympia oyster, Willapa Bay

European flat oyster, Discovery Bay

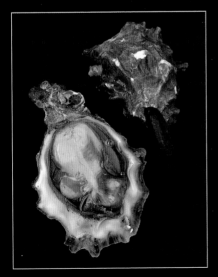

Pacific oyster, Dabob Bay
(Photos by Jean-Michel Addor)

European Flat or Belon Flat
(Ostrea edulis)
Washington coast oyster farmers grow these round, flat oysters from "seeds" imported from Europe, usually France. Once the most widely cultivated oyster, the European flat has a saline, somewhat metallic taste popular with connoisseurs. The pink flesh has a crisp yet tender texture.

Kumamoto *(Crassostrea sikamea)*
A native of Japan, these oysters are closely related to Pacifics; many argue that on the Pacific Northwest coast, the two species are genetically indistinct. Few farms in Washington raise Kumamotos, which are prized for their smooth flavor. Most are grown farther south, in Oregon and northern California.

Atlantic *(Crassostrea virginica)*
Like other oysters, the Atlantic is highly variable in shape, but generally has a smoother shell than the Pacific, and is more elongated than the Euro flat. They are grown along the East and Gulf Coasts, and today are also grown in Puget Sound.

■ What to Drink with Oysters

I accompany the oysters with chunks of dark rye bread and a rich, dark Pike Place stout. I used to insist on dry white wine with my oysters until I learned through a series of taste tests that beer and oysters are a better match.

On the other hand, dry European-style white wines may go better with European flat and native oysters. But I learned something surprising during these taste tests: red wine, rather than white, may be the perfect wine for oysters. Bill Marinelli agrees. When I told him I like Beringer Beaujolais Nouveau with oysters, Marinelli expressed his fondness for oysters and Saintsbury pinot noir from northern California's Carneros region, and for Oregon pinot noirs. This pairing is more logical than it seems. After all, many oyster aficionados dip their raw oysters into a red wine vinegar mignonette. One thing is certain: it's easier to match drink to cooked oysters than to raw ones because of the influence seasonings exert on the flavor of the dish. Back to the tasting room.

■ Shucked or in the Shell?

While I sometimes buy shucked oysters, I buy them only at the oyster farm and carry them home in a cooler, protected by ice. I asked Lee Wiegardt, manager of Jolly Roger Oyster Company in nearby Nahcotta, about the proper way to buy shucked oysters in the jar. "The oysters have to be coded," says Wiegardt. "Don't buy them if they're not coded." Oyster jars now have a pull date—14 days for most growers.

Wiegardt advises consumers to "buy the one farthest from the pull date." He adds that shucked oysters have "no smell when they're absolutely fresh." As they get older, oysters get a little sharp smell, then a "funky" smell, and then they can get downright stinky. To my nose, oysters that are too old have a whiff of overly ripe Limburger cheese. Wiegardt says shucked oysters should be stored at 28 to 31 degrees F—they contain enough salt to keep them from freezing. He also suggests that you take them home right away. Like all seafood, oysters should not just be set into a warm car but should be carried home in an ice chest.

It's equally important to find a seafood supplier you can trust, adds Wiegardt. But, he warns, you cannot smell the things that can really hurt you, such as polluted water. Willapa Bay is so pure, Wiegardt says, the federal government is using it to set nationwide water standards.

Oyster Recipes

Captain Whidbey Inn Poached Oysters

2 cups	Dry white wine
1 tbl	Dried sweet basil
1 tsp	Paprika
1 cup	Unsalted butter
6 pints	Shucked oysters
	Toasted French bread rounds

Combine wine, basil, paprika, and butter in a large, heavy skillet and bring to a boil. Add oysters all at once. Poach until oysters become firm and opaque. Immediately remove from liquid. Serve oysters on rounds of toasted French bread. Carefully skim butter off top of poaching liquid and pour over oysters. Serve with a crisp white sauvignon blanc or semillion.

Serves 8 to 12

Marinated Oysters

2 pints	Extra small oysters (shucked)
1 cup	White wine vinegar
2 tsp	Fresh French tarragon
3 tbls	Pickling spice
¼ cup	Amontillado sherry

In a large saucepan, simmer oysters in their liquor until curled at the edges (about 3 to 5 minutes). Combine remaining ingredients in a small saucepan and cook over medium heat for 10 minutes. Drain oysters thoroughly and transfer to a bowl. Strain sauce and pour liquid over oysters. Cover and refrigerate for at least 3 hours. Serve chilled with crackers.

Serves 6 to 8

Mignonette

⅔ cup	Champagne or sparkling wine
⅓ cup	Champagne vinegar
1	Large shallot, finely diced
	Liberal grind of coarse black pepper

Mix all ingredients in a nonreactive bowl. Pour into small bowls and serve with oysters on the half shell for dipping.

Serves 6 to 8

HEAVENLY
OYSTERS

■ MY FAVORITES

I've watched the Pacific Northwest oyster industry grow during the last decade, and I've eaten a lot of oysters. My favorites? Umpqua flats from Winchester Bay, the Kumamotos in Tillamook Bay, the native oysters from Willapa Bay, and the Pacifics raised in Westcott Bay on San Juan Island and in Samish Bay. This is not to say I don't like oysters from other growing regions. My mouth waters at the thought of slurping delicate Fanny Bays and Lasqueti Islands from Georgia Strait, crisp Crescent Bays from Orcas Island, richly flavored Hamma Hamma oysters from Hood Canal, assertive Quilcenes from Quilcene Bay, the flavorful Pacifics raised in Coos Bay, and last but not least, the creamy Willapas from the West Coast's largest oyster-producing bay.

ODE TO THE OYSTER

The world's oyster lovers included the satirist Jonathan Swift, who summed up his feelings in "Oysters":

> Charming oysters I cry:
> My masters, come buy,
> So plump and so fresh,
> So sweet is their flesh,
> No Colchester oyster
> Is sweeter and moister:
> Your stomach they settle,
> And rouse up your mettle:
> They'll make you a dad
> Of a lass or a lad;
> And madam your wife
> They'll please to the life;
> Be she barren, be she old,
> Be she slut, or be she scold,
> Eat my oysters, and lie near her,
> She'll be fruitful, never fear her.

(opposite) Shucked oysters being jarred, near Nahcotta on the Long Beach Peninsula.
(following page) Pike Place Market is one of the best places in Seattle to buy fresh seafood.

Buying Washington Seafood

You are driving down the coast, blissfully gazing out the window—water as far as the eye can see—and suddenly you become inspired to stock up on seafood.

Well, maybe. Just a few years ago it was pretty difficult to find fresh seafood on the coast, unless you caught, dug, or gathered it yourself. That's not because there weren't fresh fish, clams, crabs, or oysters. There were. But they went from boat to packing house, from packing house to big-city distributor, and then from the distributor back to coastal fish markets and supermarkets. Which means that you might find fresher seafood in Seattle than in fishing harbors like Bellingham or Willapa Bay.

The locals didn't care because they didn't have to buy seafood at a market. They'd catch it themselves or get it free from friends. Even today, coastal types rarely order seafood when they eat out. There's enough of it at home in the freezer. When locals dine out, they order steak. Which is why, more often than not, the steak served in restaurants up and down the coast is better than the seafood.

Oyster shells discarded after shucking are recycled as fertilizer.

HEAVENLY
OYSTERS

All that has been changing for some time. Fewer people have time to go fishing or digging for clams, which means they're now buying seafood at the market. And that means quality is up, since seashore residents know what fresh seafood is supposed to taste like. From north to south, below are places to pick up oysters at the source.

■ Bow/Bellingham

Chuckanut Drive is a narrow road that winds south from Bellingham between steep sandstone cliffs and the tide flats of Samish Bay. **Taylor Shellfish Farms** has the most scenic of all oyster farm locations in Washington. To the west, the mountainous San Juan Islands rise from the sea. The farm's small store sells different types of oysters, plus fresh crab (live and cooked), pink scallops in the shell, clams, and mussels. *188 Chuckanut Drive, Bow; 360-766-6002.*

At **Blau Oyster Company,** off the beaten path on Samish Island, you can buy fish, crab, and other seasonal seafood. *919 Blue Heron Road, Bow; 360-766-6171.*

Staked salmon is barbecued during the Makah Days festival held every August on the Makah Indian Reservation.

■ **ANACORTES**

On your way to the outer coast, if you're going by way of Fidalgo and Whidbey Islands, is the small roadside shack of **Strom's Shrimp**. The locally caught shrimp are tasty and make for a great snack while you're waiting for the Keystone ferry to take you to Port Townsend. *1481 State Route 20, Anacortes; 360-293-2531.*

■ **HOOD CANAL**

Shells are piled high at the **Hama Hama Oyster Company,** where shellfish are kept fresh in live tanks. Besides the oysters, which have an uncommonly delicate texture, there are excellent clams as well as geoduck (pronounced "gooey-duck"), the uncouth-looking giant clam of the Northwest. Never mind how it looks—the meat is delicious! The Puget Sound inlets south of Hood Canal have oyster farms, but these are difficult to find and most prefer to sell wholesale. *South of the Hamma Hamma River; 360-877-6938.*

■ **WESTPORT**

Brady's Oysters has rope-grown Pacific oysters known for their big, meaty flavor. They also have tiger prawns, shrimp, salmon, tuna, and other fresh seafood. *3714 Oyster Place East; 360-268-0077.*

Nelson Crab has excellent canned oysters in a variety of sizes in addition to crab, smoked king salmon, and coho. *3088 Kindred Avenue, Tokeland; 360-267-2911.*

■ **WILLAPA BAY**

At **R&B Oyster Company**, in Bay Center, you can buy mud-farmed and rope-grown Pacific oysters. *414-D Dike Road; 360-875-5324.*

■ **LONG BEACH PENINSULA**

Jolly Roger Oyster Company has a variety of mud-farmed Pacific Oysters, from "yearlings" to jumbo-size. *Nahcotta dock; 360-665-4111.*

Oysterville Sea Farms sells Pacific oysters in shells and shucked. *Oysterville Dock; 360-665-6585.*

NORTHWEST INTERIOR

SEATTLE AND THE OTHER CITIES on the eastern shore of Puget Sound are close to both sea and mountains. One of the area's great attractions has always been the ease with which travelers can move between the mountains and the islands in Puget Sound. From Snoqualmie Pass north to Canada, hundreds of miles of hiking trails wind through the Alpine Lakes, Glacier Peak, and Noisy-Diobsud Wilderness Areas, Ross Lake National Recreation Area, and North Cascades National Park. To the west, killer whales, ferries, kayaks, and sailboats travel through the islands. For nature lovers, the entire state is an embarrassment of riches, but this region may just be the jewel in Washington's crown.

■ NORTH CASCADES *map page 137, C-1*

The granite peaks of the North Cascades are more rugged and ancient than the eroded hills south of Snoqualmie Pass. Drive into these mountains on a cloudy day and the evergreens on the steep slopes look almost black, and the rock walls seem to rise from earth to heaven. On the lower slopes, the soil of the rocky trail may be dry as dust in the heat of summer, while patches of snow farther up linger among wildflower meadows in full bloom with white or golden lilies, bright red-orange Indian paintbrush, and intensely purple lupines. As you climb higher, ridge succeeds ridge, their misty outlines towered over by great, snow-capped volcanoes.

In the solitude of the mountains, hikers may not encounter other people, but they will certainly meet plenty of wild creatures—whiskeyjacks, juncos, buntings, pikas, chipmunks, mountain goats, and, in rare instances, cougars. The heavy snows of winter, and the rock and ice of the high country, have not made the mountains inhospitable to wildlife. Wolves, once hunted nearly to extinction in the North Cascades, are making a comeback. Threatened northern spotted owls and marbled murrelets nest here, and salmon spawn in many rivers. Grizzly bears, though rarely seen, are not uncommon in this region.

The North Cascades start at Snoqualmie Pass, due east of Seattle, and continue south all the way to California. From Snoqualmie Pass north, three paved roads

Liberty Bell Mountain looms over Washington Pass along the North Cascades Highway.

cross the mountains: I-90, the fastest, crosses the 3,022-foot pass; farther north, slower but equally scenic U.S. 2 crosses 4,061-foot Stevens Pass; and farthest north, U.S. 20, the North Cascades Highway—the slowest but most scenic of all—crosses 5,477-foot Washington Pass.

You can make a long loop through Snoqualmie and Stevens Passes or a much longer loop through Snoqualmie Pass and the North Cascades. Smaller roads, many unpaved, lead to trailheads, campgrounds, and fishing spots all along the Cascades.

■ SNOQUALMIE PASS   *map page 137, C-5*

Most transcontinental traffic between Seattle and the Eastern Seaboard gets funneled over the Cascades through Snoqualmie Pass on the fast lanes of I-90. Snoqualmie is the pass for people in a hurry; for those who aren't, there are ample roads to wander off the main highway. Some of these northerly roads lead to the half-million-acre **Alpine Lakes Wilderness Area,** a haven for hikers, fishermen, and backpackers. *425-888-1421.*

Snowfalls on the rails over Snoqualmie Pass were sometimes so heavy that rotary plows could not operate. In those instances, Chinese laborers were hired to dig the tracks clear by hand, as captured in this 1886 photograph. (University of Washington Libraries)

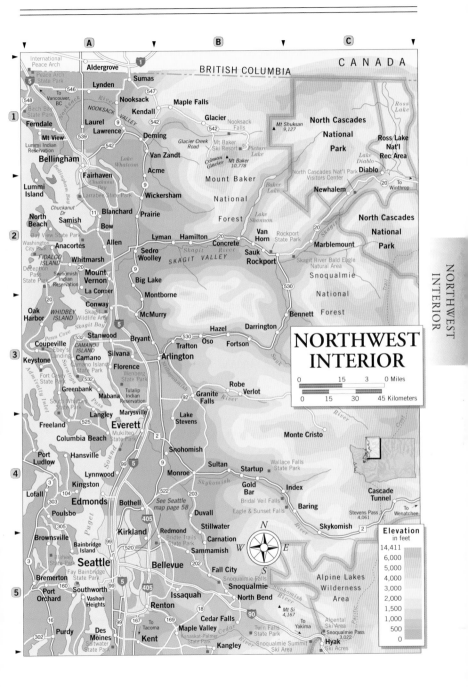

NORTHWEST INTERIOR

0		15		3		0 Miles
0		15	30			45 Kilometers

Elevation
in feet

14,411	
6,000	
5,000	
4,000	
3,000	
2,000	
1,500	
1,000	
500	
0	

The crew and passengers on an inaugural trip of the Great Northern Railway pause for a photo opportunity in the early 1890s. (Museum of History and Industry)

Despite its modest elevation, Snoqualmie Pass can easily receive 35 feet of snow a year, making this a perfect destination for skiers. Most head for the groomed slopes, abundant trails, and warm firesides of ski areas like Alpental, Ski Acres, and Summit-at-Snoqualmie. *425-434-7669.*

In the foothills west of the pass, popular trails lead through the so-called **Issaquah Alps** or climb the steep southern slope of 4,167-foot **Mount Si,** the crag that looms over the upper Snoqualmie Valley. Nearby, the Snoqualmie River plunges 268 feet over a stone ledge at **Snoqualmie Falls.**

The Northwest Railway Museum operates the **Snoqualmie Valley Railroad,** whose antique coaches wind for 5 miles through the upper Snoqualmie Valley. *38625 Southeast King Street, Snoqualmie; 425-888-3030.*

(opposite) A high climber tops a tree that will be used as a spar pole for cable logging in this 1923 Asahel Curtis photograph. (Washington State Historical Society)

■ EVERETT *map page 137, A-3/4*

Seattle's economy extends at least to the southern edge of Everett, where **Boeing** manufactures commercial aircraft in the largest space under one roof in the world. You can view aircraft in various stages of assembly on plant tours. *800-464-1476 or 360-756-0086.*

Historically a mill town, Everett lies on the shore of Port Gardner Bay, an inlet of northeast Puget Sound, bounded on the east and north by the dark waters of the Snohomish River. Lumber mills loom over Everett's waterfront, as they have for more than a century. Most have closed now, as many jobs have moved to the Boeing plant south of town.

In the late 1880s, as the Great Northern Railway inched west from Minneapolis, Port Gardner was proposed as the railroad's western terminus. (Trains, including

(above) Crowded conditions in logging camps, as seen in the bunkhouse above, led to labor unrest among loggers and miners. (Museum of History and Industry)
(opposite) Air-lifting logs out of difficult-to-reach areas is a 20th-century innovation that ameliorated harsh working conditions for loggers.

Amtrak's *Empire Builder,* still roll into Everett from the east by way of Stevens Pass—or rather *under* Stevens Pass through one of the nation's longest railroad tunnels.) Sensing the site's economic potential as a lumber source, local investors teamed up with Tacoma lumber baron Henry Hewitt and a group of eastern capitalists, including Charles Colby and John D. Rockefeller, Sr., to form the Everett Land Company (named for Colby's son Everett). The town became Everett in 1890.

Frederick Weyerhaeuser subsequently built what became the world's biggest sawmill on Everett's shore. Early-20th-century buildings decorate the downtown area. Within a few blocks, you can see the old wing of the Spanish mission–style courthouse with its clock and bell tower; the art deco City Hall; and the massive Romanesque Federal Building. Many of the mansions built by lumber barons still stand on Grand and Rucker Avenues at the north end of town. Several blocks north on 18th Street are the marina and **Marina Village,** a string of waterfront restaurants and shops. This is where you can catch the ferry to **Jetty Island** for a day of picnicking, hiking, and bird-watching. The marina is also where you can experience the popular **Everett Farmers Market** on Sundays. While in town, make sure to drop by the **Snohomish County Museum** (2817 Rockefeller Avenue; 425-259-2022), which has changing exhibits featuring the work of regional and international artists.

Darrington

Northeast of Everett, off Route 530 in the Cascade foothills, is Darrington, settled by loggers from North Carolina in 1890. A **Bluegrass Festival** (360-436-1006) held each July celebrates the town's Tarheel roots. In this scenic valley, cattle graze in wet meadows, with the crags and spires of the North Cascades rising behind them.

■ SKAGIT RIVER VALLEY *map page 137, A/B-2*

The jade green Skagit River rises in Canada and flows down through the North Cascades, entering Puget Sound in a wide delta southwest of Mount Vernon. Much of it is protected as the Skagit National Wild and Scenic River. Whistling swans, snow geese, and other birds live here. For a look at the Skagit River delta farmlands, turn off the freeway south of Mount Vernon and head west to Conway, a quiet hamlet with a white-steepled church built in 1916.

Mystic Skagit Valley

It is a poetic setting, one which suggests inner meanings and invisible connections. The effect is distinctly Chinese. A visitor experiences the feeling that he has been pulled into a Sung dynasty painting, perhaps before the intense wisps of mineral pigment have dried upon the silk. From almost any vantage point, there are expanses of monochrome worthy of the brushes of Mi Fei or Kuo Hsi.

The Skagit Valley, in fact, inspired a school of neo-Chinese painters. In the Forties, Mark Tobey, Morris Graves and their gray-on-gray disciples turned their backs on cubist composition and European color and, using the shapes and shades of this misty terrain as a springboard, began to paint the visions of the inner eye. A school of sodden, contemplative poets emerged here, too. Even the original inhabitants were an introspective breed. Unlike the Plains Indians, who enjoyed mobility and open spaces and sunny skies, the Northwest coastal tribes were caught between the dark waters to the west, the heavily forested foothills and towering Cascade peaks to the east; forced by the lavish rains to spend weeks on end confined to their longhouses. Consequently, they turned inward, evolving religious and mythological patterns that are startling in their complexity and intensity, developing an artistic idiom that for aesthetic weight and psychological depth was unequaled among all the primitive races. Even today . . . a hushed but heavy force hangs in the Northwest air: it defies flamboyance, deflates extroversion and muffles the most exultant cry.

—Tom Robbins, *Another Roadside Attraction*, 1971

Skagit Wildlife Area

Ducks and geese are most common here in spring and fall, when huge flocks stop on their way to and from wintering marshes in California's Sacramento Valley. Waterfowl, especially swans, stay all winter. There is nothing more stirring than to watch a skein of trumpeter swans flying overhead, their melodic bugling drifting across the marsh. In summer, watch for goldfinches collecting thistledown for nests. Swallows twitter in the air, and the booming "oonk-ka-ch'oonk" of a bittern may resound from the reeds. Great blue herons may wade in the shallow water, carefully measuring each step, and if you're lucky, you'll see a beaver carry sticks and twigs to a lodge. Don't forget your camera and binoculars.

To reach this bird-watcher's paradise, take the Conway–La Conner Road off I-5 heading west. After winding past fields and farms, the road crosses a bridge to the top of the Skagit River levee, where signs will point you to the park. Before you go, however, look at the current hunting regulations. You're not going to see many birds on days open to hunting.

The Skagit Valley has the largest concentration of trumpeter swans in the lower 48 states. At least 3,000 swans migrate to Skagit County annually, staying from October to March. The best place for up-close viewing is **Johnson/DeBay Swan Reserve** and the best viewing opportunities are in late January. *College Way Exit, east from I-5 in Mount Vernon, turn left at LaVenture Road, following the road until it becomes Francis Road. Turn left on DeBay Isle Road.*

Mount Vernon

Straddling the Skagit River along I-5 is Mount Vernon, whose small but bustling downtown includes a Mexican grocery, two bike shops, a good bakery, and a small bookstore with an entire shelf devoted to UFO abductions. The valley is famous for its daffodils and Dutch iris fields, but is also known for tulips. The **Skagit Valley Tulip Festival,** in April, celebrates the spring blooms with exhibits, barbecues, picnics, walks, runs, a parade, and fireworks. *From I-5, take Exits 221–231. Exit 226 takes you to the Tulip Festival office and information center; 360-428-5959.*

When festival time rolls around, everyone wants to get in on the act, including tulip lovers in Anacortes and Sedro Woolley. Don't be fooled. The only towns close to the fields are La Conner and Mount Vernon. During the annual April Tulip Festival, drop by the **Tulip Town** shops and flower fields *(15002 Bradshaw Road, 360-424-8152)* and also take in the 3-acre display garden at **Roozengarde** (15867 Beaver Marsh Road; 360-424-8531), or the splendid tulip displays at **Skagit Valley Gardens** (I-5 near Exit 221; 360-424-6760).

Between Conway and La Conner, the delta spreads out in a patchwork of fallow and green fields. Farmhouses with old barns dot the side of the road at regular intervals, and drainage ditches wind through green fields. You can tell from far off that one old clapboard building atop a levee is a country store because it advertises the usual "BAIT, AMMO, COLD BEER." On a clear day, white-topped Mount Baker presides over the landscape.

(preceding pages) Mount Vernon in the Cascade Mountains rises above fog settling in over Skagit Valley. (right) Fields of tulips in bloom, in time for the annual Skagit Valley Tulip Festival.

La Conner

La Conner lies along the eastern bank of the Swinomish Channel, a narrow inland waterway used as a marine passage from Padilla Bay to Puget Sound. Quaint "olde tyme" boutiques, craft stores, and antique marts occupy the many early-20th-century buildings along La Conner's First Street. You can browse for trinkets in the many shops, or dine alfresco in restaurants overlooking the channel.

La Conner's reputation as an artists' colony dates back to the late 1930s, when Northwest School painters Guy Anderson and Morris Graves took up residence here in a dilapidated cabin. The town got a boost in the 1970s when novelist and pop philosopher Tom Robbins became the most famous resident. La Conner is atmospheric, friendly, and relaxed.

Fine old Victorian homes and churches stand on the cliff above the commercial district, and the **Skagit County Historical Museum** (501 Fourth Street; 360-466-3365) sits atop a nearby hill. The museum's galleries display Native American crafts, tools, and art.

■ NORTH CASCADES NATIONAL PARK *map page 137, C-1/2*

The Skagit River tumbles out of some of the state's most wild and beautiful country. Upstream from the vacation town of Rockport, the **Skagit River Bald Eagle Natural Area** (360-445-4441) attracts at least 500 of the birds every winter. Beyond the eagle refuge, Route 20, the North Cascades Scenic Highway, follows the river through **Ross Lake National Recreation Area,** a buffer zone between the northern and southern units of North Cascades National Park. Campgrounds, trailheads, lodges, resorts, and boat launches abound.

The drive along the highway is truly scenic. Stop for the views from Goodall Creek Viewpoint and Diablo Lake, Ross Lake, and Washington Pass overlooks.

North Cascades National Park has an estimated 1,700 plant species, more than botanists have found in any other national park in the United States. The highway's climax is Washington Pass (5,477 feet), from which short hikes lead to Snagtooth Ridge, Cooper Basin, and the jagged peak of Liberty Bell.

The park itself is a roadless wilderness accessible only on foot. Trails connect the park and recreation area with the Pasayten Wilderness to the east, and to Glacier Peak Wilderness and Lake Chelan National Recreation Area to the south. Water taxis take hikers up 24-mile-long Ross Lake to trailheads far north of the road. Short trails starting at campgrounds or the side of the highway can easily be covered in a day or a few hours. Fishermen can rent boats and motors at **Ross Lake Resort** or **Diablo Lake Resort.**

Both Ross and Diablo Lakes were created early in the 20th century by Seattle City Light power dams. The scenic trip up Diablo Lake ends at the foot of Ross Dam. A 4-mile hike takes you to Cascade Pass and back, through acres of lupines and white-tufted beargrass. *North Cascades National Park; 360-854-7200 (visitor information) and 360-854-7245 (wilderness information).*

■ CHUCKANUT DRIVE   *map page 137, A-1/2, and page 159, B-3*

Route 11, also known as Chuckanut Drive, got its start early in the 20th century as the first highway heading south from Bellingham, Fairhaven, Skagit County, and Seattle (before the road was built, people traveled by steamer or railroad). For a dozen miles, this 23-mile road winds above Chuckanut Bay and Samish Bay. The steep and heavily wooded Chuckanut and Blanchard Mountains limit the roadway to a narrow passage along sandstone cliffs. Turnouts frame magical views across the water to the San Juan Islands.

NORTHWEST INTERIOR

A view of Diablo Lake, and the North Cascades Highway winding along its shores.

The drive south begins in Fairhaven, and after skirting the mountains and traversing the flat farmlands of the Samish Valley near Bow, joins up with I-5 at Burlington. You'll pass **Larrabee State Park** along the way, at the foot of Chuckanut Mountain. The mountain has been logged assiduously, but wooded wilderness remains. Miles of trails lead through fir and maple forests to hidden lakes and cliff-top lookouts. There are sandy beaches warm enough for summer sunning, a rocky shore with tide pools, and headlands occasionally graced by passing gray whales and orcas. The park has picnic and campground areas, and there is a small boat ramp for kayaks. Crabbing and bird-watching opportunities abound. *245 Chuckanut Drive; 360-676-2093.*

There's much else to see and do along this scenic passage. Check out the small town of Bow, just east of Samish Bay, and when you're hungry, two classic restaurants should do nicely: **Chuckanut Manor** (302 Chuckanut Drive; 360-766-6191), with its handsome, glassed-in dining room and bar; and the **Oyster Bar** (240 Chuckanut Drive; 360-766-6185), which has the best marine views of any coastal restaurant in Washington State.

■ BELLINGHAM *map page 137, A-1, and page 159, B-2*

The last big town before the Canadian border is Bellingham, whose urban core has fallen on hard times since a mall opened north of town. Cobbled together from four pioneer communities in 1903, Bellingham is mostly a fishing port, but it's also home to **Western Washington University,** whose campus rests high on Sehome Hill. From the freeway, all you see of Bellingham is a strip mall, but downtown you'll find elegant **Mount Baker Theater** (104 North Commercial Street) and the **Whatcom Museum of History and Art** (121 Prospect Street; 360-676-6981), a late-19th-century brick affair north of Champion Street. The collection here includes Native American artifacts, exhibits on pioneering and logging, and Northwest contemporary art. The museum faces Bellingham Bay from its perch atop a steep bluff.

Fairhaven

Fairhaven's downtown is filled with coffee shops, bookstores, and restaurants. Farther afield of downtown, you'll find cottages and gardens, green woods bordering a purling creek, wildflower meadows, and, along the bayfront, sandstone cliffs, tide flats, and fishing boats. The ferry to Alaska docks here, at the former site of

Mount Baker forms a vivid backdrop to the San Juan Islands.

one of the world's largest salmon canneries. In summer, passenger ferries carry visitors to the San Juan Islands and Victoria on Vancouver Island.

Fairhaven is rife with history. Ancient shell middens and stone tools, many of them thousands of years old, are proof that the mouth of Padden Creek has long been occupied by humans. The Lummi Nation once had a fishing village here, and there are legends of a fierce battle between the local tribes and Spanish pirates in Padden Marsh in the 1600s. There is no historic proof of the battle, but pioneers recorded their discovery of a Spanish chalice, dated 1640, embedded in a muddy bank.

Few historic remains of the 19th-century waterfront survive, but a local historical society has put down plaques throughout the village, marking such sites as the city's drowning pool (for dogs only, it says, where the local constable killed stray pets); the shore where Fairhaven moored its prison (a barge); the site of the town pillory (Fairhaven had one as late as the 1890s); and the place where a saloon owner died in a gun battle.

Fairhaven residents are a motley lot of fishermen, college professors, poets, shipfitters, painters, and the sons and daughters of hippies who settled here in the

1960s. They're a friendly bunch, meeting at the **Colophon Café** (1208 11th Street) for breakfast or a bowl of African peanut soup; sipping coffee at **Tony's Coffee House** (Harris Avenue and 11th Street); or browsing the shelves of **Village Books** (1210 11th Street). Come evening, folks crowd into **Stanello's** (1514 12th Street) for the best pizza in town, or congregate at Post Point to watch the red sun sink behind the San Juan Islands.

To reach Fairhaven, take Old Fairhaven Parkway off I-5 and head west toward the water. Turn right on 12th Street and then left on Harris Street.

■ NOOKSACK VALLEY AND MOUNT BAKER *map page 137, B-1*

From Bellingham, Route 542 takes you east to 10,778-foot Mount Baker and the trails of the northernmost and wildest parts of North Cascades National Park.

Beyond Glacier, the steep cliffs rise higher and higher, trees become taller, and the boulders in the north fork of the Nooksack River become bigger. A few miles south on twisting Glacier Creek Road, you will encounter the trailhead for **Coleman Glacier.** A short trail leads to the glacier's snout, where ice pushes into the alders; a longer, steeper hike brings you to the glacier's side, where you can peer down into the crevasses and listen to the ice as it grinds downhill. Take a close look at the edges, where the ice meets the land. In midsummer, pink and white wildflowers cover this fertile verge.

The next stop is Nooksack Falls, reached by a short gravel road. Notice the nearly impenetrable tangle of trees, shrubs, ferns, and deep mosses as you head down the slope. This is a typical western Washington forest. The tree-girded falls plunges over a rocky ledge 170 feet into a narrow canyon, and a nearby grove of cedars is thousands of years old. If you're driving to Mount Baker in August or September, you'll see high-bush huckleberries by the road. The shrubs are about chest-high and have smallish light-green leaves and blue-black berries.

Picture Lake, near the end of the road, high up on the east slope of Mount Baker, has great picnic spots along its shores. **Mount Shuksan** looms across the valley. The blueberries here grow on low bushes, but they're worth every stoop you make to pick them. They ripen from August until late fall. If the snow has melted, you can drive to the end of the road, past the ski lodge, and hike along alpine ridges for good views of both Mount Baker and the glacier-cut valley of Baker Creek.

Deception Pass between Whidbey and Fidalgo Islands.

■ WHIDBEY ISLAND   *map page 137, A-2/3, and page 159, A-5*

Lying in the Olympic Mountain rain shadow, Whidbey Island receives little rain even during the wet season, and its many sunny summer days bring out visitors and locals alike. Farms, woods, and native prairies cover most of this peaceful isle. The towns are small.

Deception Pass State Park

British navigator Capt. George Vancouver sighted this channel in 1792. Hoping the rock-bound passage would lead to a secure harbor, Vancouver felt deceived when he realized it didn't, so he named it Deception Pass. The park itself has 4,134 acres of campgrounds, 77,000 feet of saltwater shoreline, and 33,900 feet of freshwater shoreline on four lakes. Hiking, swimming, fishing, and boating are popular here, and the views are breathtaking. *Route 20; 360-675-2417.*

Whidbey Island changes with the year, from the wildflower-covered meadows of spring to the windy days of winter, when new colonies of lichen spread across the decaying concrete walls of the abandoned forts like so many colorful ice flowers. Not that you'd often see real ice flowers here. The climate is mild year-round. An occasional wild rose may bloom on New Year's Day; rain and snow never stay long. Turquoise cabbage fields, yellow wheat patches, lush meadows, and scattered conifers cover the low, undulating landscape of the island's center. Plowed fields, black with the fertile loam of prairies, terminate in tall sand bluffs crowned by sculpted trees and weathered snags. One of the prairies has been preserved as **Ebey's Landing National Historical Reserve** (off Route 20; 360-678-6084).

Perego's Lagoon

At the north end of the reserve, a small turnout marks the beginning of the bluff trail and beach walk to Perego's Lagoon. The trail climbs along the leading edge of the prairie until it reaches a point about 240 feet above the waters of Admiralty Inlet. The hilltop affords a sweeping view of the water and the Olympic Mountains to the west. The land just off the trail is private property, so respect the rights of the owners by treading carefully.

The lagoon and bluff take their name from George Perego, a Civil War veteran who homesteaded here in 1876. Perego never farmed the land, and today it remains a wilderness—a windswept bluff of sand, rocks, and driftwood. Many of the rocks are not native to the island. They were carried here as ballast in sailing vessels whose stewards dumped them onto the beaches before the ships loaded Puget Sound lumber. Ravens and bald eagles may fly past, and don't be surprised if you see a rare peregrine falcon. Much of Whidbey Island is a wildflower paradise in spring, especially the steep meadow at the head of Penn Cove. This is one of the few places west of the mountains where wild blue flag grows in profusion.

From the head of Penn Cove, you can drive along winding, scenic Madrona Drive to the **Captain Whidbey Inn,** a long, two-story lodge on a wooded promontory. The inn is nestled in a scenic wonderland bordered on one side by Penn Cove and on the other by a secluded saltwater lagoon. A special kind of hospitality holds sway here. Gracefully aged, surrounded by native shrubs and trees, it is the perfect hideout for those who wish to escape from the stress of the world. The bar at the Captain Whidbey is a favorite hangout of local characters. *2072 West Captain Whidbey Inn Road, Coupeville; 360-678-4097.*

Whidbey Island Bridge at Deception Pass State Park.

Coupeville

Continuing down Madrona Drive brings you to Coupeville, a village founded in 1852 and known for its well-preserved Victorian-era downtown, colorful art galleries, restaurants, and antique shops. A pier and a few historic houses sit above the tide flats on mussel-encrusted wooden stilts (the oldest dates from the early 1850s). On a clear day, Mount Baker looms to the northeast, its white glaciers reflected in the waters of the cove. **Toby's Tavern,** on the waterfront, has the best views.

The **Island County Historical Museum** has exhibits that trace the history of the island's fishing, timber, and agricultural industries. The museum also hosts tours of the town's commercial buildings and many of its fine homes. *908 NW Alexander Street; 360-678-3310.*

Whidbey Island pioneers built blockhouses in the 1850s to protect themselves against hostile forces. In 1857, for instance, a band of the Tlingit tribe from Alaska raided the homestead of Col. Isaac Ebey and took his head to avenge the killing of a Tlingit chief by U.S. Marines. Some of the log structures still stand in the town of Coupeville.

The 53-acre **Meerkerk Rhododendron Gardens,** in Greenbank, has 1,500 native and hybrid species of rhododendrons. The flowers are in full bloom in April and May. *Resort Road; 360-678-1912.*

Langley

Another attractive walking village is **Langley**, to the south, with galleries, restaurants, a bakery, and small, well-stocked shops. Tranquil and casual, Langley is a great place for biking, walking, and kayaking. The village's **Island County Fair** (360-221-4677) takes place in late August with agricultural exhibits, a parade, and logging competitions.

Fort Casey State Park

Fort Casey State Park, on the island's western shore, has fortifications built in the 1890s, including **Admiralty Point Lighthouse.** You can explore the grounds, check out the cannon, or hike on the bluff, through the woods, or on the long sand and cobble beach. Divers flock to the underwater park on the south side of the Keystone/Port Townsend ferry landing, but since the attractions here are subtidal, there's not much for the casual visitor to see. *Three miles south of Coupeville; 360-678-4519.*

NORTHWEST
INTERIOR

■ FIDALGO ISLAND *map page 137, A-2, and page 159, A-4/5*

Wooded and rural, with massive rocks that rise straight from the sea on one side and tide flats stretching across Padilla Bay on the other, Fidalgo Island is instantly appealing. Its only town, Anacortes, has ferries to the San Juan Islands. But Fidalgo itself is worth exploring. It's connected to the mainland by a bridge (Route 20) across Swinomish Channel, a winding saltwater slough. Look for terns fishing over the saltwater channels (and plunging head first into the brine), and for harbor seals sunning themselves on the sand banks at low tide.

Anacortes

The charms of Anacortes, on the island's northwestern shore, include attractive parks and sweeping views, the 19th-century residential neighborhood of **Causland Park,** and an attractive old downtown area. South of town and accessible by a paved road, Mount Erie (1,270 feet) offers views of Campbell Lake, Deception Pass, and, on clear days, both Mount Rainier and Mount Baker. Exhibitions at the **Anacortes Historical Museum** (1305 Eighth Street; 360-293-1915) focus on the cultural heritage of Fidalgo and nearby Guemes Islands.

A dense tangle of Douglas fir, cedar, madrona, and alder covers the rocky hill of **Washington City Park.** Broken now and then by clearings and meadows, the park rises from the waters of Rosario Strait and extends to the rocky crest of Fidalgo Head. You can navigate it by car on a 2.4-mile loop road, or explore it on one of the many trails winding through the woods. *Route 20; 360-293-1927.*

Fidalgo Head

Grass-covered cliffs on Fidalgo Head rise from the churning currents of Burrows Channel in a series of rocky steps that lead to forested ridges. Bedecked with wildflowers in spring, the cliffs appear to be well-tended rock gardens, but the arrangement of elements here is all nature's handiwork. Fidalgo Head is composed of serpentine and ultrabasic rocks, which also make up the southern part of Cypress Island, to the immediate north. These stones are akin to the dunite rock of the Twin Sisters at the edge of the North Cascades, but are unrelated to other boulders in the vicinity. Twisted junipers crouch on the exposed cliffs of Fidalgo Head. Their tangled roots grip the convoluted rocks, and their gnarled branches reach defiantly into the sky. Hawks and bald eagles ceaselessly patrol the shore.

NORTHWEST INTERIOR

APPLE AND CHEESE TOUR

Owing to differences in climate throughout Washington, different types of apples grow east and west of the Cascade Mountains. Most people know about eastern Washington apples but are unaware that western Washington also grows great apples.

Apples and cheese make a great duo, and it's likely that you'll find just the right cheese to enhance the flavor of the locally grown fruit. Start the tour in Whatcom County, north of Ferndale, by taking Grandview from I-5 west to Kickerville and turning left. Pleasant Valley Dairy is on your left.

Pleasant Valley Dairy   *map page 159, A-1*
The gouda and farmstead cheeses here are made from raw cow's milk and go well with Whatcom and Skagit County apples. The dairy is open on Saturdays from January through June. *6804 Kickerville Road; 360-366-5398.*

Appel Farms   *map page 159, A/B-1*
The Appels make four cheeses: gouda (aged or smoked), quark (German-style sour cream cheese), *paneer* (East Indian fresh cheese), and squeaky cheese (unpressed, unaged cheddar), named for the sound produced when you bite into it. *6605 Northwest Road, off I-5, Ferndale; 360-312-1431.*

Samish Bay Cheese   *map page 159, B-4*
Excellent aged gouda made from unpasteurized milk, a montasio, and a delightful Mont Blanchard are made here. A sign on the east side of Chuckanut Drive (south of where the road enters the flats) directs you to the cheese works. Call for hours. *15115 Bow Hill Road, Bow; 360-766-6707.*

Merrit's Apples   *map page 159, B-4*
On a clear day, with snowcapped Mount Baker looming in the eastern sky, you are likely to think you've rediscovered the Garden of Eden here. When you bite into one of the Gravenstein or Jonagold apples, you'll know you have. *8914 Bayview-Edison Road, Bow; 360-766-6224.*

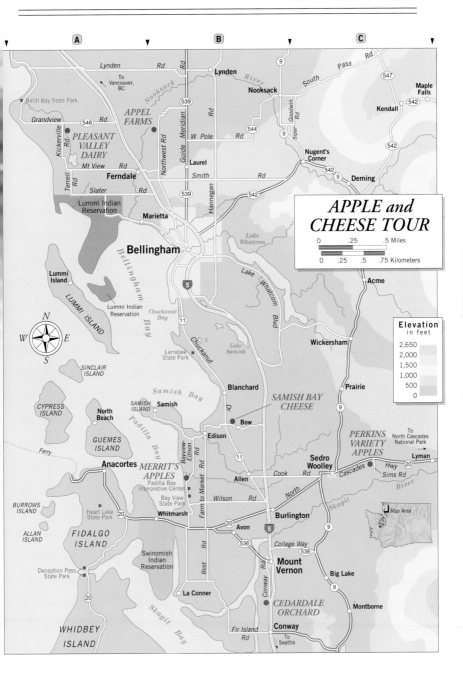

APPLE and CHEESE TOUR

0   .25   .5 Miles

0   .25   .5   .75 Kilometers

Elevation
in feet

2,650
2,000
1,500
1,000
500
0

Lynden Rd

To Vancouver, BC

Lynden

River

South Pass Rd

547

Maple Falls

Nooksack

542

Kendall

Birch Bay State Park

539

APPEL FARMS

544

Grandview

548

Rd

W. Pole

Rd

9

Siper Rd

Goodwin Rd

Nugent's Corner

542

PLEASANT VALLEY DAIRY

Northwest Rd

Guide Meridian Rd

Laurel

542

Mt View Rd

Smith

Rd

542

9

Deming

Ferndale

539

Hannegan Rd

542

Terrell Rd

Slater Rd

Lummi Indian Reservation

Marietta

Lake Whatcom

Bellingham

Lummi Island

Lummi Indian Reservation

Chuckanut Bay

5

Lake Whatcom Blvd

Acme

LUMMI ISLAND

Bellingham Bay

11

Chuckanut Dr

Lake Samish

Wickersham

N W E S

SINCLAIR ISLAND

Larrabee State Park

CYPRESS ISLAND

Samish Bay

SAMISH ISLAND

Samish

Blanchard

SAMISH BAY CHEESE

Prairie

9

North Beach

Bow

GUEMES ISLAND

Padilla Bay

Edison

PERKINS VARIETY APPLES

To North Cascades National Park

Ferry

11

Lyman

Anacortes

MERRIT'S APPLES

Bayview-Edison Rd

Sedro Woolley

Cascades Hwy

Sims Rd

Skagit River

BURROWS ISLAND

Padilla Bay Interpretive Center

Bay View State Park

Cook

North

Map Area

Heart Lake State Park

Whitmarsh

Allen

Wilson Rd

ALLAN ISLAND

20

Farm to Market Rd

FIDALGO ISLAND

20

Avon

5

Burlington

9

Swinomish Indian Reservation

536

College Way

538

Deception Pass State Park

Best Rd

Mount Vernon

Big Lake

20

La Conner

Conway Rd

CEDARDALE ORCHARD

Montborne

9

WHIDBEY ISLAND

Skagit Bay

Fir Island Rd

Conway

To Seattle

Cedardale Orchard   *map page 159, B-5*

If you're in a hurry, skip the northern leg of this tour and stock up on westside apples at Cedardale Orchard, where you'll find the diverse flavors of Akane, Gala, Jonagold, Jonamac, Melrose, and Summered. *18216 Conway Frontage Road; South Mount Vernon Exit, off I-5 on Conrad Road; 360-416-6513.*

Continue the tour by taking Route 20, the North Cascades Highway, east from Burlington across the mountains.

Perkins Variety Apples and Eagle Haven Winery   *map page 159, C-4*

Your next chance to stock up on apples comes on Route 20, the North Cascades Highway, 3 miles east of Sedro Woolley, at Perkins Variety Apples. More than 100 varieties of apples are grown here, including Akane, Jonamac, and Melrose. Lay in a good supply. Perkins also makes five grape wines and four fruit wines. *8243 Sims Road; 360-856-6986.*

NORTHWEST INTERIOR

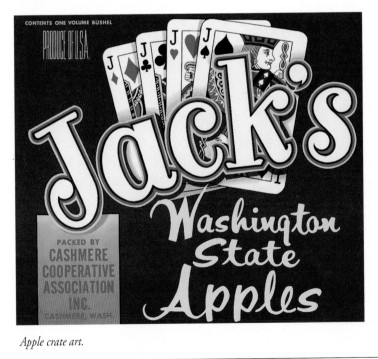

Apple crate art.

(opposite page) Apples and cheese. (University of Washington Libraries)

SAN JUAN ISLANDS

ISLANDS ARE SPECIAL PLACES, miniature continents with moods uniquely their own. In the Pacific Northwest, with its mist and fog, you sometimes wonder if they are terra firma at all, or if they float this way or that at the whim of the tide.

The inland waters of the Pacific Northwest, between the southern end of Puget Sound and the Canadian Inside Passage, contain hundreds of islands of various sizes, shapes, and elevations. Some are little more than reedy sandbars in river mouths; others have peaks that rise straight from the water for almost 3,000 feet. Some are so close to shore they have been tied to the mainland by bridges. Others are separated by deep, swift-running tidal channels or saltwater straits.

What really sets these islands apart is their exceptional beauty, which expresses itself in dramatic cliffs, lush seaside meadows, gnarled trees, and multicolored wildflowers that cling to rocks. The islands have valleys and mountains, forests filled with birds, and leafy glens where tiny island deer browse. A species of prickly pear cactus grows here, and the beaches, pebbly or sandy, are scenic. Offshore, seals splash on sandbanks and orcas patrol the deep channels.

The islands are visited by ducks and swans, herons and hawks, humans and whales. Many islands are settled; some have picturesque villages—only a few near

■ How To Get There

Although the islands are separated from the mainland (and from each other) by miles of salt water and often turbulent currents, they're easy to get to. Washington State Ferries (800-843-3779) runs several ferries each day to the four largest islands, Lopez, Shaw, Orcas, and San Juan. The ferries run frequently, but not to all the islands. Pick up a ferry schedule at the terminal. The lines are well marked and tell you where and when to catch each boat.

If you're in a hurry, and want the most out of your vacation time, take a single-engine airplane from Anacortes or Bellingham airports or hop a floatplane from Seattle's Lake Union or Lake Washington.

You can even charter a boat to explore the maze of islands. Many of the state parks have mooring buoys and docks, but get there early, they fill up fast.

Sea kayaking at Doe Bay, Orcas Island.

SAN JUAN ISLANDS

ferry landings—and some have resorts. There are campgrounds and ample beaches, places where hikers can pitch a tent. In years past, travelers could only get to the main islands, but passenger-only ferries now journey to the smaller, lesser-known, less-crowded islands.

The San Juans, the most beautiful of the Pacific Northwest's islands, lie north of the Strait of Juan de Fuca, between the northwest Washington mainland and Vancouver Island. Like the Canadian Gulf Islands to the north, the San Juans were once part of Vancouver Island, from which they were separated by the grinding action of continental glaciers during the last ice age. Because the ice—3,000 feet thick—pressed the land down into the earth's crust, the islands have been rising slowly ever since the ice melted.

Objects from archaeological digs indicate that these islands have been inhabited for at least 5,000 years. They were stopping-off points for Nanaimo and Cowichan Indians from Vancouver Island; for Salish, Musqueam, and Tsawwassen from the mainland of present-day British Columbia; and for Lummi and Samish from what is now Washington State. These tribes used the islands mostly as summer homes, camping in shelters of woven mats, and as a sort of natural supermarket, taking salmon and halibut from the reefs and harvesting camas root and berries on the land. The Indians had an ingenious fishing method—called reef netting—to catch salmon. They would string a net between two canoes in the shallow waters near the mouth of a river and wait for large groups of the fish to swim into the snare. The chief would ceremonially "welcome" the fish and thank them for their bounty, then the salmon would be scooped from the net into the canoes.

This method is still practiced today by a few traditional fishermen, though nets are now made of nylon, and the canoes might be made of plastic and equipped with an outboard motor.

It is believed that the islands were not settled permanently because they were regularly raided by Haida, Tlingit, and Kwakiutl warriors from the north, out to capture booty and slaves. In 1858, northern Indians—reportedly Stikine Tlingit from southeast Alaska—raided a Lummi summer village on the east shore of West Sound on Orcas Island. According to contemporary reports, the beach was soon littered with "over a hundred bodies." The site of that ill-fated village is still known as Massacre Bay. Raids continued long after Americans and British had settled along the inland waters and did not cease until the late 19th century. In 1846, when the Oregon Territory was divided between Britain and the United States, it was decided that the border south of the 49th parallel should run down the middle of the main channel between Vancouver Island and the mainland.

The vague language of that decision caused grief in the late 1850s, when the British decided that Rosario Strait, not Haro Strait as previously agreed, was the "main channel" separating the British from the American domain. War almost erupted between the two nations when an American settler shot a Hudson's Bay Company pig that had been raiding his San Juan Island potato patch. This so-called Pig War remained an *opera buffa* episode because cooler heads prevailed, leading to a joint occupation of San Juan Island by British and American troops until 1872, when the German emperor, Kaiser Wilhelm I, was asked to settle the dispute—he awarded the San Juans to the United States.

■ LOPEZ ISLAND *map page 164, B/C-3*

The first stop on the ferry run from Anacortes is Lopez, the flattest of the big islands. Its gentle topography has fostered agriculture since white settlers first arrived in the 1850s.

In summer, the island's 1,800 year-round residents are joined by vacationers who descend every sunny weekend. Like the rest of the San Juans, Lopez has managed to hold onto its identity and remain a unique community. Islanders are so sure of themselves they welcome visitors with open arms (unlike the more reclusive residents of some of the other islands).

Lopez Village

Lopez Village, on the island's western shore, has historic homes and buildings, some good restaurants, a winery, and a supermarket. There's also an interesting museum, **Lopez Island Historical Museum** (Weeks Road; 360-468-2049), which has maritime exhibits like reef net boats, a fish trap, and models of steam-

(above) Boats in Fisherman Bay, Lopez Island.
(preceding pages) The granite peaks of the North Cascades rise above the San Juan Islands.

boats. Displays of old utensils and horse-drawn farm machinery show how the pioneers lived. The museum's most unique object is San Juan County's first automobile. From the ferry terminal, you can reach Lopez Village by following Ferry Road south about 5 miles. You'll pass through two splendid parks, **Odin County Park** and **Spencer Spit Park.** Both are ideal for hiking, picnicking, and clamming.

Lopez Island Vineyards

Lopez Island Vineyards, a family-run winery, struggled for years growing grapes and making wine from certified organically grown estate grapes. Recent bottlings include a crisp siegerrebe that goes well with local seafood. The winery is open seasonally. Call first. *724 Fisherman Bay Road; 360-468-3644.*

■ ORCAS ISLAND *map page 164, B-1/2*

On the map, Orcas Island—the largest of the San Juan Islands—looks like a pair of well-worn saddlebags divided by long and slender Eastsound. Up close, Orcas is lush and steep, its roads narrow and contorted. Luxury homes occupy much of the coastline, but along the island's one main road the landscape is mostly rural or thickly forested with second-growth fir and alder.

At the end of the 19th century, fruit orchards and hop fields flourished in the fertile soil of Crow Valley, on the island's western side. All the crops went to market by boat, and as water transportation lost ground to railroads and then trucks, the island became commercially stranded. After irrigation projects converted the arid Wenatchee and Yakima Valleys of eastern Washington into fruit-growing centers, most of the island's orchards were abandoned.

The massive hump of Mount Constitution, the highest point in the San Juans, rises 2,409 feet above sea level on the eastern side. A steep, narrow road climbs to the mountain's summit. At road's end stands a watchtower built of hand-cut stone by the Civilian Conservation Corps in the 1930s. An open deck on top of the tower affords a spectacular 360-degree view of the area. To the east, Mount Baker's snowy cone rises over the North Cascades. The jagged ice-and-granite wall of the Cascades and the Canadian Coast Range closes out the eastern horizon, and the Olympics are etched onto the western sky.

Island artisans produce quality crafts, especially pottery and metal sculpture. One of the oldest and best-loved crafts studios is **Crow Valley Pottery & Gallery**

(2274 Orcas Road; 360-376-4260). **Orcas Island Artworks** (360-376-4408), on the Olga waterfront, sells works by local artists and has a popular café. **Howe Art Gallery** (west on Horseshoe Highway from Eastsound; Box 362; 360-376-2945) has kinetic sculptures that flutter, twist, and gyrate in the slightest breeze. **Darvill's Rare Print Shop** [Box 1387 (mail order only now); 360-376-2351] is renowned for its antique prints and maps of the Pacific Northwest and Europe.

Moran State Park

Mount Constitution is surrounded by Moran State Park, a forested 3,325-acre tract of land that covers most of Orcas Island's eastern lobe. Groves of spruce and fir—some of them 4 or 5 feet in diameter—grow near the cool, mossy gorge of Cascade Falls, a short walk from the Cold Springs trailhead.

The park was the gift of shipyard tycoon Robert Moran, who was Seattle's mayor at the time of the big fire of 1889. Moran made a fortune building steamships for the Klondike gold rush, then retreated to the San Juans, where he bought thousands of acres on Orcas. In 1906, he started construction on a 19-bedroom mansion (today the centerpiece of the Rosario resort) with two bowling alleys and an indoor pool. He donated most of his land to the state in 1921.

During the Depression, the Civilian Conservation Corps cleared the park's campsites and trails and built stone gazebos, the Mount Constitution Observation Tower, and the stone guardrails along the mountain's treacherous, winding road. *From the Orcas Island ferry, follow signs to Moran State Park; 888-226-7688.*

If you want to get a feel for what island living was like in the old days, when locally raised fruit and lamb were more lucrative than tourism, check out **Turtle-back Farm Inn** (Route 1, Eastsound, 360-376-4914 or 800-376-4914), in the shadow of Turtleback Mountain. Eighty acres of meadows, woods, and farmland, dating back to the late 1800s, create a pleasant refuge for sheep and black cattle, chickens, and ducks.

Rosario Spa & Resort (1400 Rosario Way, Eastsound; 360-376-2222 or 800-562-8820) is also a step back in time. This grand mansion, built in 1906, was the residence of shipbuilding magnate and former Seattle mayor Robert Moran. It was converted into a hotel in 1960 but soon fell upon hard times. Later renovations restored its luster, though, and the place is once again worth seeing.

(opposite) View from Mount Constitution of Rosario Strait and Mount Baker.
(preceding pages) Boats of all styles and sizes dock at Deer Harbor Marina on Orcas Island.

SAN JUAN
ISLANDS

If you want to meet locals and get involved in deep conversations on a long winter night, you should dine at **Christina's** (North Beach Road and Horseshoe Highway, 310 Main St. Eastsound; 360-376-4904), a homey waterfront restaurant.

■ SAN JUAN ISLAND *map page 164, A/B-2/3*

The most developed and second largest of the islands, San Juan is the last stop in U.S. waters on the ferry run from Anacortes and the seat of San Juan County government. San Juan's National Historic Park, vantage points for whale-watching, restaurants, hotels, and campgrounds attract droves of fair-weather visitors who disembark at the town of Friday Harbor.

A few ribbons of two-lane blacktop cross the island from coast to coast, winding past the small farms of the San Juan Valley. The roads are confusing and poorly marked, but eventually they all lead back to Friday Harbor. Traffic—both cars and bicycles—fills them every summer. Many cyclists will tell you that the best way to enjoy the islands is to leave your car in Anacortes, take ferries between the islands, then bike and camp at your leisure.

Friday Harbor

With a population of 1,600, Friday Harbor is the largest community in San Juan County. The town is named after Joe Friday, a Hawaiian shepherd who once lived here. Friday Harbor climbs the hill above the ferry landing and a neighboring marina. The town's remodeled early-19th-century homes have been converted into an assortment of chichi bistros, health food stores, and gift shops.

Friday Harbor's **Whale Museum,** a yellow, two-story building catercorner from the old brick courthouse on First Street, houses whale skeletons, models, and informational displays. Speakers in the stairwell broadcast what seem to be the sounds of creaking docks and keening seagulls. They're actually the recorded voices of local whale pods, often observed at Lime Kiln State Park on the island's west side. *Open June–September. 62 First Street North; 360-378-4710.*

San Juan Island National Historical Park

American and British troops occupied San Juan Island jointly for 12 years in the mid-19th century. American Camp, where U.S. forces lived, and British Camp, the British stronghold on the island's north end, are both administered today as San Juan Island National Historical Park.

AN ISLAND PORTRAIT

David Guterson's 1995 novel, Snow Falling on Cedars, *takes place on the fictional island of San Piedro, north of Puget Sound.*

Amity Harbor, the island's only town, provided deep moorage for a fleet of purse seiners and one-man gill-netting boats. It was an eccentric, rainy, wind-beaten sea village, downtrodden and mildewed, the boards of its buildings bleached and weathered, their drainpipes rusted a dull orange. Its long, steep inclines lay broad and desolate; its high-curbed gutters swarmed, most winter nights, with traveling rain. Often the sea wind made its single traffic light flail from side to side or caused the town's electrical power to flicker out and stay out for days. Main Street presented to the populace Petersen's Grocery, a post office, Fisk's Hardware Center, and a run-down filling station. At the wharf, a fish packing plant exuded the odor of salmon bones. Rain, the spirit of the place, patiently beat down everything man-made.

San Piedro had too a brand of verdant beauty that inclined its residents toward the poetical. Enormous hills, soft green with cedars, rose and fell in every direction. The island homes were damp and moss covered and lay in solitary fields and vales of alfalfa, feed corn, and strawberries. Haphazard cedar fences lined the careless roads, which slid beneath the shadows of the trees and past the bracken meadows. Cows grazed, stinking of sweet dung and addled by summer backflies. Here and there an islander tried his hand at milling sawlogs on his own, leaving fragrant heaps of sawdust and mounds of cedar bark at roadside. The beaches glistened with smooth stones and sea foam.

American Camp occupies most of San Juan's southern tail, 6 miles south of Friday Harbor, and includes an information center, interpretive trails, two restored military buildings, and a few miles of public beach. The open plain around the camp is honeycombed with rabbit warrens over which eagles, hawks, and owls glide, looking for dinner. **British Camp** overlooks Garrison Bay, a sheltered inlet on the island's northeast corner, a 10-mile drive from Friday Harbor. Neat, white-washed buildings, including a two-room barracks with brick fireplaces, are scattered across the manicured lawn that slopes down to the bay. A blockhouse built of whitewashed logs stands at the water's edge.

The Pig War

In 1858, about two dozen American gold seekers, returning discouraged from the Fraser River rush, settled down to farm on San Juan Island, which was claimed at the time by both the British and the Americans. One settler, Lyman Cutler, staked a claim near Bellevue Farm, property of the Hudson's Bay Company and Her Britannic Majesty. One June day in 1859, when he walked out of his cabin, he discovered a Hudson's Bay Company hog rooting in his potato patch, and he shot the pig dead. Settlers at Bellevue Farm were outraged, and British authorities threatened Cutler with arrest. Gen. William Harney of the United States responded by sending forces to occupy San Juan Island.

British Columbia's governor, James Douglas, responded in kind. The showdown quickly escalated, and by the end of August, 461 American soldiers had dug in near Bellevue Farm facing five British warships carrying 2,140 men and 167 cannons.

By the time news of the conflict reached Washington, D.C., the nation seemed poised on the brink of a war over a pig, at the same time that it was about to break apart over slavery. President James Buchanan relieved General Harney of his Northwest command, and a joint military occupation of the island was negotiated with Great Britain. In 1872, the dispute was finally referred to an independent arbitrator—the German emperor, Kaiser Wilhelm I. The kaiser ruled in favor of the United States, which is the obscure reason why today the San Juan Islands are not a part of Canada.

George E. Blankenship in his 1938 book, *Told by the Pioneers,* relates the following popular version of the war's outcome:

> The Olympia boys were preparing for their trip to Victoria when there was posted upon a bulletin board on a Western Union telegraph blank, the following purported dispatch from Washington: "Emperor William has decided to let the result of the coming baseball game between Olympia and Victoria dictate his decision of the international boundary question." Olympia won, and Emperor William decided in favor of the United States, but it is unlikely that he ever heard of the ball game. But there were those who took the above dispatch as authentic.

> *(opposite) British Camp overlooks Garrison Bay, near the site of the U.S.–British sovereignty conflict that came to be known as the Pig War.*

SOUTHERN LOWLANDS

THREE OF WASHINGTON'S GRANDEST NATURAL ATTRACTIONS punctuate the Cascade Mountain Crest between Snoqualmie Pass and the Columbia River: the snow cone of Mount Rainier; the shattered crater of Mount St. Helens; and the Columbia River Gorge, where the rugged Cascade Mountains grudgingly open to allow the West's largest river passage to the sea. Less grand but appealing for their low-key ambience and natural beauty are the small islands at the southern end of Puget Sound, and the state's capital, Olympia.

■ LOWER PUGET SOUND *map page 181, A/B-1*

Traveling through the southern Puget Sound country is a delight, with many roads shaded by trees alternating with green pastures where cattle graze contentedly; in southern Puget Sound you never know when the trees lining the road will drop away to reveal views of idyllic saltwater inlets. Peninsular roads are quiet enough to allow for enjoyable exploration by bicycle. Because few ferries travel on the southern inlets, you'll have to bring or charter a boat to explore the intricate waterways. Many local mariners do that in the same canoes they use on lowland rivers. But be aware that tidal differences are greater the farther south you travel. At Olympia, tides can be more than 16 feet high and generate strong and dangerous currents.

When Capt. George Vancouver named Puget Sound in 1792, the name was meant only for its southern end, and to commemorate the lieutenant—Peter Puget—who helped navigate Vancouver's ship through these waters. The name has since become applied to a much greater region, encompassing Admiralty Inlet to the north and even Washington Sound (Bellingham Bay and the San Juan Islands).

The bay Vancouver named after Puget is most likely Commencement Bay, where the city of Tacoma is now located. Puget's party made note of the people living along the water's edge:

> They seemed not wanting in offers of friendship and hospitality; as on our joining their party, we were presented with such things as they had to dispose of: and they immediately prepared a few of the roots, with some shell fish for our refreshment, which were very palatable. (Journal, May 20th, 1792)

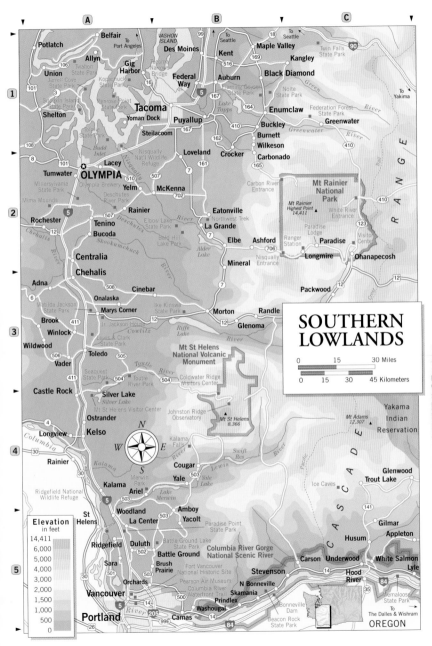

SOUTHERN LOWLANDS

0   15   30 Miles
0   15   30   45 Kilometers

SOUTHERN LOWLANDS

A Skokomish fishing camp in the lower Puget Sound area was photographed by famed frontier photographer Edward S. Curtis in the 1880s. (Museum of History and Industry)

Vashon Island is accessible only by water, although it has been populated for more than a century and once produced currants and strawberries.

In the summer, **Quartermaster Harbor,** along the island's southern shore, is filled with sailboats, speedboats, and yachts, many of which tie up at **Dockton Park.** In winter, perhaps a couple of dozen pleasure boats are moored at Dockton, along with an old gillnetter and a couple of seiners. Several rows of weather-beaten old pilings stand in the still water below the bluff where Dockton's early-20th-century buildings stand. It's hard to imagine that in 1892 this sheltered water held the only real drydock north of San Francisco. Before 1892, if a merchant ship needed repairs and the captain did not want to sail all the way to San Francisco, he would run the ship into shallow water and wait for the tide to go out. In the 1940s, the WPA guide to Washington described Dockton as a "a pale ghost, with graying remnants of wharves and ships along its waterfront." Today, you don't even find remnants.

People here aren't nostalgic for the days when Vashon lay in the mainstream of Puget

Sound commerce, and no one wants to see the island enter the mainstream. In 1992, when the state of Washington briefly revived the notion of building a bridge to link Vashon to Seattle and the Kitsap Peninsula, one-quarter of the island's population showed up at a public meeting to protest. So it's still the more leisurely car ferries that take the locals north to Seattle or south to Tacoma.

■ TACOMA   *map page 49, A-5, and page 181, B-1*

Draped dramatically over a water-bound headland between Commencement Bay and Puget Sound, Tacoma has views of Mount Rainier, excellent parks, and a downtown filled with late-19th-century buildings.

To see the city from its best angle, arrive by ferry from Vashon Island to the north. You'll be facing the tree-covered slopes of Point Defiance as you arrive, with the port stretching to the east. Most visitors, though, take the less attractive entrance, I-5 to I-705 downtown.

Shipyards at Dockton, Maury Island, *by Alice Samson (1907).*
(Museum of History and Industry)

Downtown Tacoma

Old City Hall and the headquarters of the **Northern Pacific Railway** are the portals of the north end of downtown. Up the hill, the Broadway Center for the Performing Arts, a complex of historic and new theaters, presents plays, concerts, and films in three venues: **Pantages Theater** (901 Broadway; 253-591-5894), a restored vaudeville house; the **Rialto Theater** (301 South Ninth Street; 253-591-5890); and the newer **Theater on the Square** (Broadway and South Ninth Street). At the south end of downtown, look for the domed Union Station, now part of a federal courthouse. The **Washington State History Museum** (1911 Pacific Avenue; 253-272-3500 or 888-238-4373) tells the state's story with artifacts and high-tech video displays and interactive computers. The **Museum of Glass** (1801 Dock Street; 253-396-1768), which opened in 2002, exhibits glass and other media, with an emphasis on the contemporary. The **Tacoma Art Museum** (1701 Pacific Avenue; 253-272-4258) houses a small collection of European and American art.

The Tacoma Narrows Bridge, unstable and dubbed "Galloping Gertie"
a few months after it opened in 1940, is shown here collapsing during a windstorm.
(University of Washington Libraries)

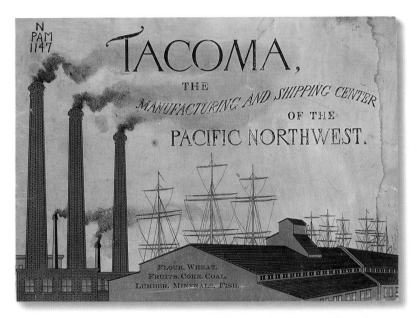

A promotional poster extols Tacoma industries. (University of Washington Libraries)

SOUTHERN LOWLANDS

If Tacoma's Stadium-Seminary and Hilltop Districts seem to have more than their share of stately Victorian homes, that's because of the building boom of the 1880s, when the Northern Pacific Railway picked Tacoma over Seattle as the Pacific Northwest endpoint for its transcontinental railroad. Fancy new homes sprouted all over town until the nationwide depression of 1883, when construction came to a screeching halt. The depression was over by the 1898 gold rush, but by then Seattle had its own railroad connections and momentum shifted away from Tacoma. The homes were preserved for the simple reason that their owners could not afford to replace them with more modern ones.

Most of the Victorian-era homes decorating hills around Tacoma can't be toured, but a few are open to the public, including **Chinaberry Hill** (302 North Tacoma

(following page) An enormous stack of cedar boards dwarfs a worker at an early-20th-century mill near Seattle. (Pemco Webster and Stevens Collection, Museum of History and Industry)

WEYERHAEUSER

Weyerhaeuser is the largest forest products company in the Northwest. Aside from its vast land holdings and timber-cutting operations, it is also a potent symbol of the logging industry in arguments over clear-cutting, preserving wildlife habitats, creating parks and hiking trails, exporting logs, and converting forest land to other uses.

Like most of the other men who started Washington timber empires in the late 19th century, Frederick Weyerhaeuser, a native of Germany, had been a lumber baron in the Midwest. He saw the pine forests of upper Michigan going fast and decided to invest in the still largely uncut woodlands of the Northwest. When his St. Paul neighbor, the railroad builder Jim Hill, offered him 900,000 acres of federal land-grant forest in Washington, Weyerhaeuser bought it for $6 an acre. The company subsequently bought more land, traded land, built mills, operated whole company towns, and started the first American tree farm in 1942.

Its ivy-draped headquarters in Federal Way, a bit north of Tacoma, is the nerve center for an organization that owns more standing timber than any other private company in the world.

Nobody stops to visit the corporate offices themselves, but the Weyerhaeuser headquarters campus contains the **Pacific Rim Bonsai Collection** (253-924-5206) **and the Rhododendron Species Foundation,** which are open to the public. The rhododendron collection is the largest in the world. *2525 South 336th Street; 253-661-9377.*

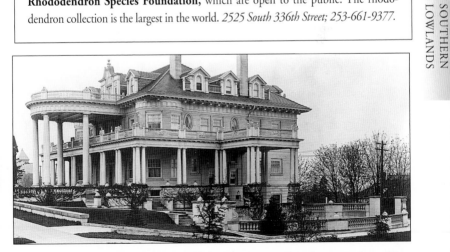

The family that built the William Rust mansion in Tacoma made its fortunes in the smelting business. (Washington State Historical Society)

Avenue; 253-272-1282), a Queen Anne–style dwelling with stained-glass windows, original fixtures, and a garden. **Anthony's at Point Defiance,** between the classic old public boathouse and the Vashon Island ferry dock, matches first rate views with fresh Northwest seafood. This is one of the few local places serving red clam chowder (and it is good!). *5910 Waterfront Drive, Tacoma; 253-752-9700.*

Point Defiance Park

This is one of the most rewarding parks you'll ever visit anywhere in the United States. On a wooded peninsula that projects into the sound, the park has miles of tree-shaded roads that wind through idyllic glens. A beach runs along the shore, and there are rose gardens, grassy slopes, and brushy ravines echoing with the song of birds. The outdoor **Camp Six Logging Museum** (253-752-0047) displays old logging equipment and has the original granary from the Hudson's Bay Company's old **Fort Nisqually** (253-591-5339). **Point Defiance Zoo & Aquarium** (5400 North Pearl Street; 253-591-5337) has a shark tank, aquariums, and elephants. *From downtown Tacoma, take Ruston Way north along the waterfront (follow signs); 253-591-5337.*

■ NISQUALLY NATIONAL WILDLIFE REFUGE
map page 181, A-1/2

On the shore of Puget Sound between Tacoma and Olympia, the fields and marshes of Nisqually Delta are preserved as the Nisqually National Wildlife Refuge. To the north, beyond the sprays of purple daisies and the brown marsh grass, the gray-green Nisqually River flows toward Puget Sound. Mallards skim the surface of the river. Upstream, water from the Nisqually Glacier above Paradise in Mount Rainier National Park glitters in the sunlight.

A wooden boardwalk loops from the visitors center through the marshes to the river and back to the center. This is a great place for observing marsh birds, ducks, and wetland wildflowers. Primeval-looking giant horsetails also grow here. (Hot tip: the refuge has the only public rest rooms on southbound I-5 between Seattle and Olympia.) *I-5 Exit 114; 360-753-9467.*

(previous pages) Mount Rainier forms a dramatic backdrop to the port of Tacoma.

■ OLYMPIA *map page 181, A-2*

Olympia sits at the junction of I-5 and U.S. 101, at the narrow extremity of Budd Inlet, the most southerly arm of Puget Sound, where the fresh water of the Deschutes River mixes with the salt of the sea. Founded in 1850 and named for the majestic mountains that loom northwest of the city on clear days, Olympia has been Washington's capital since Washington Territory was severed from Oregon in 1853.

The Capitol

The first territorial legislature met here in 1854, in a room above the Gold Bar Store and Restaurant. At the time, the town was little more than a few scattered cabins and a patch of land above a muddy bay. The domed marble capitol that stands above the modern city wasn't completed until 1928. For 74 years before that, legislators met in the Masonic Temple, a humble wooden hall, and (from 1901 to 1928) in the old Thurston County Courthouse, currently known as the Old Capitol.

You can see the current capitol dome from the freeway, rising above the trees. Up close, it's an unusually handsome building set in a nicely landscaped campus—quite beautiful in spring, when the trees are in bloom. Downhill from the capitol and state office buildings east of Capitol Way lie downtown Olympia and the old center of political gravity at **Sylvester Park.** The turreted stone mass of the **Old Capitol** building, between Franklin and Washington Streets, overlooks the park from the east. On the north stands the former **Olympian Hotel** (116 Legion Way SE), where generations of lobbyists bought politicians lavish meals, deals were made, big-time legislators set up housekeeping, and old pols hung out in the lobby. A lot of the state's real business was conducted at the Olympian until the late 1950s, when lobbyists and legislators moved to the new Tyee Motel south of town. The Olympian suffered major structural damage in the Nisqually earthquake of 2001.

The **Japanese Garden,** a symbol of the sister-city relationship Olympia shares with Yashiro, Japan, opened in 1989. Within the garden are a waterfall, bamboo grove, koi pond, and stone lanterns. *Union and Plum Streets, east of the Capitol campus.*

Downtown Olympia

Olympia's downtown is low-key but interesting, replete with used bookshops, cafés, and record stores. Old brick buildings—many a bit rundown, some stripped of their cornices by a fierce earthquake in 1949—line the streets. The town's vitality shines in the scruffy bars where the worlds of middle-age working stiffs and college kids with green hair overlap. Even around its dilapidated edges, Olympia is never threatening.

Olympia has long been known for its alternative, if offbeat, culture, perhaps because of its close proximity to aggressively unconventional Evergreen State College. The town hosts independent film festivals and supports a vigorous music scene—locals claim that Nirvana, the infamous "Seattle band," actually got its start here. But if much of the downtown pub scene seems young and hip, it's also a friendly crowd. Shoot a game of pool at the **Eastside Club Tavern** (410 East Fourth Avenue; 360-357-9985), a gathering place for students, locals, and government types, and you're sure to meet an Olympian or two.

Timber dollars fed this area from the time its first settlers built a sawmill at Tumwater Falls, in 1845, until the middle of the 20th century. Before World War II, when government was still relatively small, Olympia was primarily a Puget Sound port and mill town. In 1941, it contained 15 lumber, shingle, plywood, and furniture mills and 10 dairy and poultry processing plants. Even after the war, the port continued to cut and send lumber and plywood to the East Coast. Now, there are a pedestrian walk and a lookout tower along part of the waterfront, and a busy public marina.

Contemporary Olympia remains a government town. State and local government provide more than half the jobs in all of Thurston County. But you can get some sense of the way things used to be from the wonderful black-and-white photographs of huge trees and old-time loggers that adorn the walls of the **McMenamius Spar Café and Bar** (114 East Fourth Avenue; 360-357-6444), a historic watering hole of local mill workers and deal makers.

■ TUMWATER   *map page 181, A-2*

You know you're in Tumwater when you see signs for Olympia Brewery on the freeway immediately after exits for downtown Olympia. Immediately south of Olympia (and essentially its suburb), Tumwater was established in 1845 as the first American settlement north of the Columbia River.

Tumwater was founded by a party of Missourians led by Michael Simmons and George Bush, a black man who had fought with Andrew Jackson at the Battle of New Orleans and had traveled to the Pacific Northwest as a Hudson's Bay Company employee in the 1820s. Bush's popularity exempted him from the Missouri law

(opposite) State policemen in the lobby of the capitol building in Olympia.

barring free blacks from residence there, but when the Simmons party asked him to go west, he went. Like most settlers bound for the Oregon Country, the party planned to settle in Oregon's Willamette Valley.

Many of Willamette's first American settlers came west from the border states, often fleeing the violent tensions that eventually resulted in the Civil War. In an effort to obviate a crisis over slavery and racial issues in Oregon, the 1844 territorial legislature simultaneously outlawed slavery and required all blacks to leave the territory within three years; any black who stayed longer would be flogged every six months.

By law (that was only loosely enforced), blacks could

Michael Simmons was one of the state's earliest settlers. He and the party he led from Missouri established the town of Tumwater in 1845. (Washington State Historical Society)

not own land or vote in Oregon. On learning this, Bush and the Simmons party headed north of the Columbia River for land then claimed by the British, who were relative racial progressives. The Simmons party settled at the mouth of the Deschutes River, where the pioneers built a gristmill and a sawmill at the base of Tumwater Falls.

When Great Britain and the United States drew the international boundary at the 49th parallel in 1846, Tumwater officially became an American settlement. When Washington's first territorial legislature met in 1854, it approved a petition to grant George Bush title to his land, overriding the terms of the Donation Land Law of 1850 that allowed only "white citizens and half breeds" to file claims. Despite this victory, Bush was never allowed to vote and was never granted citizenship.

SOUTHERN LOWLANDS

Mima Mounds

To the south of Olympia lie the Mima Mounds—symmetrical, dome-shaped hills six to eight feet high and 20 to 30 feet in diameter. Rising one after another in all directions, they once covered the prairies in much of Thurston and Lewis Counties. Only a few pockets of mound prairie remain, and they are mostly covered with small trees and Scotch broom, the result of fire suppression begun in the early 20th century. The state is now trying to restore the remaining mound areas to their natural state by cutting, clearing, and burning the brush.

The origin of these strange formations, found scattered throughout Washington and other western states from Nebraska and Texas to California, remains a mystery. In 1841, explorer Charles Wilkes and his men dug up a few mounds in this area, thinking they were the graves of some early Indian people. Inside the mounds, they found no treasure, artifacts, or bones—nothing but gravelly soil.

Conflicting explanations hold that the mounds were built by prehistoric fish as spawning nests when seas covered the continent, or that they are monuments of some vanished race, or that they were formed by the freezing and thawing that occurred as the Puget Glacier retreated. The glacier might sound plausible, except that the mounds occur in areas never glaciated. The currently accepted theory is that the mounds were built by generations of pocket gophers, small but prodigious earthmovers. The regular spacing of the mounds coincides with the gophers' territorial habits. *Take Exit 95 off I-5, 10 miles south of Olympia, and head west to Littlerock. Drive through town on Waddell Creek Road until you find the entrance, on the left.*

■ **MOUNT RAINIER** *map page 181, C-2, and page 196*

Mount Rainier National Park (Route 706 off I-5; 360-569-2211) is less than an hour's drive southeast of Tacoma. The park, which climbs the slopes of the 14,411-foot volcano, encompasses broad tracts of old-growth forest, waterfalls, glaciers, and meadows smothered in summertime wildflowers. Lodges, campgrounds, hundreds of miles of hiking trails, and cross-country skiing at Paradise Lodge draw people year-round. Some approaches to the area are closed in winter because of heavy snow.

The mountain has drawn climbers since the 1830s, when a Hudson's Bay Company's doctor stationed at nearby Fort Nisqually made it part way up. In 1870, Gen. Hazard Stevens (the son of Washington Territory's first governor, Isaac Stevens) and

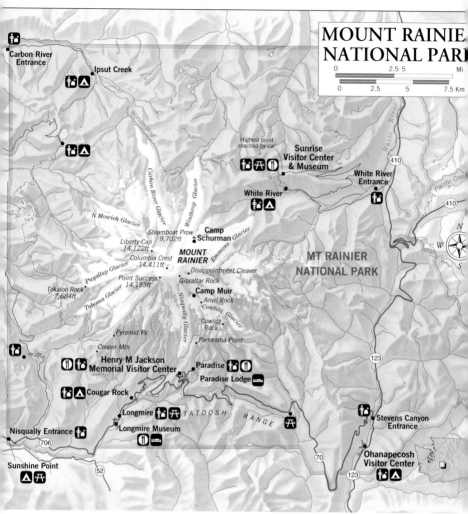

MOUNT RAINIE
NATIONAL PAR

Carbon River Entrance

Ipsut Creek

Highest point reached by car

Sunrise Visitor Center & Museum

White River Entrance

White River

N Mowich Glacier

Steamboat Prow 9,702ft

Camp Schurman

Liberty Cap 14,122ft

Columbia Crest 14,411ft

MOUNT RAINIER

Disappointment Cleaver

Point Success 14,153ft

Gibraltar Rock

Tokaloo Rock 7,684ft

Camp Muir

Anvil Rock

Cowlitz Rock

MT RAINIER NATIONAL PARK

Pyramid Pk

Panorama Point

Cooper Mtn

Henry M Jackson Memorial Visitor Center

Paradise

Paradise Lodge

Cougar Rock

Longmire TATOOSH RANGE

Nisqually Entrance

Longmire Museum

Stevens Canyon Entrance

Sunshine Point

Ohanapecosh Visitor Center

Philemon Van Trump actually made it to the top. They spent the night on the summit, where a volcanic steam cave saved them from freezing to death. Twenty years later, a teacher named Fay Fuller became the first woman to climb Rainier. Today, several thousand people make the climb every year. Complete novices can get a day of training from Rainier Mountaineering, which, weather permitting, will then lead them to the top. Old people, young people, and people with disabilities have all climbed the peak. Nevertheless, Rainier is a highly technical climb and challenges even the best climbers. Each year, some climbers are killed or injured on this mountain.

Wildflowers blanket meadows in Mount Rainier National Park during the summer.

You needn't be a mountain climber to enjoy Mount Rainier. Those who want to experience the mountain without climbing it will find roads that lead to vantage points on all sides of the mountain, each with its own celebrated views, amenities, and summertime hiking trails. Of course, driving to a viewpoint doesn't guarantee a view of the glaciers or summit: clouds frequently hide Mount Rainier from sight, even in the summer.

Note that the park suffered serious damages in the floods of winter 2006. For current road status, call 360-569-2111.

The park headquarters, including a visitors center and inn, is located in the southwest corner at **Longmire,** 2,761 feet above sea level. From there, the road climbs 13 miles to **Paradise,** at 5,400 feet. From Paradise, which offers spectacular views of the mountain, you can walk through steep flower meadows on paved trails or head toward the climbers' 10,000-foot base camp at Camp Muir. The summit that you see from Paradise stays white all year-long. The mountain and its 35 square miles of glaciers trap 156 billion cubic feet of water, comprising the largest single-peak glacier system in the nation.

At 6,400 feet, **Sunrise** is the highest point in the park that can be reached by road. From the visitors center, a trail up Burroughs Mountain climbs 1,400 feet in slightly more than 3 miles to exquisite views of Emmons and Winthrop Glaciers.

Ambitious backpackers can launch out on the 93-mile circumnavigation of the mountain on the **Wonderland Trail.** But you don't have to walk far to enjoy Rainier's wild beauty: even near a much-traveled entrance road, a brief uphill walk can give you an exhilarating look at raw nature.

If you approach Rainier from its northwestern side via Route 165, you'll find the road climbs through the old coal-mining towns of Wilkeson and Carbonado to the **Carbon River entrance,** near Ipsut Creek. From the Ipsut Creek campground, a relatively short trail takes you to the **Carbon River Glacier.** The glacier isn't way up the mountain, it's in the woods, across a swaying suspension bridge. After climbing a slope along the riverbank, get as close to the dense ice as you like—but don't stand at the base of the ice wall or even very near it, because boulders fall intermittently from the glacier's sheer face.

South of Ipsut Creek is Mowich Lake, where a trail leads to Spray Park. Here, in the bloom of the high country's late-summer "spring," you can look across acres of

Mountaineers along a crevasse of the Nisqually Glacier, Mount Rainier, ca. 1920.
(University of Washington Libraries)

A CREVASSE on NISQUALLY GLACIER,
Rainier National Park Ranapar Studio 227

Wildflowers

Like people, wildflowers need lots of sunshine to be happy, which is why the greatest floral displays are found in the sunnier parts of the state.

■ West of the Cascades

West of the Cascades, wildflowers are mostly seen in the San Juans. The small, rocky islands, accessible only by boat, seem to have the greatest variety of colors.

Mt. Rainier National Park's Paradise area is abloom with wildflowers every July.

Whidbey Island, stretched out in the rain shadow of the Olympics, also puts on spectacular displays. Look for **wild lily-of-the-valley** and **Venus-slipper orchids** in the shade of the woods, for **blue iris** at the head of Penn Cove, and admire the **rhododendrons** at Point Partridge. If you time it right (in June), you can admire **blue camas** growing in the meadows beneath outcroppings at Deception Pass. **Oxeye daisies** will soon whiten roadsides throughout western Washington, just before **fireweed** and **foxglove** paint them pink.

■ SOUTHEAST

East of the Cascades, few places can match the Yakima River Canyon for sheer scenic beauty, where the river breaks through the basalt flows of Manastash and Umtanum Ridges in a series of steep-sided cliffs. In spring, the precipitous slopes are covered with wildflowers, but you'll see even more spectacular displays at the Wenas State Game Range, along the old stage road that runs from Ellensburg to Selah via the Wenas Valley. Look for **lavender mariposa lilies** and **yellow columbines** among the brightly colored mounds of **pink phlox, purple sage,** and **blue lupine.** If you're lucky, you'll see meadows covered with **gold stars.** In spring and summer, before the start of the hunting season, the game range is also a great place to watch birds, especially bluebirds, tanagers, and orioles.

In the Palouse, drive to the top of Steptoe Butte, where the green of the flowering meadows and the golden-brown of the soil lie half-hidden beneath a sea of pink, yellow, and blue flowers. **Wild roses** pour down the slopes of Steptoe Butte into an abandoned orchard. Their fragrance fills the air.

■ OKANOGAN

The rolling meadows of the Okanogan highlands are also bedecked with wildflowers in spring and early summer. This forgotten nook is so peaceful you can hear birds sing as you drive along Route 155, which runs north from Grand Coulee Dam through the Colville Indian Reservation to Omak. For much of the summer, roadsides will be lined with bands of scarlet **skyrocket gilia** and deeply **blue larkspur.** But look for **asters, sunflowers,** and **blazing stars** as well.

flowers to the snowcapped peak, so close it fills your field of view. Small streams run through the flower meadows; clouds of insects wait to devour you along the banks.

■ CENTRALIA
map page 181, A-2

Seen from I-5, Centralia looks like a typical freeway development—a strip of gas stations, fast-food franchises, and factory outlet stores, thoughtlessly scattered a few blocks deep on either side of the highway. Off the freeway, though, the old face of Centralia remains remarkably intact. The town's commercial district along Tower Avenue is a showcase of stylish, beautifully maintained, two-story buildings of brick and

George Washington founded Centralia in 1852.
(University of Washington Libraries)

stone, most of which date back to the 1890s and early 1900s. With the decline of the timber industry in recent years, Centralia has tried to cash in on its history. Stores full of antiques stand on every block.

The fabulous **Olympic Club Hotel** (112 North Tower Avenue; 306-736-5164) is a saloon/tobacco store appointed in swank, early-20th-century style. Its colored-glass chandeliers, tile floors, stenciled ceilings, and ornate cash register are monuments to the golden age of public drinking.

Centralia was founded in 1852 by George Washington, the son of a Missouri slave. The Cochrans, a white couple, raised Washington, and the three came west together, fleeing the violent climate of the antebellum border states.

Oregon's territorial legislature granted George Washington an exemption from the law prohibiting black land ownership two months before the area north of the Columbia River became a separate territory, no longer governed by Oregon. George Washington's exemption did not apply under Washington Territory law, and the

Cochrans filed a claim for his land, which they deeded to him when the law was repealed in 1857.

The park at the corner of Main and Pearl Streets, where the old **Carnegie library** stands, was part of George Washington's original land claim. The sentinel statue standing guard before the library is a monument to the four American Legionnaires slain by radical loggers in the Centralia Massacre of 1919.

■ MOUNT ST. HELENS   *map page 181, B-3/4*

A trip to Mount St. Helens is a bit like a visit to a war zone. Although more than two decades have passed since the volcanic eruption that destroyed the mountain's top, scars of that event are still prominent everywhere you look. Until 1980, Mount St. Helens was a serene-looking 9,677-foot volcano. Visitors to nearby Spirit Lake enjoyed the reflection of the peak's perfectly symmetrical cone in the lake's blue water. Then, in the spring of 1980, geologists noticed some ominous rumblings and warned that an eruption was inevitable.

Mount St. Helens from the Smith Creek viewpoint.

Few were prepared for what happened on the morning of May 18. More than 1,300 feet of its top simply disappeared. Instead of going straight up, the blast went north, destroying everything in its path. Old-growth forests were vaporized. Big trees a little farther from the blast were scattered across the hillsides like straw or were simply killed where they stood. Soil was incinerated and nearby slopes were scoured down to bedrock. Volcanic ash fell on 22,000 square miles of land, including much of eastern Washington. The sky in many eastern Washington communities darkened at midday, and ash piled up like drifted snow on the streets and sidewalks. Snow and glacial ice melted by the blast poured down the mountain, creating rivers of mud that swelled the Toutle River, which rose 66 feet above its normal level, sweeping away homes and bridges. Mud flowed down to the Cowlitz and the Columbia Rivers, where millions of tons had to be dredged from the shipping channel. Fifty-seven people died. The devastation appeared complete.

But pocket gophers living underground survived the blast, and fireweed and other plants started recolonizing some of the blast area within a year. Soon, herds of huge brown elk wandered comfortably across the mud and the ridges above. Much of the area remains a moonscape, but life is returning. Weyerhaeuser, which owned most of the land in the path of the blast, traded some to the federal government, which included it in a Mount St. Helens National Volcanic Monument.

Before making the long drive to the mountain along Route 504, stop at the **Mount St. Helens Visitor Center at Silver Lake** (360-274-0962), where you can learn about the eruption by walking through a giant model of the volcano. You can also pick up maps and information for touring and hire guides to lead you into the blast zone.

Also on Route 504 is the **Coldwater Ridge Visitors Center** (360-274-2114), which offers spectacular views of the steaming crater and the new cinder cone inside its walls. From the **Johnston Ridge Observatory** (360-274-2140), 9 miles closer to the mountain, you can look straight down into the crater.

Or you can take a **helicopter tour** from the Hoffstadt Bluff Viewpoint (360-274-7750). From the helicopter at the crater's rim, you can look into an amphitheater of sheer gray cliffs and see a lava dome steaming in the shadows.

(preceding pages) Moments after Mount St. Helens exploded on the morning of May 18, 1980, a photographer captured the event near the town of Toledo, 30 miles west of the mountain. (Rocky Kolberg)

■ LONGVIEW   *map page 181, A-4*

The mill town of Longview is the largest planned community in the United States after Washington, D.C. The city is not laid out on the familiar grid system, but has a roundabout where the civic center is located, surrounded by curving streets that are crossed by diagonal roads, creating a somewhat off-kilter grid.

The **Civic Center**, also known as R.A. Long Park, is towered over by the **Monticello Hotel** (1405 17th Avenue), an exuberant 1923 brick and terra-cotta affair with an impressive lobby. The **Longview Public Library** (1600 Louisiana Street) is flanked by a lovely rose garden, and the **post office** (1603 Larch Street) is 1930s art deco. Downtown Longview, with its broad streets and beautiful parks, is separated from the Columbia River by levees and a grungy industrial district and port. A 1,200-foot-long bridge crosses from here to the Oregon side of the river.

No trace remains of **Monticello,** a pioneer community that made its home on the Columbia River floodplain in the mid-19th century. The town was important enough at the time for the state's constitutional convention to be held here in 1852. Monticello was washed away in the disastrous floods of 1867 and 1868.

A few miles up the Columbia River, you'll come to the old river town of **Kalama,** founded in the 1850s as a steamboat stop. Pleasant and with a compact downtown, Kalama has shops and stores that allow you to stock up on supplies for picnics and hikes. There's a small picnic area overlooking the river at the west end of town.

Kalama is famous because it was here, back in the 1980s, that Hart Brewing created **Pyramid Ale** in a storefront brewery. The brewery has since moved to larger digs in Seattle, but the ale is as good as ever. The Kalama Marina is popular with boaters. *From downtown Kalama, take Elm Street west and follow signs.*

In nearby Woodland, the **Hulda Klager Lilac Gardens** are a showcase of flowers, shrubs, and exotic trees, in addition to lilacs, whose hybridization made Hilda Klager famous. Tours of the Victorian farmhouses are available year-round by appointment and during the annual lilac festival in April and May. *15 South Pekin Road, Woodland; 360-225-8996.*

On the Columbia River near Vancouver is the **Ridgefield National Wildlife Refuge,** 5,000 acres of meadows, marshes, and woods that provide habitats for endangered species. Bald eagles, peregrine falcons, and Aleutian Canada geese flock here, along with great blue herons and sandhill cranes. Trails pass through groves of ancient white oaks. Wintering swans frequent the small lake south of the trailhead. *Off I-5, Exit 14, Ridgefield; 360-887-4106.*

WHO LIVED HERE IN 1828?

When I descended the Cowlitz in 1828… our bateau carried as curious a muster of races and languages as perhaps had ever been congregated within the same compass in any part of the world. Our crew of ten men contained Iroquois, who spoke their own tongue; a Cree half-breed of French origin, who appeared to have borrowed his dialect from both his parents; a North Briton, who understood only the Gaelic of his native hills; Canadians, who, of course, knew French; and Sandwich Islanders, who jabbered a medley of Chinook, English and their own vernacular jargon. Add to all this that the passengers were natives of England, Scotland, Russia, Canada and the Hudson's Bay Company's territories, and you have the prettiest congress of nations, the nicest confusion of tongues, that has ever taken place since the days of the Tower of Babel.

—Sir George Simpson, *Overland Journey Around the World, 1841–42*

The original fort owed its importance to early-19th-century geopolitics. After the War of 1812, Great Britain and the United States set the U.S.–Canadian border east of the Rocky Mountains at the 49th parallel, but failed to agree on a border west of the Great Divide. After much deliberation, the two countries agreed to a joint occupation of the disputed Oregon Country, a wilderness stretching from the Alaska panhandle to California, and bounded east and west by the Rockies and the Pacific Ocean respectively.

In the early years of joint occupation, Fort Vancouver was the vast territory's sole bastion of Anglo civilization, and orders from the Hudson's Bay Company were law. Indeed, the company strove for self-sufficiency, building farms, sawmills, and smithies to supply its forts and outposts. It guaranteed protection to anyone traveling to or from its forts with furs, and forbade its employees to trade liquor to the Indians (who did most of the trapping).

Pacific Northwest historian Carlos Schwantes wrote that within its 20-foot-high stockade, "Fort Vancouver constituted a small, almost self-sufficient European community." Also within the fort were a hospital, storehouses, workshops, mills, a shipyard, a dairy, orchards, and a farm of several hundred acres. "Ships from distant ports called at Fort Vancouver bringing news, books, and periodicals to stock the post's library."

Schwantes adds that:

> …An unusually cosmopolitan population collected around Fort Vancouver: Delaware and Iroquois Indians from the East, local Chinooks, Hawaiians, mixed-blood Métis from the prairies, French Canadians, and Scotsmen, and presiding over them all was the imperious John McLoughlin, harsh, brooding, and given to occasional temperamental outbursts. More than profit and loss were involved in a Hudson's Bay post: Each enclave was a visible link in a truly imperial system joining London with the vast hinterlands of the Pacific Northwest.

John McLoughlin ran the fort on the Columbia in a truly imperial manner. "Nightly," writes Peter C. Newman in a history of the Hudson's Bay Company, "the Company's traders and visiting dignitaries gathered at the officers' mess to trade tall tales in the warm light of candelabra, lolling at tables laden with crested cutlery, crystal glasses and blue earthenware dishes…with McLoughlin leading spirited exchanges of ideas that spun on long into the convivial nights."

McLoughlin's virtues as a host did not mean that he was soft on the people who worked for him or on those who strayed into the Company's sphere of influence. "What impressed the Indian chiefs who came to call was McLoughlin's sense of justice," Newman writes. "Anyone—white or Indian—caught breaking the Chief Factor's concept of permissible behavior was sentenced to be lashed while tied to the fort's cannon."

Nevertheless, McLoughlin fed American trappers who showed up hungry on his doorstep, and he gave supplies on credit to American settlers who came over the Oregon Trail, ignoring company policy against helping Americans, who rarely paid him or the company back. Although McLoughlin was later called "the Father of Oregon," he died in Oregon Territory unappreciated and bitter.

By that time, Vancouver had become part of the United States. Hudson's Bay Company governor George Simpson had foreseen the outcome of the boundary struggle between the United States and Great Britain and had relocated Company headquarters to Vancouver Island in 1843. Three years later, Britain gave up all claim to what is now Washington and Oregon. *Fort Vancouver National Historic Site, 612 East Reserve Street; 360-816-6230 or 360-816-6200.*

The Sisters of Providence toured mining camps in the late 1800s to collect donations in gold and coins to fund schools, hospitals, and Indian missions. (Courtesy Sisters of Providence Archives, Seattle)

Mother Joseph and the Sisters of Providence

In 1856, five Canadian nuns—Sisters of Providence—made a 6,000-mile sea journey to Vancouver from the cosmopolitan Montreal. Their leader, Mother Joseph, a 23-year-old with thin lips and a stubborn chin jutting beneath her nun's cowl, had learned carpentry and design as a girl from her father, a Quebec carriage maker.

Finding no home prepared for their arrival, the sisters set to work remodeling an abandoned Hudson's Bay Company building, and made their home there. In her first years in Vancouver, Mother Joseph planned and oversaw the construction of a school, a hospital, a lunatic asylum, and an old folks' home. Her building crews respected her as a fine carpenter, although her habit of praying aloud as she labored with hammer and saw, or hitching up her skirts and crawling beneath a building to inspect its foundation, may have disconcerted some workers.

In the last four decades of the 19th century, the Sisters of Providence built more than two dozen hospitals, schools, and orphanages throughout the Pacific Northwest. To finance their many good works, the sisters made heroic begging tours of the Washington Territory's remote mining camps by horseback and canoe, navigating wild rivers, rugged highlands, and vast, arid plains.

Mother Joseph herself survived into the 20th century. The American Institute of Architects later named her "the First Architect of the Pacific Northwest." Statues of her stand in the Washington State Capitol and the U.S. Capitol's Statuary Hall.

When Mother Joseph and her fellow Sisters of Providence completed Vancouver's Providence Academy (now known as the Academy) in 1874, it was the largest building west of the Rockies and north of San Francisco. Mother Joseph was the Academy's architect and contractor, and carved its elaborate wooden altars and benches herself. The big colonial brick building, partially occupied by various small businesses, still stands at the edge of downtown Vancouver. *400 East Evergreen Boulevard.*

Columbia River Waterfront Trail

The 4-mile trail follows the river from the Captain Vancouver Monument, near the I-5 bridge, to Tidewater Barge, passing Waterfront Park, Renaissance Promenade, and the plaza and a statue dedicated to Ilchee, daughter of Concomly, a famous Chinook Indian chief of the 19th century. The oldest apple tree in the state, the Marine Park Wetlands, and Kaiser Viewing Tower and Shipyards are a few of the passing points worth noting along the trail.

Pearson Air Museum

East of Fort Vancouver is Pearson Air Field, the oldest active airfield in the western United States. It's the site of several famous aviation feats, including the 1937 trans-polar flight from Moscow to Vancouver (63 hours and 16 minutes). The Pearson Air Museum, in the M. J. Murdock Aviation Center on the north side of the field, reveals this history with a 25,000-square-foot museum that includes vintage airplanes, exhibits, a cockpit simulator, and photographs of planes and their pilots. *1115 East Fifth Street; 360-694-7026.*

 COLUMBIA RIVER GORGE   *map page 181, B-5, and pages 258–259, A-5*

The Columbia River Gorge marks the spot at which the river flows west through the Cascades between basalt cliffs that are older than the mountains themselves. U.S. 14 follows the north bank of the river all the way through the gorge, although most visitors follow the freeway on the Oregon side.

When Lewis and Clark followed the Columbia through the gorge in 1805, the Native American tribes they found along its banks had been fishing these waters for perhaps 9,000 years. These waters—mostly rapids and vertiginous falls—formed impassible barriers to navigation. Lewis and Clark portaged around them, and in the early 20th century, wheat shipped downriver by steamboat from the Palouse Hills had to be unloaded, hauled around the rapids by rail, and loaded onto another boat in the calmer water below. Railroads and highways follow both banks of the river today, and a system of dams and locks enables boats to go all the way to Idaho.

The road along the Washington shore provides more dramatic views but slower driving than the freeway on the Oregon side. (The Columbia Gorge Scenic Highway on the Oregon side is also slow but spectacular.) It winds around rock walls and bores through the rock in short tunnels, passing fruit warehouses, small sawmills, and enormous rocks softened by moss. On the opposite shore, you can see the mountains plunging straight to the river, appearing and disappearing in the mist, their forested slopes split by ravines. In winter, snow dusts the upper slopes.

For a long view up and down the river, climb the series of ramps and steps up 848-foot-tall **Beacon Rock.** Beacon Rock State Park has campsites and swimming areas along the Columbia River. East of Beacon Rock, near the Hood River, windsurfers take advantage of the ideal winds. *Take Route 14 east from I-5 at Vancouver.*

Bonneville Dam was the first of the great federal dams built across the Columbia River, the irreversible step toward transforming the river and much of the region with millions of tons of concrete. In addition to the dam itself, you can see the locks where barges and tugs wait for rising or falling water to lift them up or let them down to the river level on the other side of the dam. *I-84, Exit 40 to Tanner Creek Road; 541-374-8820 or 541-374-8344.*

Before Bonneville Dam was built, this spot was known for its dangerous rapids. On November 1, 1805, Lewis and Clark "Set about takeing our Small canoe and all the baggage by land 940 yeards of bad slippery and rockey way" to avoid them. They saw "Great numbers of Sea Otters" and "got the 4 large canoes over by slipping them over the rocks on poles." This was their last portage. Less than a week later, when the river mouth widened, they thought they saw the ocean. They were wrong, but only a couple of weeks after dragging their canoes around the rapids, they were walking beside the Pacific.

Where the Dalles Dam has flooded the ancient Indian fishing site at Celilo Falls, a steep road leads downhill to the town of **Wishram,** which once stood near the north end of the falls. Long lines of freight cars wait in the railroad marshalling yards.

View from Beacon Rock up the Columbia River Gorge, looking toward the Bonneville Dam.

Kids play in the narrow streets, and people take good care of their small lawns. Behind the town, craggy cliffs reach out toward the river, an indication that the natural river might once have dropped over a falls. Drop it did, and Indians gathered here to spear or net salmon for perhaps eight millennia. Celilo Falls was one of the great fishing spots in North America.

Sam Hill, a railroad magnate and public works entrepreneur, built the first highway on the Oregon side of the gorge. He chose the Washington side for his grand home, now the **Maryhill Museum.** Hill had planned to live here amid a utopian Quaker farming colony, but then he changed his mind and moved to Seattle. A friend later convinced him it would make a great museum. The collection includes many Indian baskets, Russian icons, and small Rodins in addition to paintings by French impressionists and American realists. Hill knew the American dancer Loie Fuller, and there are various mementos of her career, including a small statue of her dancing, with veils swinging out all around. Wrote William Butler Yeats in "Nineteen Hundred and Nineteen":

Columbia River Gorge, near Wishram.

When Loie Fuller's Chinese dancers enwound
A shining web, a floating ribbon of cloth,
It seemed that a dragon of air
Had fallen among dancers, had whirled them round
Or hurried them off on its own furious path....

Hill was also friendly with Queen Marie of Romania, and the museum contains objects that once belonged to her, including gilt furniture and the rhinestone-studded brocade gown she wore to the coronation of Russia's Czar Nicholas II. *35 Maryhill Museum Drive, Goldendale; 509-773-3733.*

On a cliff overlooking the river, Sam Hill built another improbable monument: **Stonehenge**—not quite the Stonehenge you see on England's Salisbury Plain, but a slightly scaled-down model with the same number of stones, the circle unbroken. It is a memorial to the soldiers who died in World War I. *Stonehenge Road off Route 14, east of U.S. 97.*

N O R T H E A S T

NORTHEASTERN WASHINGTON IS A LAND OF VIVID CONTRASTS, of parched sagebrush and lush meadows, rushing rivers and dry creeks, expansive alpine peaks and terse canyon escarpments. The valleys cutting into the eastern slopes of the northern Cascades—Wenatchee, Chelan, Methow, and the Okanogan—sometimes look arid and lifeless, yet they produce some of the best apples, cherries, apricots, nectarines, and peaches you'll ever taste.

A rugged territory of heavily glaciated valleys and steep-sided mountains of granite, sandstone, and metamorphic rock, this expanse has some of the Pacific Northwest's most spectacular scenery. Farms, villages, and fruit orchards are sprinkled throughout the flat bottoms of the valleys or sit on the banks of the mighty Columbia River, which skirts the area. One of the longest of these valleys, Chelan, is filled with the deep waters of Lake Chelan.

Despite the agricultural bustle of vast irrigated stretches and dryland wheat fields on the Columbia Plateau, northeastern Washington is a quiet range. North of the Columbia, wild woods alternate with farms in one of America's most beautiful rural settings. In the heart of the region, the Columbia River backs up behind Grand Coulee Dam, forming Franklin Delano Roosevelt Lake. The city of Spokane, to the east, is the cultural and economic capital of the Inland Empire.

There is much to do here. You can run river rapids, fish on a placid lake, ski across rolling uplands, climb precipices, sip microbrews at a streamside pub, or pick fruit at an orchard all on the same day. Best of all, the exceptionally friendly residents welcome visitors with open hearts.

■ HISTORY

As remote as this expanse is from today's metropolitan centers, it was one of the first areas of Washington State to be settled. When David Stuart and Alexander Ross of John Jacob Astor's Pacific Fur Company arrived in 1811 to build Fort Okanogan at the confluence of the Okanogan and Columbia Rivers, seminomadic Yakima and Okanogan Indians roamed the valleys on hardy ponies. Prospectors poured into the area in the late 1850s after surveyors discovered gold in the Similkameen River, but the region's mining boom did not take off until

Aspens in resplendent fall color at the edge of Banks Lake.

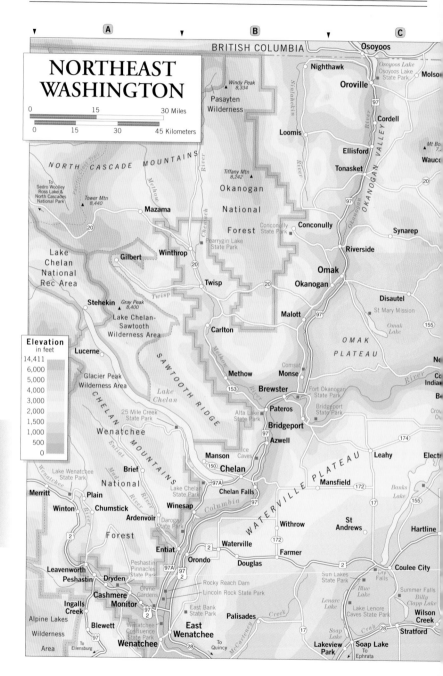

NORTHEAST WASHINGTON

0   15   30 Miles

0   15   30   45 Kilometers

Elevation
in feet

14,411
6,000
5,000
4,000
3,000
2,000
1,500
1,000
500
0

BRITISH COLUMBIA

Osoyoos
Nighthawk
Osoyoos Lake
Osoyoos Lake
State Park
Molso
Oroville
Windy Peak
8,334
Pasayten
Wilderness
Cordell
Loomis
Ellisford
Mt Bo
7,
Wauco
Tonasket
Tiffany Mtn
8,242
Okanogan
National
Conconully
Conconully
State Park
Synarep
Pearrygin Lake
State Park
Forest
Riverside
To
Sedro Woolley
Ross Lake &
North Cascades
National Park
Tower Mtn
8,440
Mazama
Winthrop
Omak
Gilbert
Okanogan
Lake
Chelan
National
Rec Area
Twisp
Disautel
Stehekin
Gray Peak
8,400
Malott
St Mary Mission
Omak
Lake
Lake Chelan-
Sawtooth
Wilderness Area
Carlton
OMAK
PLATEAU
Lucerne
N
Glacier Peak
Wilderness Area
Methow
Monse
Co
India
Comsat
Brewster
Be
153
Fort Okanogan
State Park
Lake
Chelan
25 Mile Creek
State Park
Pateros
Bridgeport
State Park
Crov
Ou
Wenatchee
Alta Lake
State Park
Bridgeport
174
Manson
Ice
Caves
Azwell
Leahy
Electr
150
Chelan
Mansfield
172
Banks
Lake
155
Brief
97A
Plain
Chelan Falls
St
Andrews
Hartline
Merritt
Chumstick
Winesap
Withrow
17
Winton
Ardenvoir
Daroga
State Park
Columbia
National
Entiat
Waterville
Farmer
172
Coulee City
Leavenworth
Peshastin
Peshastin
Pinnacles
State Park
97A
Orondo
Douglas
Sun Lakes
State Park
Dry
Falls
Dryden
Rocky Reach Dam
Blue
Lake
Summer Falls
Billy
Clapp Lake
Forest
Cashmere
Ohme
Gardens
Lincoln Rock State Park
Lenore
Lake
Lake Lenore
Caves State Park
Wilson
Creek
Ingalls
Creek
Monitor
East Bank
State Park
Palisades
Creek
Stratford
Alpine Lakes
Blewett
Wenatchee
Confluence
State Park
Soap
Lake
Soap Lake
28
Wilderness
Area
To
Ellensburg
Wenatchee
East
Wenatchee
To
Quincy
McCartney
Lakeview
Park
To
Ephrata

NORTHEAST

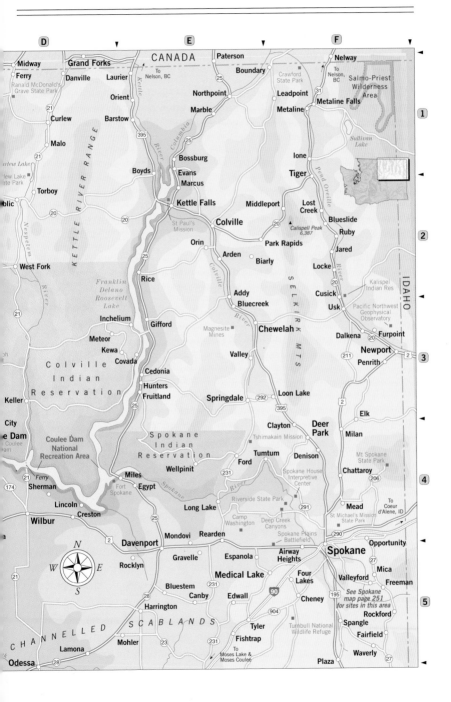

CANADA

Midway
Ferry
Ranald McDonald's
Grave State Park
Danville
Laurier
Orient
Curlew
Malo
Barstow
Torboy
blic
West Fork

Grand Forks
To
Nelson, BC
Paterson
Boundary
Northpoint
Marble
Bossburg
Evans
Marcus
Kettle Falls
St Paul's
Mission
Orin
Arden
Rice
Addy
Bluecreek
Gifford
Meteor
Kewa
Covada
Cedonia
Hunters
Fruitland

Paterson
Boundary
Crawford
State Park
Leadpoint
Metaline
Metaline Falls
Ione
Tiger
Middleport
Lost
Creek
Calispell Peak
6,387
Park Rapids
Biarly
Locke
Cusick
Usk
Chewelah
Valley
Springdale
Loon Lake

Nelway
To
Nelson,
BC
Salmo-Priest
Wilderness
Area
Sullivan
Lake
Blueslide
Ruby
Jared
Dalkena
Furpoint
Newport
Penrith
Elk
Milan

KETTLE RIVER RANGE

Columbia River

Colville
Colville River
Pend Oreille
Metal River

SELKIRK MTS

Franklin
Delano
Roosevelt
Lake

Magnesite
Mines

Nespelem River

Colville
Indian
Reservation

Keller
City
e Dam
Coulee
am
Sherman
Lincoln
Wilbur
Creston

Miles
Egypt
Fort
Spokane
Long Lake

Spokane
Indian
Reservation

Wellpinit
Ford
Tumtum
Denison
Mt Spokane
State Park
Chattaroy

Spokane House
Interpretive
Center

Riverside State Park

Camp
Washington
Deep Creek
Canyons

Mondovi
Rearden
Davenport
Gravelle
Rocklyn
Espanola
Medical Lake
Bluestem
Canby
Harrington
Edwall

Mohler
Lamona
Odessa
Tyler
Fishtrap
To
Moses Lake &
Moses Coulee

Spokane Plains
Battlefield
Airway
Heights
Four
Lakes
Cheney

Mead
St Michael's Mission
State Park
To
Coeur
d'Alene, ID
Opportunity
Mica
Valleyford
Freeman
See Spokane
map page 251
for sites in this area
Rockford
Spangle
Fairfield
Waverly
Plaza

Turnbull National
Wildlife Refuge

IDAHO

Kalispel
Indian Res
Pacific Northwest
Geophysical
Observatory

CHANNELLED   SCABLANDS

Deer
Park

Clayton
Tshimakain Mission

Keller
City

N
W   E
S

D   E   F

1
2
3
4
5

the 1880s, when gold and silver ore were discovered in the mountains. By then, ranchers driving herds of cattle north had staked out most of the valuable grazing lands. Sheep arrived in the valleys in 1898, causing almost instant conflict between sheepherders and cattlemen. More often than not, these resulted in senseless slaughter of sheep by resentful cowboys. Today, backpackers and horse trekkers use the old sheep trails to reach the mountains. The first farmers arrived in the 1880s, establishing orchards that still flourish today.

■ EASTERN SLOPES OF THE CASCADES

Where the Okanogan River flows into the Columbia River the landscape takes on a dramatic cast. Eons ago, this combined force cut its way through deep layers of basalt that had flowed in from the southeast and then solidified in vertical columns. As the river toppled these rock columns and reduced them to rubble, it carved a deep, steep-sided canyon of the type known in Washington State as a "coulee." Examples of this dramatic landform can be found east of the rivers at Moses Coulee, Grand Coulee, and Dry Falls.

This is a stark landscape, with high canyon walls devoid of vegetation except for scraggly sagebrush and clumps of sere grasses rising above the Great River of the West. Surrounding the river are the orchards that make Washington a preeminent apple-producing region. This land lies in the rain shadow of the North Cascades and receives so little precipitation that life would come to a virtual halt without the Columbia and its western tributaries—the Okanogan, Methow, and Wenatchee—gushing from the glaciers of alpine peaks.

To the west rise the North Cascades, first in low, brown hills, then pine-clad mountains, and finally in serried ranks of jagged, snow-clad ridges. The mountain valleys are U-shaped, like the coulees, but their geologic origin is different. They were carved by the ice of a cooler age, when mountain glaciers covered the valley floors. The most scenic of these glaciated troughs is Lake Chelan, which reaches deep into the alpine heart of the mountains. The Methow Valley to the north and the Wenatchee Valley to the south are beautiful swales where clear rivers skirt sheer rock walls and flow through wildflower meadows and past apple, cherry, pear, and peach orchards.

U.S. 2 connects Seattle to eastern Washington and Spokane via the Cascade Crest and scenic Stevens Pass. As mountain crossings go, Stevens Pass is more interesting than Snoqualmie Pass (I-90) to the south. Colorful towns and villages, each one happily outfitted with at least one good bakery and café, punctuate the landscape between Snohomish and Stevens Pass, and the scenery between each is breathtaking. The landscape is particularly impressive in spring, when wildflowers cover canyon walls and apple, apricot, and peach trees are in bloom. In winter, Stevens Pass, a tad higher than 4,000 feet, closes occasionally for snow removal, but rarely for more than an hour or two.

Leavenworth   *map pages 220–221, A-5*
The former logging town of Leavenworth has been transformed over the past few decades into a faux Bavarian village, complete with Bavarian restaurants, a German dance club, and a wildy popular Oktoberfest. For a while, these trimmings seemed more fake than inspired, but recent efforts to incorporate Bavarian-style architecture throughout the town have been successful.

From Leavenworth, U.S. 2 descends east from the alpine backcountry past apple orchards, wending its way to the Chelan County town of Wenatchee, on the banks of the Columbia River. Before the town of Dryden, look for a sign directing you to **Peshastin Pinnacles State Park,** which has climbable spires (experts only) and moderately challenging trails for hikers. Trails open onto areas with views of surrounding orchards, the Enchantment Mountain Range, and Wenatchee River Valley. *North Dryden Road off U.S. 2.*

Wenatchee   *map pages 220–221, A-5*
The compact towns in the Wenatchee River Valley region cater to apple farmers, loggers, and visitors. Wenatchee itself, on the west bank of the Columbia River, is considered the capital of Washington apple country. The town was billing itself "the home of the big red apple" as early as 1905, and it still holds an apple blossom festival every spring.

Wenatchee is a shipping point for apples and apricots from local orchards and a shopping center for surrounding farmlands. Its pleasant downtown contains beautifully restored buildings, many of them occupied by restaurants and boutiques. The Beaux Arts–style **County Courthouse** (350 Orondo Street), built in 1924, is an architectural gem. Packinghouses, where you can buy apples by the box, line the main road north of town.

Wenatchee rests on the site of an ancient village of the Wenatchi Indians, who may have lived here 11,000 years ago. Orchards surround **East Wenatchee,** a

(following pages) The Cascades loom over the Wenatchee Valley at sunrise.

growing suburb across the Columbia River that the high cliffs of the Columbia Plateau overlook.

Four miles south of Wenatchee is **Rock Island Railroad Bridge,** erected by the Great Northern Railway in 1893. Forged in the Edge Moore Bridge Works at Wilmington, Delaware, the bridge was shipped west in sections and assembled on location. **Rock Island Dam** (Route 28), built in the 1930s, 2 miles south of East Wenatchee, was the first dam built on the Columbia River.

■ Up the Columbia River

North of Wenatchee, U.S. 97A and U.S. 97 travel parallel to each other along opposite banks of the Columbia River. U.S. 97A, which heads north along the west bank of the Columbia, is the more scenic of the two routes. U.S. 2, signed as U.S. 2/97 until Orondo, heads east from there into a sagebrush canyon and the wheat fields of the Waterville Plateau.

About 3 miles north of Wenatchee is the **Ohme Gardens Park.** The gardens look like a series of coniferous towers perched atop rocky parapets. From here, you'll get unobstructed views south over the confluence of the Columbia and Wenatchee Rivers; west to the snowcapped peaks of the North Cascade Mountains; and east to the sharp rim of the Columbia Plateau. The views, though, are not the park's claim to fame. What makes Ohme Gardens a treasure are the horticultural efforts that have transformed a once barren hill into one of the most famous alpine gardens in America.

Stone paths wind around waterfalls and through 9 acres of shady glens, sunny meadows, and evergreens. The gardens are patterned on the natural plant associations of the mountain peaks above Wenatchee Valley, so trees and low-growing alpine shrubs and perennials blend into existing rock formations, as they do in valley forests and alpine meadows.

Herman Ohme and his wife, Ruth, began the gardens in 1929. The couple had no intention of creating a public garden and wanted merely to build a tranquil retreat for their small family. But as Herman and Ruth kept expanding their refuge, curiosity grew. The gardens were officially opened to the public in 1939. Over the years, the Ohme family increased the gardens to their present size. *3327 Ohme Road (look for signs off either U.S. 97 or 97A), Wenatchee; 509-662-5785.*

A short ascent through dry canyons on U.S. 2 east of Orondo takes you up a steep two-lane road that curves around Easter Island–like outcroppings and hill-

APPLES OF ENDLESS VARIETY

Washington State and apples are synonymous. Apples grow almost everywhere, both east and west of the Cascade Mountains. Once known only for the much-maligned Red Delicious (because it turns mushy very quickly), the state's growers have expanded their harvests to include such rarities as Rhode Island Greening, Arkansas Black, and Bramling. All over the state, farmers markets, farm stands, and small-town markets sell such rarities as the Braeburn, Cox Orange Pippin, Winter Banana, Russet, Criterion, Jonagold, Idared, Fuji, Mutsu, and Spitzenberg, besides the more widely commercially grown Newton Pippin, Golden Delicious, and Gravenstein. Of the latter two, the Golden Delicious is the ideal storage apple. When grown in orchards near Lake Chelan, it achieves an unequalled crispness of flavor matched only by the finest dessert wines. The Gravenstein is a cool climate apple and, like the Golden Delicious, grows best near water, as it does in Skagit County, where orchards overhang the tide flats of Padilla Bay. The Gravenstein does not keep well and should be eaten fresh, in season. It is inimitable in applesauces and pies. Both of these golden apples are perfect with a well-aged, sharp Washington cheddar.

sides quilted with bunchgrass. On top, the land flattens into brilliant green wheat fields. Wheat has been planted from the canyon's rim to the edge of the blacktop. Nearby Waterville has a great downtown filled with early-20th-century buildings. Beyond it, you drive for miles through seemingly endless fields of wheat.

Rocky Reach Dam   *map pages 220–221, A-5*
A few miles north lies an oasis in a desert of volcanic rock and sagebrush. Rocky Reach Dam is an example of what careful landscaping and irrigation can achieve in an area of little or no rainfall. Perfectly manicured, tree-shaded lawns invite picnickers, and a splendid collection of perennials attracts garden enthusiasts. But the greenery here is famous for another attraction: rabbits. Many dozens of the furry creatures settled here (or were abandoned by former owners) and multiplied in the brush. Fences deter predators, but these rabbits are not afraid of anyone or anything, least of all people. *U.S. 97A, 7 miles north of Wenatchee; 509-663-7522.*

NORTHEAST

■ LAKE CHELAN   *map pages 220–221, A/B-3/4*

Lake Chelan is known as much for its scenery as its apples. The lake's narrow basin, gouged by ice-age glaciers, snakes 55 miles from the Columbia River to the North Cascades. The Stehekin River feeds the lake on Cascade glacier melt, and a dam at the lake's southeast end, built in 1927, keeps the water level high. Unlike Ross Lake to the west, Chelan is a natural lake, but without the dam its water level would fluctuate, rising when the Cascade snows melt in the late spring and summer, and falling later in the year.

Chelan's waters retain the ice-blue cast of their glacial sources, a cobalt transparency that combines with the dry climate of eastern Washington and the blazing heat of summer to give it a Mediterranean aura. Unlike the Mediterranean Sea, however, Lake Chelan's waters retain a glacial chill even on 90-degree July afternoons.

Lakeview condos and houses crowd the lake's south end, spreading out from the crowded vacation town of **Chelan,** shadowed by high, rounded hills and peppered with interesting old buildings. A grassy waterfront park is the perfect setting for the town's summer Bach festival.

Roads wind around both shores of the lake northwest from Chelan until national forest land begins and the mountains close in. The road on the western shore, Route 971, ends at **Twenty-Five Mile Creek State Park,** north of the campground on the lake's west side. From here, only boats and seaplanes can take you farther up the lake. Boaters beware of the strong north winds; fierce storms can come out of nowhere. *Lakeshore Road off Route 971; 509-687-3710.*

Here and there, abandoned orchards and dilapidated cabins recall the lake's pioneer days, when dairy farms and fruit trees stood on the northern shores, and miners and trappers worked the creeks and drainages of surrounding mountains.

Manson   *map pages 220–221, B-4*

On Route 150, on Lake Chelan's eastern shore, is Manson, known to many as Village on the Bay. The 8-mile Manson scenic loop drive, which starts downtown and winds through apple orchard country, is a memorable journey, especially at the end of May, when trees are in bloom. Look for signs. Each May (second weekend), Manson holds its Apple Blossom Festival. The event typically includes a carnival, parade, beauty pageant, pancake breakfast, and a ball. Manson can be reached either by road or on the *Lady of the Lake* ferry from Chelan.

NORTHEAST

Stehekin   *map pages 220–221, A-3*

Pricey restaurants and boutiques do brisk summer business in the pretty town of Stehekin, at the north end of Lake Chelan. In the shadow of the North Cascades, Stehekin is a popular point of departure for climbers and hikers and an ideal day-trip destination for Lake Chelan tourists. Three scheduled boats make the 110-mile round-trip from Chelan each day, carrying passengers, mail, and supplies. The ferry operation (509-682-4584) also runs a shuttle bus from the center of town up a steep mountain road to the Pacific Crest Trail.

Stehekin has few roads and is only accessible by boat, plane, or mountain trails. The Chamber of Commerce (800-424-3526) has information on hiking, mountain climbing, swimming, and dining.

(above) Apple crate art, ca. 1920, promotes Lake Chelan fruit.
(following pages) Lake Chelan retains its glacial chill even in 90-degree summer weather.

Apples, peaches, and apricots thrive in the moist air of the lakeside slopes during the long, hot summers. Apple orchards above the lake grow some of the most flavorful apples in Washington.

■ METHOW VALLEY *map pages 220–221, B-3/4*

The town of **Winthrop** has captured the essence of the Old West with a colorful main street, false-front buildings, wooden sidewalks, and old-fashioned street lamps. The author Owen Wister lived here in the early 1900s, and more than a few of the sights and people from his book *The Virginian* were inspired by the town's early incarnation. Winthrop is now mostly a retreat for hikers and bikers, who keep hotels and restaurants here hopping all summer. Winter brings cross-country skiers, who find great slopes by day and warm chalets by night.

You can drive to Winthrop from Chelan via the Methow River north along Route 153 and then take Route 20 west. (If you're coming from western Washington, follow the North Cascades Scenic Highway (Route 20) east across the mountains from the Skagit Valley.)

The Methow Valley in fog near Winthrop.

The **Shafer Museum** (285 Castle Avenue; 509-996-2712), a historical village, has the largest collection of early mining equipment in the Pacific Northwest. Chinook salmon are raised at the **Winthrop National Fish Hatchery** (453-A Twin Lakes Road; 509-996-2424), where you can also see other fish species.

Pasayten Wilderness   *map pages 220–221, B-1*

Trails into the southern part of the Pasayten Wilderness start nearby. The Pasayten Wilderness covers 520,000 acres of varied terrain east of the Cascades and south of the Canadian border. It's a huge tract that includes Manning and Cathedral Parks in Canada, and the North Cascades Complex, which encompasses North Cascades National Park, Glacier Peak Wilderness, Ross Lake, and Lake Chelan National Recreation Areas. The Pasayten landscape has open, rolling meadows and steep ravines, thickly forested with pine and larch. Sharp, snowy peaks stand out from the bare, wind-bitten ridges, and the vastness and unmanaged quality of the area are striking. Weather in these highlands is unpredictable. Violent summer storms may strike with little or no warning.

■ THE OKANOGAN   *map pages 220–221, B/C-2/3*

The Okanogan River meets the Columbia River above the town of Brewster, where U.S. 97 picks up the path of the old Cariboo Trail, forged first by Indians and used later by Hudson's Bay Company fur traders.

Fort Okanogan was built by the Pacific Fur Company in 1811. The Hudson's Bay Company took control of the fort in 1821 and ran it as a supply post until the British gave up their claim to the Oregon Country south of the 49th parallel in 1846. **Fort Okanogan State Park** memorializes the fur-trading era. *From Brewster, drive north to the intersection of U.S. 97 and Route 17. Turn east on Route 17 and drive half a mile to the park entrance; 509-689-6665.*

The parched sagebrush steppes of the Columbia Basin extend up the Okanogan Valley, making the landscape stark but beautiful. The treeless, rolling hills that rise on both sides of the river lie four months under snow, turn beautifully green in late spring, and soon settle under the straw blanket of summer.

The river flows slowly between its many dams, and Rainbird sprinklers tick in the pastoral geometry of orchard rows. Cottonwood and willow trees grow along the Okanogan's banks, and farmhouses scattered on exposed low hills are shielded from strong winds by groves of poplar trees.

Four miles southwest of **Okanogan,** where Route 20 follows the hillside above the river's west bank, the site of the Curtis Sheep Slaughter recalls the hostility that existed all over the West between cattlemen and sheepherders. A herder named Curtis awoke one morning in 1903, after numerous threats from local cowboys, to find hundreds of his fleecy charges bludgeoned to death.

Long after the range wars ended, when the federal government started building massive hydroelectric dams along the Columbia and its tributaries, eastern Washington became a battleground between public and private utility companies. Today, these battles seem as archaic as those between sheepherders and cattlemen, but they are not entirely forgotten. Okanogan, for example, still proclaims itself a "Public Power Community," and its sidewalk clocks bear the motto "Live Better Electrically."

The Spanish Mission–style **Okanogan County Courthouse** (149 Third Avenue), built in 1915, is a grand building, and the nearby Methodist church isn't bad either. Okanogan has pleasant cafés, and a Saturday farmers market takes place on the library lawn.

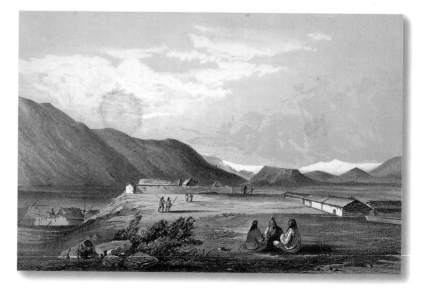

(above) Fort Okanogan was established by the Pacific Fur Company in 1811, then changed hands several times before coming into ownership by the Hudson's Bay Company in 1821. (University of Washington Libraries). (opposite) North Cascades Highway.

This early miners' supply and way station near Omak was one of the area's first permanent structures. (University of Washington Libraries)

Agriculture is big in Okanogan County, which depends on it for nearly a third of its jobs, and though apples wear the crown in this valley, the Okanogan remains cow country. Most roads that branch off U.S. 97 cross open rangeland, and the steel grates of cattle guards bisect gravel and blacktop. (Drive with caution: if a cow jumps in front of your car here and you hit it, you'll pay for damage to the cow and the car.)

Cattle still roam the hills, but the valley floor and benchlands are covered with orchards of apples. The cherries here are Washington's best. Huge sorting sheds and mountains of wooden fruit crates stand on the riverbanks, and small trees, their fertile branches propped with wooden stakes, grow row upon evenly spaced row along the road. Nearly 15 percent of Okanogan County's population is of Hispanic descent, and towns throughout the valley stock tomatillos and green chili sauce in their supermarkets.

■ GRAND COULEE DAM   *map pages 220–221, D-4*

Grand Coulee Dam is one of the largest man-made structures in the world. Its four-fifths of a mile of concrete backs up the Columbia River into a 151-mile-long lake. Rising 550 feet above bedrock, you don't realize how tall the dam is until you drive across it and look down at the trees and rooftops in the town of Grand Coulee, which was built mostly to house the workers who labored on the dam.

From the dam's northern end, you can see the 12-foot pipes that carry irrigation water up the cliff on the south side, gleaming in the sun like silver organ pipes. Up close, you can see that they're segmented like stalks of marsh grass. The water for more than a half million acres in the Columbia Basin Project gets pumped up that cliff.

Outside the generator plant, you hear the hum of distant transformers. Inside, behind glass doors, a gallery of great pumps—a line of huge, institutional-green cylinders, each with a little metal cupola on top—runs the length of a huge empty room. A catwalk along one side runs past a bank of gauges and switches for each pump. A lone workman walks along the catwalk checking the gauges. The huge room is spotless and still. There is no dirt, no noise, no visible motion. This room—this whole place—can be considered a kind of hymn to the ideal of technological progress embraced during the first half of the 20th century.

Grand Coulee was by far the largest of the dams that transformed much of the Northwest during the New Deal era and the years that followed World War II. It has nearly one-third the generating capacity of the entire vast Columbia River hydro system, and more generating capacity than any two of the other dams. It remains the largest single producer of hydroelectricity on this continent. It is also the greatest of the river's many fish killers, walling off 1,100 miles of salmon-spawning streams. People had to make a choice. At other dams, engineers designed fish ladders to help salmon get upstream. But Grand Coulee was considered too tall for fish ladders, and when it was built people knew they were trading electric lights and irrigation for fish. The first fish that found the dam in their paths battered themselves to death against its concrete base.

On the other hand, irrigation water and electricity saved some people who had been trying for years to wrest a living from an arid land. For his 1956 book *The Columbia*, Pacific Northwest historian Stewart Holbrook drove through the area around Grand Coulee, finding:

> No human being, though occasionally a reminder that some poor soul had tried to live here until one desperate day when he could stand it no longer and walked away, leaving his house as it stood, or leaned, complete with a rusting cultivator in the yard, and a mile or so of barbed wire between pitiful posts supported by little piles of stones.

When under construction, the Grand Coulee Dam required enormous amounts of lumber for its framing forms. (Museum of History and Industry)

■ THE GRAND COULEE AND SUN LAKES

map pages 220–221, C/D-4/5

Grand Coulee and the surrounding regions to the west are as various as they are austere and commanding. **Banks Lake,** in the upper Grand Coulee, is an artificial lake created by water pumped uphill from Franklin Delano Roosevelt Lake into the Grand Coulee. A holding basin for the Columbia Basin irrigation project, the lake is more than a mile wide in places and almost 30 miles long.

Steamboat Rock State Park, near the northern end, has trails, campgrounds, and swimming areas, miles of horse trails, and a trail to nearby Northrup Lake. You can't miss the park. A 600-acre-surface-area basalt rock at one end is visible for miles around. *From Coulee City, take Route 155 north 16 miles; 888-226-7688.*

The upper Grand Coulee ends on a flat near **Coulee City,** where the walls of the canyon recede and merge into the rolling uplands of the Waterville Plateau. The drive from Wenatchee to Coulee City is dramatic, as U.S. 2 takes you through the rolling wheat fields of the Waterville Plateau before rising several thousand feet to the Columbia Plateau.

In summer and fall, the snowcapped peaks of the North Cascades loom in the west beneath blue skies streaked with cumulus clouds. The landscape is mostly brushy creek beds, water towers, and grain silos. Hawks and eagles circle overhead, and the cries of curlews and trills of meadowlarks drift over a sea of grain and bunchgrass. Deer rest in moist dells, and coyotes and bobcats skulk through the dry brush.

The small country town of **Waterville** has several interesting late-19th- and early-20th-century buildings, including the 1905 **Douglas County Courthouse** (203 South Rainier Street).

Where the upper Grand Coulee merges into the lower Coulee, the landscape is flat, like a wide shelf split by low channels. This is the result of flood waters that spilled over a wide basalt shelf in the area now called Soap Lake (off Route 28). The erosion of this waterfall-cliff stopped at **Dry Falls** (south of U.S. 2), a few miles below Banks Lake.

The bluffs on U.S. 2 west of Dry Falls Dam offer great views of this enormous canyon. To the north, the banks of Banks Lake are hemmed in by steep, almost vertical basalt cliffs. Below Dry Falls, steep, barren cliffs rise from green meadows,

(following pages) The medicinal waters of Soap Lake near Ephrata draw people from around the state.

GEOLOGY AND THE COLUMBIA PLATEAU

Millions of years before humans inhabited and farmed the Columbia Plateau, fissures opened up all over the region east of the Cascade Mountains and lava poured forth. The molten rivers, sometimes as deep as 200 feet, flowed at speeds of up to 25 miles per hour. Rapidly covering hundreds of square miles, the lava flows eventually moved west to the Columbia Gorge and, finally, to the Pacific Ocean.

As the lava cooled, it turned to basalt. Over time, the rock eroded into pebbles, sand, and dust, and then the ever-blowing winds of the plateau blew the dust into dunes, which piled up on top of the basalt in a thick layer of fine-grained soil called loess. The dunes eventually turned into hills, and grass grew, producing an extremely fertile topsoil. Now known as the Palouse—the name derives from the river that skirts the hills—the area has developed into a wheat-growing region.

Some 12,000 to 19,000 years ago, during the last ice age, glaciers covered much of northern North America. One glacier pushed south from the Canadian Rockies into what is now Washington State. Its huge ice mass was about a mile thick at the Canadian border, but its advance was stopped by the high basalt cliffs rising above the southern banks of the Spokane and Columbia Rivers.

Only on the Waterville Plateau, west of the Grand Coulee, did it overcome this barrier. Its farthest advance is marked by the Withrow Hills, west of the Grand Coulee. Huge boulders, called erratics, rising darkly from the wheat fields, attest to the power of the ice flows. Some of these rocks, called "haystack" rocks by locals, are composed of Okanogan granite, but the largest of them consist of chunks of basalt torn from the Columbia River's cliffs by the advancing ice.

The ice field not only deflected the course of the Columbia River south through the Grand Coulee, but also dammed the Clark Fork River to the east, creating a vast lake. Every few thousand years, the dam gave way to the force of the water, unleashing giant floods. The torrents raced downslope toward the Wallula Gap, the only outlet to the sea for this enormous quantity of water.

The floods left behind a ravaged landscape of deep coulees, steep-sided canyons with flat floors, and channeled scablands—a cut-up landscape where the rocky plateau was reduced to freestanding walls of basalt that range in width from several miles to a few short feet. These remnants of nature's handiwork take on the shapes of crumbling city walls and decaying castles.

marshes, and lakes bordered by trees. Eagles and ravens soar along the cliffs, and songbirds, ducks, and geese patrol the bottomlands.

Dry Falls is a huge amphitheater of stone, a horseshoe of dark cliffs with pools of water at its base, 400 feet below. Climb down a trail along the fractured rock. Sunlight on the far cliffs brings out the rust and gold of lichen. There is a great stillness here, and all is quiet except for the songs and cries of birds floating up from deep inside the amphitheater.

At one time, this may have been the greatest waterfall in the world. (Victoria Falls is slightly taller but less than one-third as wide.) Ice dammed the Columbia River, flooding much of Idaho and Montana. Then the ice dam broke, and flood-waters rushed out, scoring the landscape, gouging out the coulees, pouring over what is now Dry Falls. Successive floods swept across the landscape and over these cliffs. A sign at the site tells you that at the peak of the flooding, the water plunging over the falls may have equaled the combined flow of all the rivers in the world.

Presentations at the **Dry Falls Interpretive Center** survey the area's geology and floods. *Route 17, 7 miles southwest of Coulee City; 509-632-5214.*

After Dry Falls, Route 17 winds down the cliffs in a series of switchbacks that make for scenic touring. **Sun Lakes State Park** is a high point in the lower Coulee. Campgrounds, picnic areas, and a state-run golf course attract visitors all year; in summer, lakes are filled with boaters. At Park Lake, a narrow road runs into the park and below the cliffs east of the lake. Picnic areas along the shore allow visitors to linger, and they make great places for watching redheads, canvas backs, scaups, and other ducks.

At Lenore Lake, farther south, are the **Lake Lenore Caves,** rock shelters used by Native Americans as long as 11,000 years ago. The caves were formed during the ice age and were used by nomadic peoples looking for shelter from the elements. Typically, they'd be used only for short stays. Travelers brought little with them that they couldn't carry away, though they often left behind small scrapers used in the making of protective skins. These artifacts tell the human history of these other-worldly hollows. *Eight miles south of Sun Lakes on Route 17; 509-632-5583.*

At **Soap Lake,** a gravel road runs into the hills to the site where the lava cast of a rhino was found. After skirting the lakes and passing through steep-walled clefts in the coulee, the road comes to the dusty town of Soap Lake. The landscape widens here, encroaching on a plain of dusty sagebrush that stretches almost all the way south to Moses Lake.

■ CRESTON AND WHEAT COUNTRY   *map pages 220–221, D-4/5*

Stewart Holbrook's description of this previously desolate region (see page 237) hangs in the air as you drive uphill through sage and rock on the road from Grand Coulee toward Wilbur. But it evaporates when you see the brilliant green of winter wheat growing almost to the drainage ditch beside the road.

At Creston, a grain elevator stands by the railroad tracks, and semis are parked in the unpaved lot outside the cafés and dance hall. Not much is happening. It's quiet on the main street, except when traffic goes by. A woman behind the counter complains to a trucker about how much she just paid for a small lot in town. He says he paid more for a lot in his own hometown. Yes, she says, but "there's nothing here!" Actually, in a weedy lot, there is a faded wooden sign announcing that this was where the outlaw Harry Tracy met his death.

The name may evoke blank stares now, but in the early 1900s Harry Tracy was a famous desperado. In 1902, he broke out of the Oregon State Penitentiary in Salem and made his way to Olympia, Seattle, and finally eastern Washington, eluding police and state militiamen and killing seven people along the way. A small group of well-armed locals surrounded him in a wheat field outside Creston. After a brief shoot-out, night fell, and they watched the wheat field all night. In the morning, they found that Tracy had killed himself with his own gun. Tracy's death was big news all across the country. "The first piece of business after discovery of the body," Holbrook writes, "was to pose the dead thug on his left side, gun in hand, finger on trigger, with the tall wheat as background, to make a picture that was to sell in postcard size by the hundred thousand."

If the area's small agricultural towns are somewhat depressed economically, people still find satisfaction in the spaciousness of a huge landscape, far from the cities. One evening not long ago, a man and woman who farmed 2,000 acres of dryland wheat southwest of Creston were saying that they were in it for the way of life, and they wanted to see the way of life continue. The man had been sitting by the living room window, looking out over a field that sometimes was bright green with new wheat and sometimes was covered with plowing dust; today, it was unplowed and unplanted, and he was busy with two calculators trying to figure out whether it would be more profitable to plant wheat this year or let the land lie fallow.

He and his wife couldn't have afforded this place if his father hadn't given it to them years ago. They hadn't had an easy time of it. In addition to the long days of plowing and planting, they had battled federal bureaucrats. One day, while clean-

Undulating fields of winter wheat in eastern Washington.

ing out a moving combine, the man lost an arm to the machine. Still, they liked the lifestyle and hoped, *really* hoped, that they could pass the farm along to one of their kids. After all, the man said, "that's what it's all about."

■ PEND OREILLE AND COLVILLE RIVER VALLEYS

Salmo-Priest Wilderness Area   *map pages 220–221, F-1*

Few people visit the Salmo-Priest Wilderness, a remote region east of Metaline Falls, but many wild creatures traverse its rugged terrain. Virgin forests of western red cedar, western hemlock, Douglas fir, grand fir, and larch cover the mountainsides. The area is linked to wilderness in Idaho and British Columbia, and the critters—cougars, bobcats, elk, black bears, bighorn sheep, moose, badgers, wolves, and white-tailed deer—don't stop at the border. The grizzly bear is another frequent visitor to these parts, and the Salmo-Priest remains one of the few places in North America where you'll see woodland caribou.

Kettle Falls   *map pages 220–221, E-2*

The Colville River meets the Columbia near the town of Kettle Falls. Lodgepole pines darken the hills, and the brighter greens of hay fields and pasture line the valley floor. Mills cut pine lumber in Colville and Chewelah. Log trucks rumble down roads, and near the bridge that crosses the Columbia, a power plant burns sawdust to produce electricity. Until Grand Coulee Dam was built, the river was relatively narrow here. Early in the 20th century, the scattered inhabitants of the region crossed it on small ferries. West of the bridge, in the front yard of a small motel, a gravestone marks the final resting place of a Colville Indian chief.

East of the bridge, a turnoff takes you to one of the richest historical areas in Washington. Upstream from the bridge, the river once tumbled over Kettle Falls, where local tribes speared salmon for perhaps 8,000 years. After Grand Coulee was built, Franklin Delano Roosevelt Lake flooded the falls and they ceased to exist. The old town of Kettle Falls, which used to stand beside the river, also wound up under 30 feet of water. The inhabitants moved to higher ground.

St. Paul's Mission   *map pages 220–221, E-2*

Before the dam and highways were built, people traveling up or down the river had to move around the falls. Traditionally, they walked up over a pine-covered bench on the south shore, where Catholic missionaries built St. Paul's Mission in 1837. The mission building, with its wide, pegged floorboards and heavy, hand-hewn crossbeams, is still here. When M. J. Lorraine portaged past the spot in 1924, he made note of the "former Jesuit mission, empty and with its doors and windows gone. It had been built in 1837 of the most evenly-sized and smoothly-hewn logs I ever saw, and although not a single nail held the structure together, the walls were still upright, sound and substantial."

Walk toward the water through woods of second-growth ponderosa pine. In late spring, the forest floor is sprinkled with wildflowers: bright blue larkspur and yellow and purple daisies. In a fenced-off area, old headstones mark a cemetery where traders, settlers, and Indians are buried.

At dusk, the mission interior is lost in shadows, the interpretive center is closed, and no one is around. Nothing moves among the pines. The water is still. A black boulder lies on the bluff, its weight of human history dating back eight millennia. The spot isn't really quiet—you can hear traffic whipping by—but it is serene. *Three miles northwest of Kettle Falls off Route 395; 509-633-9441.*

■ SPOKANE   *map pages 220–221, F-4/5, and page 251*

At the break of dawn, as I leave Moses Lake southwest of Spokane, the water lies dark and quiet like pewter, its silence interrupted only by the hysterical squabble of ducks, the occasional roar of a semi on I-90, and the croak of a great blue heron. The wheat fields to the east gleam like gold in the wan early light, and the basalt formations along the road remind me of sleeping dragons. The wheat soon gives way to dun grasslands and somber pines, but as the freeway tops a low ridge, a glorious vista opens up: the sun has just risen above the mountains to the east and bathes the valley of the Spokane River in an almost unearthly golden light—the hills, the pines, the river and falls, the downtown towers, the spire of St. John's Cathedral.

Driving through this landscape brushed with the ethereal beauty of the rising sun, I suddenly understand why the native Spokane Indians called themselves *Spokanes*, or "children of the sun." They also called the river, which once teemed with salmon, *Senahomana*, or "the river of salmon." Spokane Falls, actually two steep cataracts—the lower one dropping 70 feet and the upper one 60 feet—did not stop the salmon from migrating upstream but slowed their progress, so that the falls became an important fishing station. Here, people would meet in season to net or trap fish, trade, and fraternize.

(above) Downtown Spokane, ca. 1900. (University of Washington Libraries)

(above) This 1904 map reveals the city's growth pattern. (Library of Congress)

■ HISTORICAL SPOKANE

In 1872, modern Spokane's founding father, James N. Glover, purchased a sawmill from two squatters. Glover knew what he was doing—there's nothing a growing town needs more than milled timber. He also had a keen eye for beauty, choosing a spot for his mill on the south side of the river.

In the 1880s, the infant city received a boost when the railroads moved in. The Northern Pacific was first to lay tracks, followed by the Union Pacific, the Great Northern, the Canadian Pacific, and the Central Washington lines. All this activity turned Spokane into a major railroad hub. By 1889, the year Washington Territory became a state, the town's population had grown to nearly 20,000, and banks, hotels, blacksmiths, flour mills, breweries, and saloons flourished here.

In the early days, the settlers had to row across water to visit and trade with each other, but in 1881, individual citizens pledged enough money to build the first bridge. A mere four years later, the first hydroelectric plant in Washington was built beside the falls. (A successor, the blocky Upper Falls Powerhouse, erected in 1922, still generates electricity on the river's southern bank. You'll know if you're near it, because you can hear it hum.)

The city started with a lowly sawmill, but as with so many other Washington towns, its residents soon concentrated on the more lucrative business of mining gold, silver, copper, lead, and zinc in the mountains to the northwest, north, and east.

Mining began in earnest with the discovery of the Old Dominion Mine in Colville in 1885. By World War I, when San Francisco and East Coast financiers had captured the mining profits and concentrated smelting in Idaho and Montana, Spokane's economy had diversified.

In 1941, Grand Coulee Dam was completed on the Columbia River. It provided electricity and irrigation water to a vast new farming region, the "Inland Empire," and Spokane became its capital.

During the last half of the 20th century, as more manufacturers shipped their products by truck instead of train, highways superceded the rails. Several east-west and north-south roads were constructed that pass through the heart of Spokane, including I-90.

With a central location and easy accessibility, Spokane remains a shopping mecca for eastern Washington's farmers, loggers, and miners. The metropolis that emerged from the sawmill by the river has evolved into one of the most beautiful cities in the American West.

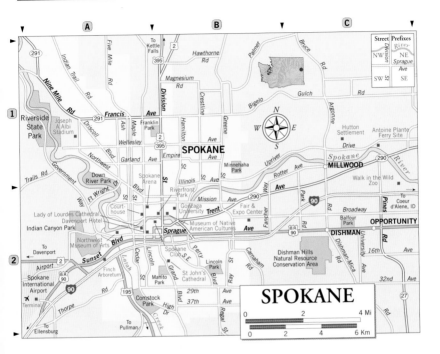

■ MODERN SPOKANE: CITY ON THE RIVER

The city of Spokane unfolds like a huge flower, with the falls, Riverfront Park, and downtown as its heart, surrounded by river terraces that grow like petals into the low hills of the countryside. The big windows of the downtown library provide spectacular views of water cascading over gray bedrock. On the south bank, parents with young children head for a century-old carousel with carved horses in full gallop, elaborate woodwork, and lightbulbs gleaming off mirrored backdrops. Loud organ music drifts through the open doors.

On a nearby island, the old Great Northern Railway station clock tower rises above the weeping willows at its base. At the southern end of the park stands a monument to the city's annual Bloomsday Run: a steel sculpture of 20 runners caught midstride. Spokane artist David Govedare created these slightly larger-than-life sculptures. The Bloomsday Run, which draws runners from the state each May, is part of the Spokane Lilac Festival, several days of exhibits, flower shows, and concerts. The river has always been the heart of the city.

(following pages) Riverfront Park and railroad station clock tower.

Downtown

One unique aspect of Spokane is that its downtown hasn't died, as did those in Bellingham, Bremerton, and Tacoma. Though challenged by unsightly malls, downtown Spokane thrives in part because its parking garages, office buildings, and department stores are connected by an ingenious system of sky bridges that allow for easy walking even during a winter blizzard. Or maybe the vitality of downtown Spokane is the result of the extensive citywide cleanup the city underwent in preparation for Expo 74—a mini world's fair—when ugly remnants of railroad yards were removed and Riverfront Park was laid out.

One of the city's major attractions, the 100-acre **Riverfront Park** sprawls across several islands in the Spokane River, near the falls. One of the modernist buildings that went up during Expo 74 now houses an IMAX theater, a skating rink, and an exhibition space. The Opera House occupies the former Washington State Pavilion, and the stone clock tower of the former Great Northern Railway Station, built in 1902, stands in sharp contrast to the Expo building. A miniature train chugs around the park in summer, and at the park's south edge a carousel, hand-carved in 1909 by master builder Charles I. D. Loof, beckons riders. *507 North Howard Street; 509-625-6600.*

A 15- to 20-minute walk west from Riverfront Park brings you to **Northwest Museum of Arts & Culture,** until recently known as the Cheney Cowles Memorial Museum. Exhibits here trace the historical development of the Inland Empire, including the mining, timber, and farming industries. Also noteworthy is the extensive collection of Plateau Indian arts and handicrafts. *2316 West First Avenue; 509-456-3931.*

Fine old commercial buildings are among the first things people see in downtown Spokane. Some are grander versions of the brick commercial blocks that line main streets in towns throughout eastern Washington, and some are truly ornate affairs. The old **Davenport Hotel** (10 South Post Street)**,** once the grandest hostelry in eastern Washington, is a Moorish fantasy. The fancy brickwork of the **Spokane Club** (1002 West Riverside Avenue) complements the exterior of nearby Our Lady of Lourdes Cathedral. The brick face of the *Spokesman-Review* building curves along West Riverside Avenue, and the **Spokane County Courthouse** (1116 West Broadway) has turrets at the corners, more turrets surrounding a central tower, and windows topped with arches and masonry scallop shells.

Other Sights

On the hill south of downtown rises lofty **St. John's Cathedral** (127 East 12th Avenue), one of the finest examples of Gothic architecture in the United States. Built with sandstone from Tacoma and Boise and limestone from Indiana, this Episcopal house of worship, designed by Harold Whitehouse, is a work of remarkable craftsmanship both inside and out.

Farther up the hill, **Manito Park** shows how pleasant an urban park can be, with informal landscaping, playing fields, a Japanese garden, a conservatory, and a duck pond. Many fine homes built in the 1920s surround the park. *South Grand Boulevard between17th and 25th Avenues; 509-363-5422.*

Despite growing urban sprawl, orchards and farms still preside over the rural landscape outside Spokane, and day trips to the upper Spokane River Valley are likely to produce some of the state's best tree fruits (notably cherries and peaches) as well as splendid melons. Look for roadside stands selling luscious strawberries in May and June.

The 41-mile **Centennial Trail,** which winds along the Spokane River (and through Riverfront Park), begins in Nine Mile Falls, northwest of Spokane, and ends in Idaho. It connects to trails crisscrossing the hills around Spokane. Maps are available at the visitors center (201 West Main Avenue).

You might also want to visit the **John A. Finch Arboretum,** a mile-long patch of green along Garden Springs Creek. The garden has paths that take you through an extensive botanical garden of 2,000 labeled trees, shrubs, and flowers, rhododendrons, hibiscus, magnolias, dogwoods, hydrangeas, and more. *3403 West Woodland Boulevard; 509-624-4832.*

South of Cheney, you'll find **Turnbull National Wildlife Refuge,** a sanctuary for as many as 50,000 ducks, geese, swans, and other migratory waterfowl. The refuge offers a 5-mile, self-guided auto tour that covers most of the shelter's 15,468 acres of lakes, marshes, and pine forests. Keep your eyes open for the beavers, otters, muskrats, elk, and other creatures that live here. *Smith Road off Cheney-Plaza Road, Cheney; 509-235-4732.*

S O U T H E A S T

EAST OF THE SOUTHERN CASCADE MOUNTAINS, spring-green ridges turn gold under the summer sun. The Yakima River could be called Washington's river of life because its waters irrigate the state's most important agricultural valley, a place where almost everything is grown, from apples to zucchini to grapes. The dry, open woods of the southern Cascade Mountains lure hikers, rivers teem with trout, and the berry bushes of the higher slopes are loaded with sweet fruit in summer and autumn. The tall volcanic cone of Mount Adams looms over hills and valleys, and along the southern edge of the region, the Columbia River forces its way through the Cascade Mountains to the sea in a spectacular gorge. Near the point where the Yakima and Snake Rivers flow into the Columbia stand the cities of Richland, Pasco, and Kennewick, also known as the Tri Cities.

Walla Walla was among the first American settlements in Washington, and even today it has some of the state's most productive farms, growing asparagus, melons, sweet onions, and grapes. Shielded from chilling winds by the Blue Mountains to the east and the tall hills of the Palouse to the north, the southeastern portion of the state has an uncommonly mild climate. The Snake River—part dammed, part wild—cuts through the territory in a steep-sided canyon. The Blue Mountains are rich in wildlife and flowers, and the deep soils of the Palouse are among the richest wheat lands in the world.

■ HISTORY

The native people of the Yakima Valley and the Palouse belonged to the Plateau Civilization, one of the great horse-based cultures of Native Americans. Horse ownership and horsemanship moved north through the Plains and west across the Rocky Mountains by way of the Utes of southern Utah. The horse then moved north to the tribes of southern Idaho, eastern Oregon, and eastern and central Washington and British Columbia. The Utes mastered the horse early in the 18th century; the tribes of the inland Northwest were using them by about 1750.

The rolling hills of the Palouse region.

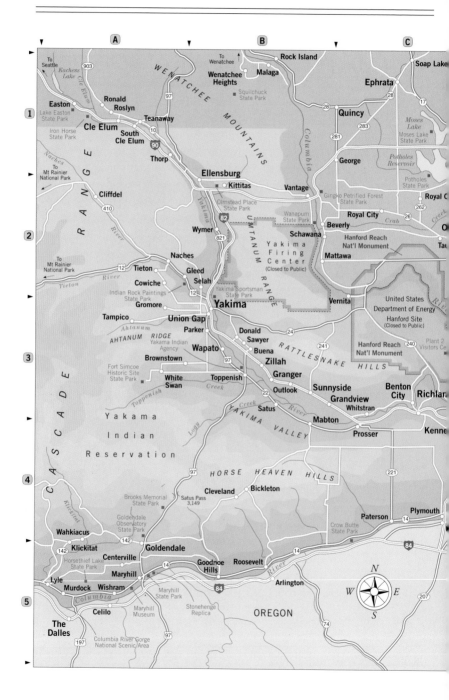

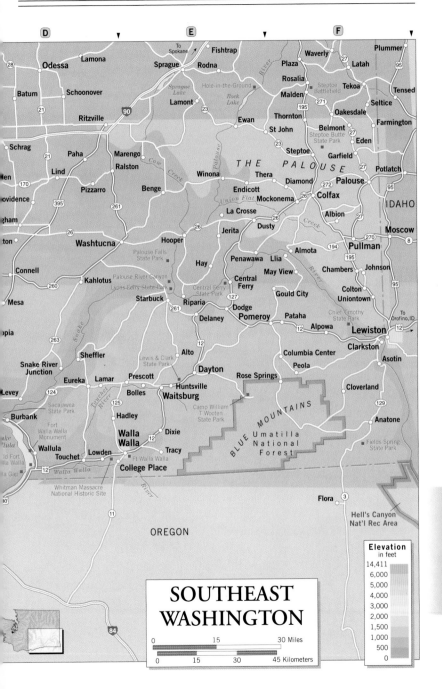

D   E   F

28   Odessa   Lamona   To Spokane   Fishtrap   Waverly   Plummer

Sprague   Rodna   Plaza   Latah   27   95

Schoonover   Rosalia   Tekoa   Tensed

Batum   Sprague Lake   Hole-in-the-Ground   Malden   Steptoe Battlefield   Seltice

21   Rock Lake   271   Oakesdale   Farmington

Ritzville   90   Lamont   23   Ewan   Thornton   195

Schrag   St John   Belmont   Steptoe Butte State Park   Eden   27

Paha   Marengo   Ralston   Steptoe   Garfield

Lind   Cow Creek   Winona   Thera   THE PALOUSE   27   Potlatch

170   Pizzarro   Benge   Endicott   Diamond   Palouse   95

ovidence   395   Union Flat   Mockonema   272   Colfax   IDAHO

gham   261   La Crosse   26   Albion   27

26   ton   Washtucna   Hooper   Jerita   Dusty   Creek   Moscow   8

Connell   Palouse Falls State Park   Hay   Penawawa   Llia   Almota   194   Pullman

260   Kahlotus   Palouse River Canyon   May View   Chambers   195   Johnson

Lyons Ferry State Park   Central Ferry State Park   Central Ferry   Colton   95

Mesa   Starbuck   127   Gould City   Uniontown

opia   Riparia   Dodge   Pataha   Chief Timothy State Park   To Drofino, ID

263   Snake   Delaney   Pomeroy   12   Alpowa   Lewiston   12

Sheffler   261   12   Columbia Center   Clarkston

Snake River Junction   Lewis & Clark State Park   Alto   Peola   Asotin

Eureka   Lamar   Prescott   Dayton   Rose Springs   Cloverland

124   Levey   Bolles   Huntsville   129

Burbank   125   Waitsburg   Camp William T Wooten State Park   BLUE MOUNTAINS   Anatone

Fort Walla Walla Monument   Hadley   Umatilla National Forest   Fields Spring State Park

ke ula   Wallula   Walla Walla   Dixie   12

d Fort lla Walla   Touchet   Lowden   Tracy   Ft Walla Walla

la Gap   12   Walla Walla   College Place

30   Whitman Massacre National Historic Site   Flora   3

11   OREGON   Hell's Canyon Nat'l Rec Area

SOUTHEAST

84

Elevation in feet

14,411
6,000
5,000
4,000
3,000
2,000
1,500
1,000
500
0

SOUTHEAST WASHINGTON

0   15   30 Miles

0   15   30   45 Kilometers

A fanciful ideal of life in the state of Washington. (University of Washington Libraries)

SOUTHEAST

When the first white explorers arrived, buffalo still roamed in southern Idaho, but they were wiped out in the early 19th century. Tribes of the inland Northwest followed the declining buffalo herds east, making annual treks to hunt them on the Great Plains. Besides buffalo and other game, the natives of the area also had easy access to camas and other roots, and to salmon, which ran as far upriver as the Rocky Mountains. Food was easily obtainable, allowing native tribes time for things besides hunting, such as sewing clothing and building dwellings.

In the 1850s, the free-roaming people of the region were subdued in a series of brutal wars and sent to reservations. Farmers began homesteading in the area, and, after the advent of irrigation and cold storage, the Yakima Valley became a prime fruit-growing region. The first commercial apple trees were planted in 1870, and the valley shipped its first carload of apples in 1894. It has been growing and shipping fruit and other crops ever since.

■ FROM ROSLYN TO GEORGE

The descent from the Cascade Crest (I-90) is a lazy trip through forests of alpine firs and pines. Ponderosa pines dominate the landscape, interrupted now and then by massive rock formations and meadows bordered by tall cottonwoods. In spring, the golden glow of sunflowers highlights the bright green of grass and trees. You'll pass the old coal towns of Roslyn and Cle Elum, but unless you leave the freeway you won't see Roslyn at all and you'll get only a glimpse of Cle Elum's backyards.

Roslyn *map pages 258–259, A-1*

Roslyn enjoyed brief celebrity as the setting of television's *Northern Exposure*. One can understand why this town was selected for that show's mythic clime. It's surrounded by densely wooded mountains and seems yet to have shaken its past as Washington's most bustling mining town. Until recently, old cottages and empty buildings gave Roslyn the look of a ghost town, but new construction has changed all that as commuters from Bellevue and Seattle are building weekend homes on the slopes.

Migrant workers harvest Washington apples about a century ago.
(University of Washington Libraries)

Much of southeastern Washington receives less than 10 inches of rainfall a year.
Were it not for irrigation, most of the area would look like this.

Highlights of the town's architectural treasures include **The Brick** (100 Pennsylvania Avenue; 509-649-2643), Washington's oldest operating tavern. In the early years, the basement served as the town jail—the cells are still there—and the back of the building was the courtroom. The Brick pours some of the best beers brewed by **Roslyn Brewing Company** (208 Pennsylvania Avenue; 509-649-2232), a block down the street.

Ellensburg   *map pages 258–259, B-2*

Farther east, you'll pass through the university and rodeo town of Ellensburg, one of many eastern Washington communities with hundred-year-old downtown commercial blocks. Its Labor Day weekend rodeo, first held in 1923, is one of the largest in the Northwest. But the presence of **Central Washington University** (400 East Eighth Avenue) has made cafés and bookstores as popular as saddles and spurs. In recent years, horse fanciers have established stud farms in the Kittitas Valley, and new orchards have been planted on the slopes. East of Ellensburg, the country turns dry and trees give way to bunchgrass, sagebrush, and rabbit brush.

SOUTHEAST

Ginkgo and Wanapum State Parks   *map pages 258–259, B-2*

Off I-90 as it heads east toward Vantage, stone columns of petrified tree trunks lie in the sagebrush of Ginkgo and Wanapum State Parks (509-856-2700). A bridge then spans the Columbia River, blue beneath the basalt cliffs, and the road beyond climbs from the river up the side of a steep escarpment leading to the top of the Columbia Plateau. A vast stretch of land that was once a near desert, the plateau is now lush with the green of irrigated fields, where thousands of people go to the Gorge Amphitheatre to hear rock and blues concerts in summer. On the way, a turnoff to the right takes you to an area inhabited by wild horses. Rust brown, silhouetted against the sky, manes and tails flying in the wind, the horses race along a flat ridge overlooking the river.

■ YAKIMA VALLEY   *map pages 258–259, B-3/4*

The high ridges crossed by I-82 on the way to Yakima are dry, rugged, sagebrush-covered rangeland. On an overcast day, the misty folds of the hills stand out clearly in patterns of light and dark, like the colors in a Cézanne painting.

As you descend into the Yakima Valley, the transition from wasteland to cornucopia is abrupt. One minute you're in sagebrush and the next you're driving through orchards and vineyards and hop fields.

In the early 20th century, the Yakima Valley was a treeless plain, and famed Supreme Court Justice William O. Douglas, who grew up here, recalled that "the land around town was mostly bleak sagebrush, occupied only by jackrabbits and rattlesnakes." Orchards and shade trees were just starting to grow, and he relished the unobstructed views of Mount Rainier and Mount Adams. "With no trees to block the view, we could look west from our front porch on the outskirts of town and see thousands of sunsets over the Cascades—sunsets which tinged the dominant glaciers of Adams and Rainier with reds and golds."

In spring, wild asparagus flourishes in roadside ditches, hop shoots wind around fence posts, and flowers bedeck hills. The valley and the nearby Columbia Basin produce more asparagus than any state but California, most of the nation's spearmint, and most of its hops. The Yakima Valley also produces many of the state's apples and most of its cherries, apricots, raspberries, and wine grapes. All in all, more than 70 different crops flourish here.

Yakima itself is a sprawling agricultural metropolis with tree-shaded residential neighborhoods and cottonwood- and willow-lined trails along the river. The

Yakima Valley Food and Wine Tour

The Yakima Valley is Washington's food basket and wine vat. Most people either travel here via Portland and the Columbia Gorge, coming up U.S. 97, or begin the trip in Seattle, crossing the Cascade Mountains on I-90. Interstate 82, which starts in Ellensburg, runs the length of the Yakima Valley. Or you can reach the valley on U.S. 12, which skirts the southern flanks of Mount Rainier.

■ COUNTRYSIDE

The Yakima River flows southeast from its source in the Cascades, cutting steep canyons through serried basalt ridges. After merging with the Naches River, it crosses the Ahtanum Valley as it passes the city of Yakima. At Union Gap, the river breaks through Ahtanum Ridge and enters the long valley bearing its name. Throughout its course, the Yakima is a rocky river, with many rapids. It was once a major salmon stream. A few salmon, undefeated by dams, still ascend the river to spawn.

Grass-covered hills, where the Yakama people freely roamed little more than a century ago, rise above green fields, orchards, and vineyards. Horses still run wild in the Horse Heaven Hills on the Yakama Indian Reservation.

Apples and other fruits took hold in valley orchards in the 1890s, with the first irrigation schemes. Grapes came much later. Concord grapes were planted first, and finally vinifera grapes used in making fine wines. Three decades ago, there were virtu-

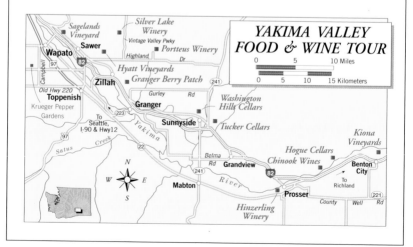

ally no vinifera vineyards in the valley; today, they dominate the local wine industry. This is more than just another wine valley, though. The Yakima Valley grows most of the nation's hops, and some of its best asparagus—it's so tender you can eat it raw, straight from the field. Tomatoes and chilis ripen to perfection in the long, hot summer days, and melons take on extra sweetness.

There are apricot, cherry, peach, and apple orchards as well. Their quality is good, though not as outstanding as the fruit grown in the east-facing valleys of the North Cascades. Yakima Valley apples get better farther west, in the foothills of the Cascades. Which is why Selah, west of Yakima, is the apple capital of south-central Washington.

Conversely, the grape quality improves the closer you get to the mitigating influence of the Columbia River. Which is why Prosser and Benton City are at the heart of the Yakima Valley wine country.

■ TOURING THE VALLEY

Because the valley's vegetables are as good as the wines, we'll start at a Wapato farm before visiting our first vineyard. The serious wine touring starts just beyond Union Gap at I-82, Exit 40, about 7 miles east of the town of Yakima.

Krueger Pepper Gardens

This exceptional farm is known for high-quality peppers—more than 60 varieties are grown here. Bring your own container, though, it's strictly u-pick. The peppers are at their peak when the grape harvest starts, as are the tomatoes, eggplant, squash, and melons. Pick up a free recipe booklet at the farm office. *462 Knights Lane, Wapato; 509-877-3677.*

Sagelands' Vineyard

The valley's westernmost winery occupies a beautiful spot on a south-facing slope. Sagelands' umbrella-shaded picnic area frames great views across the valley and nearby hills. While sipping an excellent cabernet or merlot, you can watch turkey vultures, hawks, and eagles soar against the backdrop of snow-capped Mount Adams. In a valley where most wineries have adopted a utilitarian, rustic style that makes it difficult to distinguish them from barns and farm sheds, Sagelands is most definitely an architectural high point—a feast for the eyes as well as the palate. *71 Gangl Road, Wapato; 509-877-2112.*

SOUTHEAST

Silver Lake Winery at Roza Hills

In August 2001, Silver Lake acquired the former Covey Run Winery building adjacent to Silver Lake's Roza Hills Vineyard. This winery is famous for its panoramic views of the Whiskey Canyon vineyards, the Yakima Valley, and Mount Adams. The cabernet sauvignons and merlots are uniquely flavorful. *1500 Vintage Road, Zillah; 509-829-6235.*

Hyatt Vineyards

Hyatt Vineyards has earned national attention, especially for its merlots and cabernet sauvignons. The late-harvest Riesling is also worth tasting. Hyatt sits on 97 acres and has spacious grounds for picnicking. On clear days, you can take in views of the Cascades and the Yakima Valley. *2020 Gilbert Road, Zillah; 509-829-6333.*

Portteus

Before making its own wine, Portteus gained fame as a grape grower, its grapes going into some of Washington's best reds. Taste the cabernet and merlot as well as the spicy zinfandel—yes, zinfandel. Portteus was the first Washington winery to vinify this noble grape. *5201 Highland Drive, 5 miles north of Zillah; 509-829-6970.*

Sheridan Vineyard

A young winery producing outstanding reds. Friendly and helpful staff. Affable winery dog. *2980 Gilbert Road, Zillah, WA; 509-829-3205.*

Apex Cellars

Winemaker Brian Carter has a reputation second to none. His winery divides its products into two brands: Apex for the top of the line wines, and W. B. Bridgman for quaffing wines. Any respectable wine cellar should have some Apex wines, especially the cabernets, merlots, and chardonnays. *111 East Lincoln Avenue, Sunnyside; 509-839-9463.*

Tucker Cellars

Tucker produces refreshingly fruity Rieslings and chenin blancs. The red varietals and reserve chardonnays are sold only at the winery. In spring, you can buy delicious asparagus; in summer, perfect melons and vegetables; and in fall, incredibly sweet corn. At any time of year, you can sample Tucker's white popcorn, pickled vegetables, and wines. *70 Ray Road, Sunnyside, east of Route 241, Exit 69; 509-837-8701.*

Hyatt Vineyards in Zillah.

Hinzerling Winery

Mike Wallace, a Washington wine industry pioneer, has produced some superb wines, particularly reds and port-style wines. He also has a talent for bringing out the complex flavors of gewürztraminer. *1520 Sheridan Avenue, Prosser; 509-786-2163 or 800-727-6702.*

Chinook Wines

The happy marriage of viticulturist Clay Mackey and wine-maker Kay Simon has resulted in exceptional chardonnays, sauvignon blancs, semillons, cabernet francs, cabernet sauvignons, and merlots. Unfortunately, these wines are always in short supply. But chances are you'll find some at the winery when they're unavailable anywhere else. *Wine Country Road off I-82, Prosser; 509-786-2725.*

Hogue Cellars

The Hogue winery has been acquired by an international conglomerate, but the wines are still good and the winery is well worth visiting. The Hogue fumé blanc has gained a regional reputation; the dry chenin blanc is everyone's favorite summer afternoon wine; and the reds go well with most foods. *Wine Country Road off I-82, Prosser; 509-786-4557.*

SOUTHEAST

A picture-perfect Yakima Valley vineyard near the town of Zillah.

Terra Blanca Vintners

Terra Blanca is the most exciting winery on Red Mountain, at the eastern end of the Yakima Valley. Be sure to try the red: cabernet sauvignon, merlot, and syrah. The riesling and gewürztraminer are also excellent. *34715 North DeMoss Road, Benton City; 509-588-6082.*

Other Wines of Note

Be sure to taste the Gordon Brothers' merlots from their **Snake River Vineyards** and the semillons by **L'Ecole No. 41,** made from Walla Walla Valley grapes. The Walla Walla cabernet sauvignons made by **Leonetti Cellar** and **Woodward Canyon** are good too. And by no means neglect the delicious cabernets of **Quilceda Creek.** Look for them in wineshops or ask for them in restaurants. (The restaurant at Yakima's Birchfield Manor Inn has an excellent selection of rare local bottlings.)

One last note: summer days in the Yakima Valley can get very hot. Don't leave wine or fresh produce in your car. The produce will cook, and the wine bottles may pop their corks.

SOUTHEAST

Central Washington Fair is held here in fall. Yakima has more than its share of resort motels because Puget Sounders, chilled by their region's often cool summer climate, flock here to lie in the sun and soak up the warmth, which is why the city calls itself the Palm Springs of Washington.

The **Yakima Valley Museum and Historical Association** is a must-see destination for history buffs. In addition to extensive displays on local history, the museum also has a comprehensive collection of horse-drawn vehicles, early motorcars, and a model of Supreme Court Justice William O. Douglas's office in Washington, D.C. The old-fashioned soda fountain is especially popular. *2105 Tieton Drive; 509-248-0747.*

The **Yakima Electric Railway Museum** is a big draw for railroad buffs. This "museum on wheels" has original trolley cars, streetcars, and displays. Some vehicles are used for public rides around town. *306 West Pine Street; 509-575-1700.*

Off I-82, south of town, is **Yakima Area Arboretum & Botanical Garden.** More than 2,000 species of native and exotic trees, shrubs, and flowers from around the world grow here on 46 acres. The arboretum is a place where visitors can break from the rigors of hiking to hear birds and marvel at nature's variety. Fans of the hummingbird will love this place: in summer, three different types of hummers—black-chinned, calliope, and rufous—congregate here. *1401 Arboretum Drive; 509-248-7337.*

Yakama Indian Reservation *map pages 258–259, A/B-3/4*

The nearby Yakama Indian Reservation, the largest in Washington, includes irrigated orchards and fields, miles of commercial forest, a cultural heritage center, and much of 12,276-foot Mount Adams, the state's second-highest peak. The tribal government is in Toppenish. The name was written "Yakima" until 1994, when it was changed to reflect actual pronunciation. The tribe has treaty rights to salmon in the Yakima and Columbia Rivers, though the Yakima no longer contains enough water year-round to irrigate all the valley's farms and orchards and still ensure survival of the fish.

A must-see at the reservation is the **Museum at the Yakama Nation Cultural Heritage Center**, which has one of the best Native American archives in the state.

(preceding page) Ballooning over the Yakima River.
(right) Teapot Dome, near Zillah, is one of the country's oldest gas stations.

The permanent exhibit tracing the life of the Yakamas since prehistoric times, "The Challenge of Spilay," is not to be missed. The center also has a restaurant, a gift shop, a library, and a theater for the performing arts. *280 Buster Road; 509-865-2800.*

Toppenish   *map pages 258–259, B-3, and page 264*
Toppenish, off U.S. 97, is known for the outdoor murals adorning more than 30 historic buildings. Every year, the town hosts a "Mural in a Day" festival, for which artists collectively create a painting that is then moved to a building wall.

Toppenish's **American Hop Museum** has displays on the history of the American hop industry from 1805 to the present in addition to old photographs, hop memorabilia, antiques, and a gift shop. *22 South B Street; 509-865-4677.*

Zillah   *map pages 258–259, B-3, and page 264*
A small town surrounded by vineyards and orchards, Zillah has a unique main street that runs at the edge of a bluff overlooking I-82 and the Yakima River. The most notable local landmark is an old wooden community church near the junction of First and Fifth Streets.

South of town, near the junction of I-82 and U.S. 12, the Wine Country Road, stands a unique political statement, the Teapot Dome gas station which is, indeed, built in the shape of a teapot, no doubt to commemorate the political scandal of the 1920s. Yes, you can fill up your car here.

Sunnyside   *map pages 258–259, B-3, and page 264*

Sunnyside, the lower Yakima Valley's commercial center, was once known as Holy City because it was a community of church people. Local deeds contained a clause stating that if property owners pursued vices such as dancing, horse racing, and gambling, their holdings would revert to the township company. Things have changed since those days, but Sunnyside's downtown still has old-time touches. The surrounding countryside, filled with vineyards and wineries, is attractive and grows some of Washington's best asparagus.

It wasn't always like this. Pioneer settler Roscoe Sheller described in his book *Blowsand* what it was like in the early 20th century, when the completion of the Sunnyside Canal brought water for irrigation: "In arranging her spring weather program, Nature was especially generous with her allotment of winds. They came in an assortment of velocity and bluster, from zephyr to gale, but no matter how light the breeze, it could pick up and carry the floury volcanic ash soil, called blowsand, to block any view beyond a few rods."

Nearby **Bickleton** is a small village in eastern Klickitat County known to many as the bluebird capital of the world. Could be hyperbole, but thousands of bluebirds spend most of the year here, apparently because of the tender climate. Most of the avian guests are mountain bluebirds, though western bluebirds are known to convene near the forest. Town residents, about 90 people, put birdhouses atop fence posts to attract the birds. To reach Bickleton, follow signs from Mabton.

Prosser   *map pages 258–259, C-4, and page 264*

The Benton County seat, Prosser, is changing slowly from a farm town into a winery town. Even so, the tree-shaded downtown, on the south bank of the Yakima River, has not changed much over the years, save the addition of several wineries and a burgeoning wine culture. Not long ago, the idea of wine tours here would have seemed out of place; now they are de rigueur.

Rodeo mural in Toppenish.

No Place Like Home

When you mention home to a man from Washington there is no telling what he may be thinking of....

He could be thinking of the Horse Heaven Hills, caught snug in the sharp bend of the Columbia, and could be hearing the creak of his saddle and the light music of the bit-rings. He could be remembering himself at the wheel of a fishing boat in waters off Point Roberts....Or it could be down by Dungeness, watching the stern rise and fall in the swell that is rolling up old de Fuca from the greatest of the oceans....

Yet "home" need not mean the waterfront at all. A Washingtonian may never have gazed at the sea, and he may die east of the Cascades without seeing Puget Sound or the San Juans or the Queen City whose towers were built on more than seven hills. Mention home to him, and he may think only of the rolling fields of wheat or rye grass and the Blue Mountains behind them in the haze. He may be thinking of an old house built tall and grey with narrow windows that is the only house visible around the whole horizon, and therefore the only house in the world to his young eyes.

—Nard Jones, *Evergreen Land: A Portrait of the State of Washington*, 1947

■ HORSE HEAVEN HILLS *map pages 258–259, B-4*

East of Prosser, between the Big Bend of the Columbia and the Yakima River, is a region known as Horse Heaven Hills, a series of hills, mountains, and rolling plateaus that separate the Yakima Valley from the Columbia, to the south. The region got its name because so many horses once crowded the hills. Many of these trotters were shipped to South Africa in the late 19th century to help the British army win the Boer War.

Two main roads cross the hills from the Yakima Valley to the Columbia River, and several minor roads run from west to east along the ridges. U.S. 97 crosses from Toppenish to Goldendale via Satus Pass, passing through the pine-clad spurs of Mount Adams. Farther east, off I-82, Route 221 rises from Prosser in a series of switchbacks to rolling hills where wheat has replaced the native bunchgrass. As the road descends to the Columbia, grapevines replace the wheat. This is prime vineyard country. When you reach the river, a left turn on Route 14 takes you toward I-82, a right turn down the river to the Columbia River Gorge.

SOUTHEAST

■ ABOVE THE COLUMBIA RIVER GORGE

Driving downriver from the Tri Cities, first on U.S. 12 and then on U.S. 730, takes you through some of Washington's most sculpted landscapes. Except for a few orchards and lonely farmhouses, the dry slopes to either side of the river still look much like they did when Lewis and Clark paddled down the Snake River and the Columbia on their way to the ocean two centuries ago. You'll cross the Snake River shortly after you leave Pasco. The mouth of the Walla Walla is next, where Fort Walla Walla (also known as Fort Nez Perce) stood in the early 19th century.

Wallula Gap   *map pages 258–259, D-4*

Stop at the Wallula Gap and look at the cliffs. Similar to those downstream from here in the Columbia Gorge, they are mostly barren and devoid of soil and vegetation, having been stripped down to bedrock by the torrential Spokane Floods. You'll also notice two curiously cylindrical buttes towering over the road. The Indians called them the Two Sisters and tell a story of how an old coyote married three sisters and loved them so dearly he could not bear to part from them, so he changed two of them into columnar basalt forms, and the third into a nearby cave. There's a small parking area at the left side of the road (at Milepost 4); a stile crosses over a barbed wire fence to a short trail leading to the base of the rocks; another trail winds through sand dunes that overlook the river.

A few miles down the road, you'll cross into Oregon. At Umatilla, take the I-82 freeway bridge back to the Washington side of the river and turn west on WA 14 toward Maryhill, the Columbia River Gorge, and Vancouver. But if time permits, cross into Oregon, to Hemiston, and stock up on that town's splendid melons— look for them at produce stands along U.S. 395.

Route 14 winds through shockingly primeval terrain. The cliffs become steeper, the road more twisted, and the landscape looks so raw you half expect to stumble across a dinosaur. But the only monsters you'll encounter are big produce trucks that hog the road. Stop from time to time to watch hawks soar in the updrafts generated by the cliffs. If you're lucky, you may spot a golden or bald eagle.

As you drive along the highway, you're not likely to realize that the river around you is dammed. The shores are a vivid green, and power generators and an aluminum plant blend into the landscape. A few miles beyond the plant, on a high cliff overlooking the river, you'll encounter the Maryhill Museum (see page 216) and Stonehenge (see page 217).

SOUTHEAST

Mount Adams forms the backdrop for the Triple L Farm near Goldendale.

U.S. 97 leads north from Maryhill toward Goldendale, through rolling hills of wheat and stubble before it climbs into a landscape of pines and woods broken up by spectacular rock formations. The town contains some nice Victorian houses and several blocks of early-20th-century commercial buildings.

The **Goldendale Observatory Interpretive Center,** which opens on many summer evenings (and a few winter ones) for public stargazing programs, stands on a high point near Goldendale. The largest telescope here is 24.5 inches in diameter. *Observatory Drive off North Columbus Avenue; 509-773-3141.*

Klickitat   *map pages 258–259, A-5*

From Goldendale, you can return to the river on U.S. 97 or follow narrow, twisting Route 142 down the valley of the Klickitat River. The road into the canyon from the high plateau offers great views, but it's a nail-biting ride. Down lower, you pass through the town of Klickitat, a "community supported by perpetual forest resources," with houses occupying a few wide spots on the canyon floor. The road runs through scattered pines and thickets of oak with lichen-crusted branches, always staying close to the rapids.

West to Bonneville

Heading west along the Columbia from Klickitat, you pass enormous rocks softened by moss, and the trees change from pine to fir. On the opposite shore, mountains plunge straight to the river, appearing and disappearing in the mist, their forested slopes broken by rock and split by ravines. A high waterfall cascades down a cliff. In winter, snow dusts the upper slopes. The road along the Washington shore provides a better view than the freeway on the Oregon side, but also slower driving. It winds around rock walls and, in some places, bores right through them in short tunnels. Eventually, east of 848-foot-high **Beacon Rock,** you reach **Bonneville Dam,** the first of the great federal dams built across the Columbia. Below Bonneville, the river widens out.

■ TRI CITIES *map pages 258–259, C-3/4*

The Yakima River enters the Columbia River at Richland, the largest of what nearly everyone in Washington calls the Tri Cities. The Snake River joins the Columbia downstream, below the cities of Pasco and Kennewick, the second and third legs of the triangle. In addition to shipping agricultural products by barge and train, these towns manufacture huge cranes and titanium golf club shafts.

Since World War II, they have been the bedroom communities, headquarters, and sources of labor and supplies for the Hanford Atomic Works, which produced the materials for the atomic bomb prototype that was exploded in New Mexico in 1945 and the bomb that destroyed Nagasaki. Because of Hanford's mission, the federal government never built a dam near the Tri Cities, preserving the last free-flowing stretch of the river above Bonneville Dam. Chinook salmon still spawn at Vernita Bar, in what is known as the river's Hanford Reach.

Richland and Kennewick

The riverfront in Richland and Kennewick is bordered by a number of almost continuous parks, riverside meadows, and willow thickets that are great for walking, picnicking, and bird-watching.

If you visit in autumn and walk along the river in Richland, you'll be treated to an enormous range of colors: the bright gold of ginkgo trees, the dark indigo-gray of the river, the brown of the riverside willow trunks, and the gray-green of distant hills—all under a cerulean sky. Oh, yes, and the singing of birds in the trees and the squabble of ducks and geese on the water.

Washington's 9,000-Year-Old Fisherman

Reconstruction of Kennewick Man's face, courtesy of James Chatters.

Kennewick has a pretty waterfront area, and Columbia Park here is hardly a place where you'd expect to come across a homicide victim. But two college students thought they had stumbled over exactly that when they discovered a human skull half-buried in the shallows of the Columbia River. They called the police, who called the county coroner, who in turn called in James Chatters, a forensic anthropologist. Chatters quickly assessed that the skull was not Native American in origin, that it had too many "Caucasoid" features—structural features shared by such diverse people as Europeans, Persians, and the Ainu of Japan, but not necessarily meaning "white" or "European."

Chatters went down to the river to look for additional bones and came away with a nearly complete skeleton. Determining that the deceased was male, between 40 and 55 years old, about 5 feet 9 inches—much taller than most prehistoric Native Americans of the Northwest—and well nourished, he deduced that these were the remains of a 19th-century trapper or pioneer. Then he noticed a gray object embedded in the hipbone strongly resembling a projectile point used widely in the Cascades between 4,500 and 9,000 years ago. Radiocarbon dating confirmed that the bones in his lab were 9,300 years old. Despite the age, Chatters and other anthropologists maintain he is not of a typical Native American origin. The local Umatilla tribe believes otherwise, and, under the Native American Graves Protection and Repatriation Act, wants to halt further study and bury the remains.

Some anthropologists believe that "Kennewick Man" might have been part of a small group that wandered about hunting, fishing, and gathering plants. Isotopic-carbon studies indicate that he ate a lot of seafood; perhaps he fished for salmon on the Columbia. Chatters believes that with his Caucasoid features, the man could have moved through the streets of contemporary Seattle without standing out. But whoever he was, his discovery is a fascinating and mysterious twist in the complex history of human migration to North America.

Sacajawea State Park, at the confluence of the Snake and Columbia Rivers, provides a pleasant contrast to the dry hills across the river. The 284-acre park occupies the site of Ainsworth, a railroad town that flourished from 1879 to 1884, and is named for Sacajawea, the Shoshone Indian woman who helped guide the Lewis and Clark expedition over the Rocky Mountains and down the Snake River. The two explorers camped here in 1805. The visitors center has information about their expedition and a display of Native American tools. A boat launch, a picnic area, and a children's playground round out the facilities. The beach, sand dunes, marshes, and ponds are great places for watching wildlife, including coyotes, deer, raccoons, ducks, geese, eagles, hawks, herons, and the occasional white pelican. *Off U.S. 12, 5 miles southeast of Pasco; 509-545-2361.*

A few miles south on U.S. 12, after crossing the Snake River, the highway is bordered by the reedy ponds and marshes of the **McNary National Wildlife Refuge.** Look for a sign directing you to the park headquarters, a quarter-mile east of the highway. In winter, the refuge is a shelter and feeding area for up to 100,000 migrating Canada geese, mallards, and wigeons. The main attractions are a self-guided, 2-mile trail that winds through marshes, and a blind (built like a small cabin) hidden in tall reeds that allows you to watch yellow-headed blackbirds, ducks, grebes, and geese up close. With luck, you may also spot long-billed curlews and white pelicans. *64 Maple Road, Burbank; 509-547-4942.*

■ WALLA WALLA COUNTY

Walla Walla, at the edge of the Blue Mountain foothills, has been a wheat town for more than a century. It is also a prison town. Early legislators, dividing up the spoils of state government, gave Olympia the capital, Seattle the university, and Walla Walla the pen. This is also a college town—Whitman College is one of the most highly regarded liberal arts schools in the state. In the mid-19th century, Walla Walla prospered as a supply center for mining rushes farther east; by 1870, the mining booms had made it the largest city in Washington. But for generations, wheat has paid most of the bills.

Whitman Mission National Historic Site *map pages 258–259, D-4*
The history most people associate with Walla Walla, the Whitman Massacre, happened about 12 miles west of the city at what is now the Whitman Mission National Historic Site.

(following pages) Pea and wheat fields in Walla Walla County.

RIDING LIKE CENTAURS

Thursday, May 24th [1855]

About 2500 of the Nez Percé tribe have arrived. It was our first specimen of this Prairie cavalry, and it certainly realized all our conceptions of these wild warriors of the plains…. Going out on the plain to where the flag staff had been erected, we saw them approaching on horseback in one long line…. Trained from early childhood almost to live up on horseback, they sat upon their fine animals as if they were centaurs. Their horses, too, were arrayed in the most glaring finery. They were painted with such colors as formed the greatest contrast; the white being smeared with crimson in fantastic figures, and the dark colored streaked with white clay. Beads and fringes of gaudy colors were hanging from the bridles, whiles the plumes of eagle feathers interwoven with the mane and tail fluttered as the breeze swept over them….

—Lawrence Kip, *The Indian Council in the Valley of the Walla-Walla*, 1855

---

grass. Did anyone know their names when they died? Did mothers, fathers, friends, lovers, ever know where they had gone? Or did each of these people simply head west one day—on impulse, out of desperation, following a dream—and simply disappear? *Off Route 12, west of Walla Walla; 509-522-6360.*

Walla Walla   *map pages 258–259, D-4*

Downtown Walla Walla is full of 19th-century commercial brick buildings, streets, and houses. Things here look very much as they did 50 or 100 years ago, only newer buildings now nestle in among the old ones. Walla Walla has gone to great lengths to preserve its architectural history. The most recent effort, begun in the early 1990s, is a research project for which plaques are placed on significant historic structures. Plaques have been going up all over Walla Walla, calling attention to such impressive edifices as **Naimy's Furniture** (200 East Main Street) and the **Whitehouse-Crawford Planing Mill** (212 North Third Street).

Walla Walla's restored downtown earned it the 2001 Great American Main Street Award from the National Trust for Historic Preservation. The town does look great, but what really makes Walla Walla special are its friendly people and welcoming atmosphere.

SOUTHEAST

■ BLUE MOUNTAINS   *map pages 258–259, E/F-4*

In 1878, Lucy Ide arrived in Dayton, east of Walla Walla, with a wagon train from Wisconsin. Ide and her relatives and friends had left home on May 1, passed through parts of Nebraska, Wyoming, Utah, Idaho, and Oregon, and reached Walla Walla on September 13. Two days later, they followed the Touchet River into Dayton, where they were greeted by the town's founder, Jesse Day. Some planned to stay in Dayton. Others planned to go farther east into the Palouse Hills. All were nearly out of money and food. "Aunt Sallie's prayer has been answered," Ide wrote in her diary for September 15, "her prayer was, that she might be permitted to live to see her new home and children once more settled; coming over the Blue Mountains, now and then could be seen lonely graves close by the roadside; and when she began to be sick, she prayed that she might not die on the mountains, the graves looked so lonely to her."

Astonishing though it may be that people once came out here to live, it is equally astonishing that within a generation or two, towns, farms, and wheat fields were producing goods for the whole nation. Drive east from Walla Walla on U.S.

Highway 129 winds its way through the Blue Mountains near the Grand Ronde River.

Wheat fields surround a Palouse Hills granary.

12 and you find yourself among steep hills bright green with young winter wheat. People once plowed the hillsides with teams of horses or mules. Up to 44 animals would pull a single combine over the hills. The threshed wheat would be loaded into sacks, which were then sewn shut by hand. It was unimaginably hard work. Internal combustion engines do most of it now, but one can still see the grain silos of yesterday, rising above small towns like medieval church towers.

Downtown Dayton *map pages 258–259, E-3*

People stop in Dayton mostly for its history. Dozens of Victorian houses here speak to the town's early prosperity. There's also the 1881 railroad depot, now restored as a museum. And Dayton also has the state's oldest high school, at 614 South Third Street, with pink stone columns and patterned brickwork. It's still in use. Don't miss the **Columbia County Courthouse** (341 East Main Street), a three-story Italianate structure with an outrageous cupola. Inside the 1887 building, you can climb either side of a splendid double staircase to the second-floor courtroom and see the spectators balconies, wooden railings, and shelves of old law books—plus a VCR and screen for presenting evidence the 21st-century way.

Farmland

The Blue Mountain foothills contain some of the richest farmlands in eastern Washington. Rainfalls here can be roughly twice as much as in the western part of the state. Historically, the areas with greater rainfall supported denser growths of native grasses. Over the centuries, as rain fell the grass grew, only to die back, decompose, and turn into soil. The first farmers who homesteaded the gently rolling hills of the Blue Mountain foothills found black topsoil that in places was 4 to 5 feet thick. Working the hillsides with their horses or mules, they raised enormous quantities of wheat. Their descendants, working those same hillsides with big tractors, still raise amazing crops. Whitman County often produces more wheat than any other single county in the United States.

The farmers of Walla Walla County have always shipped wheat to market down the Snake River. Today, dams and locks along the Snake and Columbia Rivers allow tugs to push their barges all the way to Idaho. Originally, there were rapids and falls that no boat—and certainly no boat laden with sacks of wheat—could safely pass. Simply getting wheat down to the river was a challenge: the Snake River winds through the hills of southeastern Washington sometimes *thousands* of feet below the farmland. Early farmers eased wagons down to wheat landings on the riverbank, dragging logs as brakes or using heavy ropes snubbed around immovable objects on the slopes above. Then, as Stewart Holbrook described in *The Columbia*:

> "In 1879, at a Snake wheat landing, shippers built a wooden pipe, four inches square, and laid it from the canyon rim to the river. At the first trial the wheat went down with such speed that it was ground into coarse flour. It also cut holes in the pipe. The chute was rebuilt with a series of upturns or baffles.... This was the answer to getting grain down to the stern-wheelers."

Getting the wheat down to the riverbank was, of course, only the first step. Beyond lay the rapids through which the Snake and Columbia poured until the big dams transformed both waterways into chains of lakes. Essentially, the sacks of grain had to be carried around every rapid. Even starting from the relative convenience of

(following pages) Wheat harvesting in the 1920s. (Pemco Webster and Stevens Collection, Museum of History and Industry)

Walla Walla, wheat had to be handled and rehandled many times. From the railroad warehouse in Walla Walla City it went by rail, Holbrook wrote:

> "...to Wallula, where it was transferred to a boat and taken to Umatilla; at Umatilla Rapids it was transferred to another boat for Celilo; at Celilo it went through a warehouse and to a car of the Portage railroad and was wheeled to The Dalles, and stored again even if briefly; then it was put aboard a boat and taken to Upper Cascades, and there transferred by Portage railroad to Lower Cascades. Here it was put into the hold or on the deck of another boat for Portland. At Portland it was stored again, and at last was loaded into an ocean-going vessel."

■ THE PALOUSE *map pages 258–259, E/F-1/2*

The Palouse landscape invites comparison to the ocean. Driving through these rolling hills of wheat you sense a vast expanse opening before you. The hillsides are all wheat, brilliant green when the crop is young, golden when it matures, pale straw and dust after it's been harvested.

Researchers from the universities of Washington and Idaho reported in 1981 that most farmers here have "either operated the same farm most of their life or, if they are younger, have grown up in one of the local communities and are now taking over the family farm or that of a neighbor." Even absentee landlords tended to be "older people who inherited their land or became owners through kinship ties. Nearly 30 percent reported they (or their spouse) had once farmed the land."

After generations of plowing, the hills have lost tons of topsoil. Until recently, some farms in the Palouse were probably losing 20 tons per year. This is no dust bowl, but when the topsoil is gone, farmers can either stop planting or spend large sums of money on nitrogen fertilizer. The last 20 years have seen an interest in "conservation tillage" that will save the soil. Now, in the hills of bright green wheat, occasional strips of pale stubble run horizontally along planted slopes, separating the swaths of green. Once upon a time, the stubble would have been considered a sign of poor farming; any thrifty farmer's field would have been turned over so that nothing showed but soil. To the west, where less rain falls, farmers leave stubble on fallow fields to keep the wind from blowing soil away.

Hidden in the hollows of these Palouse wheat fields are trees, houses, and whole towns. Rosalia, site of the 1850s Steptoe battlefield, in which Indians chased off the U.S. Cavalry, sits in a hollow among the wheat fields. The town of Colfax, with its old brick downtown blocks, lies below rocky bluffs.

Pullman   *map pages 258–259, F-2*
Pullman, where Washington State University spills over a hill overlooking downtown, is the Palouse's largest town. It has long been a wheat town, which explains the presence of old grain elevators along the railroad tracks. The university remains a center of research and education on raising crops and livestock—the Cougar Gold cheese produced on campus has a wide following—but most of the faculty works in other areas. The Edward R. Murrow School of Communications commemorates the pioneer radio newsman who provided much of the nation's news from World War II London not long after he graduated from WSU.

North of the Palouse
Most of Washington's dryland wheat grows in much harsher country than the Palouse. You see rocks among the fields, and sagebrush in uncultivated patches beside the road. The smooth hillsides are broken by basalt bluffs, and areas of sand and sage appear among the wheat, but this is certainly no wasteland. Fields of ripe wheat look golden in the sunlight, and blooming canola crowns a hill with bright yellow. All this land is naturally desert, yet this is fertile ground that has been producing crops for more than a century.

Ritzville, on I-90 east of Spokane, has been a wheat town since the 1880s, and whole blocks of old brick buildings line the streets downtown. The wooden gallery of an old hotel building—wood with a brick veneer—lends its part of the main drag a Wild West look. Past the main street, past the art deco marquee of the Ritz movie theater, past an agricultural office at which wheat rates are posted on a chalkboard, and past big grain elevators, a road rises straight into the wheat fields.

Irrigation changes the character of the landscape. As you enter the Columbia Basin Project near **Othello,** for example, the greens take on a new intensity, cattails grow in roadside ditches where irrigation runoff collects, and the scent of mint fills the air. (Eastern Washington grows most of the nation's spearmint and is a leading peppermint producer.) In the fields, circle irrigators create perpetual rainbows as they swing through the crops.

(following page) Man poses with salmon, ca. 1912. (University of Washington Libraries)

Wt 44 lbs
3 ft 9 in long

caught by
Roy Weidner
and Ed Taro

PRACTICAL INFORMATION

■ AREA CODES AND TIME ZONE

The area code in Seattle is 206; 425 for Everett and south Snohomish County, Bellevue and east King County; 360 for Olympia and the San Juan Islands; 253 for Tacoma, Puyallup, and the south Puget Sound area; and 509 for Spokane and eastern Washington. The 360 area code shares some territories with 564. The state is in the Pacific time zone.

■ METRIC CONVERSIONS

1 foot =   .305 meters
1 mile =   1.6 kilometers
Centigrade =   Fahrenheit temperature minus 32, divided by 1.8

■ CLIMATE

It rains a lot in Washington west of the Cascades, but little rain falls in many places east of them. Summers west of the Cascades tend to be dry. Even when it rains, though, it seldom rains hard. Cascades weather is cold and snowy in winter and generally cool in summer. Year-round, there are distinct west slope and east slope climates; if it's cloudy west of a pass, the sun might be shining in the east.

CITY	FAHRENHEIT TEMPERATURE			ANNUAL PRECIPITATION	
	Jan. Avg. High/Low	July Avg. High/Low	Record High/Low	Average Rain	Average Snow
Mt. Rainier N. P.	33 21	64 44	92 -22	106"	582"
Omak	30 15	90 55	114 -23	10"	36"
Port Angeles	42 34	62 51	80 11	24"	10"
Quillayute	46 34	68 49	99 5	104"	15"
Seattle-Tacoma	44 33	75 54	100 0	38"	13"
Spokane	30 20	82 55	108 -30	17"	51"
Yakima	38 20	87 53	111 -25	8" ·	24"

The coast is the rainiest part of the state. Temperatures rarely fall below freezing here, but if you're driving over coastal mountain passes or the I-5 pass near the Oregon border in winter, you should check on snow and ice conditions.

■ GETTING THERE AND AROUND

◆ BY AIR

Seattle-Tacoma International Airport (SEA) is served by most of the major air carriers and their affiliates. Horizon Air and San Juan Airlines serve cities throughout the state. *17801 Pacific Highway South; 206-431-4444 or 206-433-5388, www.portofseattle.org*

Spokane Airport (GEG) is served by Horizon Air, Northwest, and United/United Express. *9000 West Airport Drive; 509-455-6455, www.spokaneairport.net*

◆ BY CAR

The main routes into Washington include I-82 from Idaho, I-5 from Canada and Oregon, and I-84 from Oregon. The main north-south route through the state is I-5. Regional chapters in this book contain additional touring information.

◆ BY BUS

Greyhound. This company has the greatest number of scheduled bus routes in the state but runs mainly along I-5 and I-90. *800-231-2222, www.greyhound.com*

◆ BY TRAIN

Amtrak. *800-872-7245, www.amtrak.com*

◆ BY FERRY

Washington State Ferries. Most ferries carry cars, though some smaller boats that run between Seattle and Bremerton or Bainbridge and Vashon Islands carry passengers only. All ferries carry bikes. At commuting hours and on summer weekends, cars line up well in advance of the scheduled departure time. *Outside Washington and British Columbia, 206-464-6400; inside Washington and British Columbia, 888-808-7977, www.wsdot.wa.gov/ferries*

■ NORTHWEST CUISINE

Washington is a land of gustatory riches. Expect restaurant fare to include the freshest seafood and lamb you've ever tasted, the crunchiest apples, sweetest cherries, zestiest grapes, and tangiest goat cheeses. Chances are your first conversations with Washington natives will be about food, commonly expressed as "the bounty."

Washingtonians are great cooks, know how food tastes when at its best, and go to great pains to seek out the choicest fish, meat, vegetables, and fruits. Cooks here often grow their own fruits and vegetables or buy shellfish, mushrooms, herbs, and other products directly from Washington-area fish markets and farmers. Some chefs have exclusive contracts with specific gardeners to raise produce just for their establishments.

You can easily tell the difference between Dungeness crab fresh from the water and crab that has been cooked a few days prior to serving, or was frozen. With oysters, you can tell the difference almost by the hour; if they have been shucked, by the minute. (Never eat oysters that are not shucked fresh with each order. A few restaurants, annoyingly, shuck theirs in the afternoon, during the slow time, then serve them for dinner. Send those back!)

Clams and mussels are a bit hardier, though Washington's largest clam, the geoduck (pronounced "gooey-duck"), spoils rapidly if it is not cooked immediately after shucking. The geoduck is best when served sliced extremely thin and cooked for just a few seconds.

Having acquired new techniques from their Japanese and Chinese compatriots, Washington restaurant chefs and home cooks have learned to appreciate unusual harmonies in food and wine. For instance, at a wine and food tasting I once attended, the host broke two rules of standard culinary practice, yet the results were so delicious they served to remind that Washington cuisine conforms to its own rules.

The first rule our host broke was to serve red wine, and from only one vintage. Many wine connoisseurs know that Washington makes good white wines, but some believe that the state's vineyards lie too far north to produce reds of distinction. The cabernet sauvignons poured at the gathering—all from a dozen Washington wineries—were not only big but possessed uncommon finesse.

The other no-no was the food served with the wine. Typically, raw and smoked oysters, smoked steelhead, cold poached fillet of Chinook salmon, and prawns steamed in ale would be served only with dry white wines. But, surprisingly, it all worked with the reds. The tastes didn't clash because Washington reds are high in natural acids and complex enough in flavor to complement a variety of foods.

Many types of mushrooms grow in Washington. Delicate oyster mushrooms, robust morels and chanterelles, and distinctive boletus and chicken-of-the-wood add texture to many dishes. In some restaurants, chefs try different combinations of morels and beef, while at others, wild mushrooms and smoked duck are blended into a consommé. On the coast, boletus mushrooms grow so large they are often served as entrées rather than as vegetables or condiments.

Wild duck, grouse, deer, elk, and bear are popular in Washington. Don't be surprised if a menu in a rural pub offers delicacies like bear sausage and beaver salami. Don't be nervous about sampling them. They're delicious, as is buffalo, which might come prepared as a simple burger or a luscious chop.

Whether you're eating oysters and smoked salmon or a rib-sticking buffalo dinner, think about accompanying your meal with a beer from one of the state's many microbreweries. If beer isn't your thing, try some wine: effervescent sparkling wine, sauvignon blanc, pale semillon, golden chardonnay, cabernet sauvignon, or merlot. A sweet Riesling or gewürztraminer will provide a great finish to your meal.

You'll encounter many of the state's fruits long before you're ready for dessert. Blackberries or dried cherries are frequently combined with lamb, raspberries or cranberries with sturgeon, apples with venison sausage, and blueberries with quail. But don't limit fruit to the main course. You can certainly finish with it too, especially when the strawberries are topped with fresh cream, the apples or cherries are baked in a pie, and pears are poached in red wine. A perfectly ripened pear or apple also goes well with a Washington cheddar or farmstead cheese.

■ ACCOMMODATIONS

Hotels and motels throughout the state, both chains and independents, tend to be plain and ordinary. They're fancier in the downtown areas of cities like Seattle, Bellingham, and Spokane. In the Cascade Mountains, along the Columbia River, and near the ocean, motels and hotels emulate cozy lodges. Many of these accommodations emphasize views and proximity to water over comfort and luxury.

The state has many good B&Bs, in the bigger cities and areas near the rain forests and ocean. Most of these, especially those in the San Juan Islands, cater to upscale travelers. Washington also has a lot of country inns, a vaguely defined category. These lodgings are similar to B&Bs but usually have more rooms, or perhaps a restaurant and a bar—"B&Bs with attitude," say some folks.

Mount Rainier and Olympic National Parks have classic park lodges: big yet atmospheric, with fireplaces, cozy rooms with views, a restaurant, excellent service, and great location. Several state parks rent yurts, small, usually domed tents of skins or felt. Other parks, like Cape Disappointment, Fort Columbia, Fort Casey, Moran, and Sun Lakes, have cabins and lighthouse keepers' quarters.

With advance planning, visitors can also rent cabins and houses along the coast, on islands, or in the mountains. Curiously, first-rate lodging is still hard to find in Washington's wine country, but this is changing, with Walla Walla running ahead of the Columbia River and Yakima Valleys.

◆ RESERVATIONS SERVICES
Karen Brown's Guides. *www.karenbrown.com/pnw*
A Pacific Reservation Service. *206-439-7677 or 800-684-2932,*
www.seattlebedandbreakfast.com
Unique Northwest Inns. *877-286-4783, www.uniqueinns.com*

◆ HOTEL AND MOTEL CHAINS
Best Western. *800-528-1234, www.bestwestern.com*
Choice Hotels. *800-424-6423, www.choicehotels.com*
Days Inn. *800-329-7466, www.daysinn.com*
Doubletree. *800-222-8733, www.doubletree.com*
Embassy Suites. *800-362-2779, www.embassysuites.com*
Fairmont Hotels. *800-257-7544, www.fairmont.com*
Holiday Inn. *1-888-HOLIDAY, www.6c.com*
Hyatt. *800-233-1234, www.hyatt.com*
La Quinta. *800-531-5900, www.laquinta.com*
Marriott. *800-228-9290, www.marriott.com*
Radisson. *800-333-3333, www.radisson.com*
Ramada. *800-272-6232, www.ramada.com*
Renaissance. *888-236-2427, www.marriott.com*
Sheraton. *800-325-3535, www.starwoodhotels.com/sheraton*
Travelodge. *800-835-2424, www.travelodge.com*
W Hotels. *877-946-8357, www.starwoodhotels.com/whotels*
WestCoast. *800-325-4000, www.westcoasthotelpartners.rdln.com*
Westin. *800-228-3000, www.starwoodhotels.com/westin*

■ CAMPING IN WASHINGTON

Most campgrounds here are fairly developed, with showers and other facilities. Many campgrounds have picnic shelters adjacent to the campsites (some with electrical outlets and fireplaces). National Forest and Bureau of Land Management sites are generally more primitive (pit toilets), more remote, and less expensive.

National Park Service. *877-444-6777, www.recreation.gov*
National Recreation Reservation Service (for facilities managed by the U.S. Forest Service and Army Corps of Engineers). *877-444-6777, www.recreation.gov*
Recreation.Gov (for sites managed by the Bureau of Land Management and other federal agencies). *www.recreation.gov*
U.S. Forest Service. *202-205-8333, www.fs.fed.us*
Washington State Parks. *360-903-8844, www.parks.wa.gov*

■ OFFICIAL TOURISM INFORMATION

Washington Tourism. *800-544-1800, www.experiencewashington.com*
Bellingham/Whatcom County. *360-671-3990, www.bellingham.org*
Edmonds. *425-670-1496, www.edmondswa.com*
Everett/Snohomish County. *425-257-3222, www.everettchamber.com*
Kitsap Peninsula. *360-297-8200 or 800-416-5615, www.visitkitsap.com*
Lake Chelan. *509-682-3503 or 800-424-3526, www.lakechelan.com*
Long Beach Peninsula. *360-642-2400 or 800-451-2542, www.funbeach.com*
North Olympic Peninsula. *800-942-4042, www.olympicpeninsula.org*
Ocean Shores County. *360-289-2451 or 800-762-3224, www.oceanshores.org*
San Juan Islands. *888-468-3701, www.guidetosanjuans.com*
Seattle. *206-684-2489, www.ci.seattle.wa.us*
Seattle/King County. *206-461-5800, www.seeseattle.org*
Spokane. *888-Spokane, www.visitspokane.com*
Tacoma/Pierce County. *800-272-2662, www.traveltacoma.com*
Tri Cities. *509-735-8486 or 800-254-5824, www.visittri-cities.com*
Wenatchee Area. *800-572-7753, www.wenatcheevalley.org*
Yakima Valley. *800-221-0751, www.visityakima.com*

■ USEFUL WEB SITES

American Indians of the Pacific Northwest Digital Collection. Super site with historical info and many photos; *content.lib.washington.edu/aipnw*

City of Seattle. Official city site has info about parks, neighborhoods, resources, arts, and entertainment; *www.ci.seattle.wa.us*

Go Northwest. Learn about outdoor activities, from wall climbing to mountain hiking to skiing; *www.gonorthwest.com*

Pike Place Market. Fun, informative site about Seattle's famous marketplace; *www.pikeplacemarket.org*

Seattle Post-Intelligencer. Daily's state and local coverage; *www.seattlepi.com*

Seattle Times. Seattle's largest daily newspaper; *www.seattletimes.com*

Seattle Weekly. Alternative weekly has entertainment and other listings; *www.seattleweekly.com*

Spokesman Review. News, features, and information from Spokane's biggest regional daily newspaper; *www.spokesmanreview.com*

University of Washington Libraries Digital Collections. Photos and documents about politics, industry, history, and other topics; *content.lib.washington.edu*

Washington State Apple Commission. Festivals, facts, recipes, other apple info; *www.bestapples.com*

Washington State Department of Transportation. Road conditions, ferries, trains, and other info, plus statewide highway cams; *www.wsdot.wa.gov*

Washington State Facts. Government site has information about state's climate, population, geography, politics, and more; *access.wa.gov/statefacts/index.asp*

Washington State Parks. Directions, history, other info; *www.parks.wa.gov/parks*

Washington Wine Country. Everything you need to know about the state's wineries; *www.washingtonwine.org*

■ Festivals and Events

◆ January

Bald eagle count. *San Juan Island.*

Fire and Ice Winterfest. Chili cook-off, snow sculpting, snowmobiling, ice fishing, and cross-country skiing. *Chelan; 800-424-3526 or 509-682-2381.*

◆ January to February

Chinese New Year celebration. Hosted by the International District community. *Seattle; 206-323-2700.*

◆ February

Fat Tuesday. Parade, pub run, Spam-carving contest. *Seattle; 206-622-2563.*

Northwest Flower and Garden Show. Unusual flowers and plants from all over are on display at this big-deal show. *Washington State Convention Center, Seattle; 206-789-5333.*

Upper Skagit Bald Eagle Festival. Celebration of eagle migration. Festivals are held in Concrete and Rockport. *Marblemount; 360-853-7009.*

◆ March

Gray whale migration. *Westport.*

◆ April

Skagit Valley Tulip Festival. See the blooms and enjoy exhibits, salmon barbecues, picnics, walks, runs, a parade, and fireworks. *Mount Vernon; 360-428-5959.*

Washington State Apple Blossom Festival. Parades, arts and crafts, musical performances, and carnival. *Wenatchee; 509-662-3616.*

Yakima Valley Spring Barrel Tasting. Late April. *Yakima County; 800-258-7270.*

◆ May

Rhododendron Festival. City's most popular event. *Port Townsend; 360-385-2722.*

◆ MAY TO JUNE

Northwest Folklife Festival. Immensely popular music festival. Crafts, clothing, and incense vendors. Memorial Day weekend. *Seattle; 206-684-7300.*

Ski-to-Sea Festival. Street fair and relay race from Mount Baker to salt water. Memorial Day weekend. *Bellingham; 360-671-3990.*

◆ JUNE

Bust Your Butte Ball Drop. Rolling of a 6-foot ball down Steptoe Butte. How long does it take to reach the bottom? *509-397-9103.*

Wildflower Festival. Second weekend in June. *Darrington.*

◆ JULY

Darrington Bluegrass Festival. Music festival celebrating the town's early settlers from North Carolina. *Darrington; 360-436-1179.*

Festival of American Fiddle Tunes. *Port Townsend; 360-385-3102 or 800-733-3608, ext. 118.*

Loganberry Festival. Greenbank Berry Farm. *Whidbey Island; 360-678-7700.*

Seafair. Parades, hydro races, crowds. *Seattle; 206-728-0123.*

◆ AUGUST

Makah Days. Traditional dancing and singing, salmon bakes, and canoe races; *Olympic Peninsula, Neah Bay; 360-645-2201.*

Omak Stampede and Suicide Run. The largest rodeo in northeastern Washington. *Omak; 800-933-6625 or 509-826-1002.*

Skagit River Shakespeare Festival. In Edgewater Park on the north shore of the Skagit River. *Mount Vernon; 360-770-7748.*

Washington State International Kite Festival. Held the third full week of August each year. *Long Beach; 360-642-4020.*

◆ **September**

Bumbershoot. Music and arts fest. Labor Day weekend. *Seattle; 206-281-7788.*

Western Washington State Fair. *Puyallup; 206-845-1771.*

Wooden Boat Festival. Races, rides, craft shows. *Port Townsend; 360-385-3628.*

◆ **October**

Annual Cranberrian Fair. Food booths, musical entertainment, and tours through the cranberry bogs. *Ilwaco; 360-642-3446.*

West Coast Oyster Shucking Championship and Seafood Fest. *Shelton; 360-426-2021.*

◆ **November**

Winery open houses. Wineries serve samplings of their wines, paired with the right food. *Yakima Valley.*

◆ **December**

Lighted Boat Parade. Children's activities and music. *Bellingham; 360-671-3990.*

Sunnyside Lighted Farm Implement Parade. Tractors, combines, and floats decorated with holiday lights parade through downtown. *Sunnyside; 509-837-5939.*

Eagles return to the Skagit River. *Marblemount.*

Holiday Open House. At the Redmen Hall Interpretive Center: music, crafts, cookies. *Skamokawa; 360-795-3007.*

New Year's Powwow. Traditional Native American food, dancing, and games. From December 30 until New Year's Day. *White Swan; 509-865-5121.*

Buckhorn Beach and Raccoon Point, Orcas Island.

RECOMMENDED READING

■ History

Alexander, Carmela, and Ruth Kirk. *Exploring Washington's Past: A Road Guide to History.* Seattle: University of Washington Press, 1990. An interesting historical guide written for those traveling the state by car.

Alvin, John A. *Between the Mountains: A Portrait of Eastern Washington.* Bozeman, Montana: Northwest Panorama Publishing, 1984.

Bergon, Frank, ed. *The Journals of Lewis and Clark.* New York: Penguin, 1989. The journals of the classic early-19th-century journey of exploration.

Brewster, David, and David M. Buerge, eds. *Washingtonians: A Biographical Portrait of the State.* Seattle: Sasquatch Books, 1989. Short profiles of historical figures.

Brown, John A., and Robert H. Ruby. *Indians of the Pacific Northwest.* Norman: University of Oklahoma, 1981. A detailed portrait of the culture and history of the tribes from this region.

Doig, Ivan. *Winter Brothers: A Season at the Edge of America.* New York: Harcourt Brace Jovanovich, 1980. Meditations on the mid-19th-century experiences of James Swan, and Doig's contemporary experience of the same places.

Edwards, G. Thomas, and Carlos Schwantes, eds. *Experiences in a Promised Land: Essays in Pacific Northwest History.* Seattle: University of Washington Press, 1986.

Egan, Timothy. *The Good Rain: Across Time and Terrain in the Pacific Northwest.* New York: Knopf, 1990. A personal exploration of the regional essence.

Frederick, Richard, and Jeanne Engerman. *Asahel Curtis: Photographs of the Great Northwest.* Tacoma: Washington State Historical Society, 1983. A series of pictorial essays featuring the photographs of Pacific Northwest photographer and mountaineer Asahel Curtis. Exceptional insights into regional history and development.

Gates, Charles Marvin, ed. *Readings in Pacific Northwest History: Washington 1790–1895.* Seattle: University Bookstore, 1941. Anthology of memoirs from a variety of Washington's founding fathers.

Holbrook, Stewart H. *The Columbia.* New York: Holt, Rinehart and Winston, 1974. The river itself and the inland Northwest.

Hunn, Eugene S., and James Selam. *Nch'i-wana, The Big River, Mid-Columbia Indians and their Land.* Seattle: University of Washington Press, 1990. Ethnography and history of inland peoples who lived and fished along the Columbia.

Kirk, Ruth, with Richard D. Daugherty. *Exploring Washington Archaeology.* Seattle: University of Washington Press, 1978. Major pre-1980 archaeological sites.

Lavender, David. *Land of Giants: The Drive to the Pacific Northwest, 1750–1950.* Lincoln: University of Nebraska Press, 1979. This classic ties historical developments in Washington to those of other Northwest states.

Morgan, Murray. *Puget's Sound: A Narrative of Early Tacoma and the Southern Sound.* Seattle: University of Washington Press, 1979. Emphasis on 19th-century explorers and development; some wonderful descriptions.

Morgan, Murray. *Skid Road: An Informal Portrait of Seattle.* Sausalito, California: Comstock Editions, 1978. Examines 19th- and early-20th-century Seattle.

Sale, Roger. *Seattle, Past to Present.* Seattle: University of Washington Press, 1978. A history of the city with emphasis on progressive politics and urban design.

Swan, James G. *The Northwest Coast, or, Three Years' Residence in Washington Territory.* Seattle: University of Washington Press, 1972. Swan's classic account of life on the Washington coast in the 1850s.

◼ NATURAL HISTORY

Alt, David D., and Donald W. Hyndman. *Roadside Geology of Washington.* Missoula, Montana: Mountain Press, 1984. A nonspecialist's look at state geology.

Beres, Nancy, Mitzi Chandler, and Russell Dalton. *Island of Rivers: An Anthology Celebrating 50 Years of Olympic National Park.* Seattle: Pacific Northwest National Parks and Forest Association, 1988. A thoughtful assemblage of historical, contemporary, nonfiction, and creative writing about the state.

Chasan, Daniel Jack. *The Water Link: A History of Puget Sound as a Resource.* Seattle: Washington Sea Grant Program, distributed by University of Washington Press, 1981. An economic and environmental history of Puget Sound.

Kruckeberg, Arthur R. *The Natural History of Puget Sound Country.* Seattle: University of Washington Press, 1991. The basics of much of western Washington.

Paulson, Dennis. *Shorebirds of the Pacific Northwest.* Seattle: University of Washington Press, 1993. One of the best books ever written on shorebirds.

Pyle, Robert Michael. *Wintergreen: Rambles in a Ravaged Land.* New York: Scribner, 1986. A naturalist's fond but outraged portrait of southwestern Washington.

Whitney, Stephen. *A Field Guide to the Cascades & Olympics.* Seattle: Mountaineers, 1983. The basic flora and fauna of the state's two main mountain ranges.

■ FICTION AND POETRY

Guterson, David. *East of the Mountains.* New York: Random House, 1999. A widowed doctor in the Columbia River Basin who has terminal colon cancer sets out on his last hunt.

Guterson, David. *Snow Falling on Cedars.* New York: Vintage Books, 1995. The PEN/Faulkner Award winner, which takes place in the 1950s on an island above Puget Sound, reflects on the area and the relations between Anglo- and Japanese-Americans in the Pacific Northwest.

Robbins, Tom. *Another Roadside Attraction.* New York: Ballantine Books, 1971. Pop-philosopher Tom Robbins offers provocatively twisted, beautiful, and insightful descriptions of his home state.

Sund, Robert. *Bunch Grass.* Seattle: University of Washington Press, 1969. Poems about wheat country.

Sund, Robert. *Ish River.* San Francisco: North Point Press, 1983. Poems about the wet side of Washington.

■ GENERAL

MacDonald, Betty. *The Egg and I.* Philadelphia: Lippincott, 1945. A Seattle socialite adapts to life in the Olympic Mountains in this story that made Ma and Pa Kettle famous.

McCarthy, Mary. *How I Grew.* Orlando: Harcourt Brace Jovanovich, 1987. A wry, sophisticated, and entertaining autobiography of a young woman growing up during the 1920s in Seattle's social circle.

INDEX

COMPASS AMERICAN GUIDES

Alaska (5th Edition)
978-1-4000-0736-3

Alaska's Inside Passage (1st
Edition) 978-1-4000-1480-4

American Southwest (3rd
Edition) 978-0-679-00646-6

Arizona (6th Edition)
978-1-4000-1265-7

Boston (3rd Edition)
978-0-676-90132-0

California Wine Country (5th
Edition) 978-1-4000-1783-6

Cape Cod (1st Edition)
978-1-4000-1310-4

Chicago (3rd Edition)
978-0-679-00841-5

Coastal California (3rd
Edition) 978-1-4000-1538-2

Colorado (6th Edition)
978-1-4000-1204-6

Connecticut and Rhode
Island (1st Edition)
978-0-676-90492-5

Florida (2nd Edition)
978-0-676-90494-9

Georgia (3rd Edition)
978-1-4000-1617-4

Gulf South: Louisiana,
Alabama, Mississippi (1st
Edition) 978-0-679-00533-9

Hawaii (6th Edition)
978-1-4000-1482-8

Idaho (2nd Edition)
978-0-679-00231-4

Kentucky (2nd Edition)
978-1-4000-1661-7

Las Vegas (8th Edition)
978-1-4000-1244-2

Maine (4th Edition)
978-1-4000-1237-4

Manhattan (4th Edition)
978-0-676-90495-6

Massachusetts (1st Edition)
978-0-676-90493-2

Michigan (2nd Edition)
978-1-4000-1483-5

Minnesota (3rd Edition)
978-1-4000-1484-2

Montana (6th Edition)
978-1-4000-1662-4

Montreal (1st Edition)
978-1-4000-1315-9

New Hampshire (1st Edition)
978-0-676-90151-1

New Mexico (5th Edition)
978-1-4000-1393-7

North Carolina (4th Edition)
978-1-4000-1616-7

Ohio (1st Edition)
978-1-4000-1394-4

Oregon (5th Edition)
978-1-4000-1587-0

Oregon Wine Country (1st
Edition) 978-1-4000-1367-8

Pacific Northwest (4th
Edition) 978-1-4000-1867-3

Pennsylvania (2nd Edition)
978-0-676-90141-2

Santa Fe (5th Edition)
978-1-4000-1866-6

South Carolina (4th Edition)
978-1-4000-1485-9

South Dakota (3rd Edition)
978-1-4000-1243-5

Tennessee (2nd Edition)
978-1-4000-1618-1

Texas (3rd Edition)
978-0-676-90502-1

Utah (6th Edition)
978-1-4000-1416-3

Vermont (2nd Edition)
978-0-679-90139-9

Virginia (4th Edition)
978-1-4000-1241-1

Washington (4th Edition)
978-1-4000-0738-7

Wisconsin (3rd Edition)
978-0-679-00433-2

Wyoming (5th Edition)
978-1-4000-0737-0

■ AUTHOR

John Doerper has worked as a food and wine columnist and editor for numerous publications. His articles about food, wine, and travel have appeared in *Travel & Leisure* and *Pacific Northwest Magazine,* among others. He is also the author of several books, including *Shellfish Cookery: Absolutely Delicious Recipes from the West Coast* and Compass American Guides' *Wine Country, Pacific Northwest,* and *Coastal California.* John lives in Bellingham, Washington.

■ PHOTOGRAPHERS

Bruce Hands has had his work published in *Countryside, Outdoor Photographer, Modern Maturity,* and *Bon Appétit.* He has also provided photographs for many books, including the "Beautiful Cookbooks" series. He has earned several awards of distinction in international competitions, and his photography has been displayed at Kodak's Professional Photographers' Showcase in Disneyland's EPCOT Center.

Greg Vaughn's award-winning imagery has appeared in *National Geographic, Outside, National Wildlife, Sierra, Natural History,* and *Travel & Leisure,* and he was the principal photographer for two books about Hawaii and Compass American Guides' *Oregon* and *Pacific Northwest.*